A former federal prosecutor, **Paul Butler** provides legal commentary for MSNBC and NPR and writes for the *New York Times* and the *Washington Post*. A law professor at Georgetown University, he is the author of *Let's Get Free: A Hip-Hop Theory of Justice* (The New Press) and lives in Washington, D.C.

ALSO BY PAUL BUTLER

Let's Get Free: A Hip-Hop Theory of Justice

CHOKEHOLD

POLICING BLACK MEN

Paul Butler

THE
NEW
PRESS

NEW YORK
LONDON

© 2017 by Paul Butler
Preface © 2018 by Paul Butler
All rights reserved.
No part of this book may be reproduced, in any form,
without written permission from the publisher.

Requests for permission to reproduce selections from this book should
be made through our website: https://thenewpress.com/contact.

First published in the United States by The New Press, New York, 2017
This paperback edition published by The New Press, 2018
Distributed by Two Rivers Distribution

ISBN 978-1-59558-905-7 (hc)
ISBN 978-1-62097-483-4 (pbk.)
ISBN 978-1-62097-498-8 (e-book)
CIP data is available

The New Press publishes books that promote and enrich public discussion
and understanding of the issues vital to our democracy and to a more
equitable world. These books are made possible by the enthusiasm of our
readers; the support of a committed group of donors, large and small; the
collaboration of our many partners in the independent media and
the not-for-profit sector; booksellers, who often hand-sell New Press books;
librarians; and above all by our authors.

www.thenewpress.com

Composition by dix!
This book was set in Electra LH

Printed in the United States of America

In memory of my father, Paul Butler

CONTENTS

Preface to the Paperback Edition

In the Trump era the Chokehold is in full effect. The police go on killing as they did during the reign of Barack Obama, the first African American president. In 2017, the first year of Donald Trump's presidency, the police ended the lives of 1,129 people, mostly by shooting them, but also by beating them up or deliberately running them over with their squad cars. There were only fourteen days in 2017 in which U.S. cops did not take a life. Eighty-seven men and women got killed after being stopped for a traffic infraction. In other words, it was a typical year in American policing.

Donald Trump, speaking to a group of police officers in July 2017, signaled that a new sheriff was in town. He told the assembled cops, "We have your backs 100 percent. Not like the old days." The president said that in the same way he wanted "a rich guy at the head of [the U.S.] Treasury [Department]," he wanted "rough guys" as police officers. Trump said that when he was interviewing a candidate for a top law enforcement job, "they said he looked very nasty, he looked very mean. I said, that's exactly what I am looking for." The transcript of the speech notes that the audience laughed.

Near the end of his remarks to the police, Trump said, "You see these thugs being thrown into the back of a paddy wagon— you just see them thrown in, rough—I said, please don't be too nice. (Laughter.) Like when you guys put somebody in the car and you're protecting their head, you know, the way you put their hand over? Like, don't hit their head and they've just killed somebody— don't hit their head. I said, you can take the hand away, okay?" The transcript of the event notes: "Laughter and applause."

The Trump administration has practiced what its leader preached. The United States Department of Justice shut down federal oversight of the country's 18,000 police departments. In a memo to federal prosecutors, Attorney General Jefferson Beauregard Sessions wrote, "It is not the responsibility of the federal government to manage non-federal law enforcement agencies."

Trump signed an executive order fully reinstating the 1033 Program, in which the Pentagon provided surplus military equipment to local police departments. Trump gave the police back their tanks, bayonets, weaponized airplanes, and grenade launchers.

Is the Chokehold worse in the post-Obama era? Things could hardly have gotten worse. The cops shoot and beat up African American men regardless of who is in the White House. The previous administration refined, but chose not to end, the 1033 Program, so even when Barack Obama was in the White House the Pentagon offered U.S. cops weaponry intended for enemies of the state, including Humvees, drones, manned aircraft, explosives, and battering rams. Certainly, the Trump Justice Department's retreat from its watchdog role over local police departments sent a clear message of disdain for the victims of police violence; but, as explained in chapter 6, those federal takeovers had limited effects. The main problem has never been bad apple cops. The main problem is that the system is working the way it is supposed to, and that does not change regardless of who is the president.

What is different is that the force of white supremacy can no longer be denied. When neo-Nazis marched in Charlottesville, Virginia, carrying torches and chanting, "Jews will not replace us," Donald Trump said the marchers included some "very fine people." The president called Latino gang members "animals," described African nations as "shithole countries," said that people who support the removal of monuments to the pro-slavery Confederacy are "trying to take away our culture," and, during the campaign, called for "a complete and total shutdown of Muslims entering the United States."

If people don't get it now, they never will. The "productive apocalypse" described in chapter 8 is ascendant. What remains to be seen is the form the resistance takes, including whether it settles for removing Trump from office or, alternatively, demands the more extreme change described in the introduction to this book. As *Chokehold* makes clear, for people of color to be safe and free, the old ways of thinking about "reform" and "civil rights" are not only insufficient, they can get in the way of the transformation that the United States desperately needs. In this moment of extreme crisis, with white supremacy as transparent as it has ever been, here's to the revolution.

CHOKEHOLD

Introduction
Broke on Purpose

Here are some of the things that police did to African American people, during the time of the country's first African American president: in Ferguson, Missouri, arrested a man named Michael for filing a false report because he told them his name was "Mike." Locked up a woman in Ferguson for "occupancy permit violation" when she called 911 to report she was being beat up by her boyfriend and the police learned the man was not legally entitled to live in the house. Killed a seven-year-old girl in Detroit while looking for drugs at her father's house. Shot Walter Scott in the back in North Charleston after stopping him for a traffic infraction. Severed Freddie Gray's spinal cord in Baltimore. Unloaded sixteen bullets into seventeen-year-old Laquan McDonald while he lay cowering on a Chicago street. Pushed a teenage girl in a bikini to the ground in McKinney, Texas. Shot twelve-year-old Tamir Rice in Cleveland within two seconds of seeing him in a public park. Pumped bullets into Philando Castile in Minnesota while his girlfriend livestreamed it on Facebook, with her four-year-old daughter in the backseat.[1]

If the police did these things to African Americans during Barack Obama's presidency, what should we expect in the era of Donald Trump? During the 2015 protests in Baltimore following the death of Freddie Gray, Trump tweeted, "Our great African American President hasn't exactly had a positive impact on the thugs who are so happily and openly destroying Baltimore!"

Trump has called police officers "the most mistreated people in this country" and suggested that activists who protest police violence should be investigated by the Justice Department.[2]

Cops did not treat African Americans better when Obama was in office, and they will not treat them worse during the era of Trump. The ascendency of Donald Trump might embolden a racist cop, but racist cops are not the main problem. Most police officers are decent working-class men and women with no more racial hang-ups than teachers, doctors, or anyone else. As we will see, the crisis in law and order in the United States stems from police work itself rather than from individual cops.

There has never, not for one minute in American history, been peace between black people and the police. And nothing since slavery—not Jim Crow segregation, not forced convict labor, not lynching, not restrictive covenants in housing, not being shut out of New Deal programs like Social Security and the GI Bill, not massive resistance to school desegregation, not the ceaseless efforts to prevent African Americans from voting—nothing has sparked the level of outrage among African Americans as when they have felt under violent attack by the police.[3] Most of the times that African Americans have set aside traditional civil rights strategies like bringing court cases and marching peacefully and instead have rioted in the streets, destroyed property, and attacked symbols of the state have been because of something the police have done. Watts in 1965, Newark in 1967, Miami in 1980, Los Angeles in 1992, Ferguson in 2015, Baltimore in 2016, Charlotte in 2016—each of these cities went up in flames sparked by the police killing a black man.[4]

The problem is the criminal process itself. Cops routinely hurt and humiliate black people because that is what they are paid to do. Virtually every objective investigation of a U.S. law enforcement agency finds that the police, *as policy*, treat African Americans with contempt. In New York, Baltimore, Ferguson, Chicago, Los Angeles, Cleveland, San Francisco, and many other cities, the

U.S. Justice Department and federal courts have stated that the *official* practices of police departments include violating the rights of African Americans.[5] The police kill, wound, pepper spray, beat up, detain, frisk, handcuff, and use dogs against blacks in circumstances in which they do not do the same to white people. It is the moral responsibility of every American, when armed agents of the state are harming people in our names, to ask why.

The work of police is to preserve law and order, including the racial order. Hillary Clinton once asked a room full of white people to imagine how they would feel if police and judges treated them the way African Americans are treated.[6] This is not a difficult question in a country that was founded in response to an oppressive occupation by armed agents of a remote government. If the police patrolled white communities with the same violence that they patrol poor black neighborhoods, there would be a revolution. The purpose of this book is to inspire the same outrage about what the police do to African Americans, and the same revolution in response.

A chokehold is a maneuver in which a person's neck is tightly gripped in a way that restrains breathing. A person left in a chokehold for more than a few seconds can die. The former police chief of Los Angeles Daryl Gates once suggested that there is something about the anatomy of African Americans that makes them especially susceptible to serious injury from chokeholds, because their arteries do not open as fast as arteries do on "normal people."[7] The truth is any human being will suffer distress when pressure on the carotid arteries interrupts the supply of blood from the heart to the brain. Many police departments in the United States have banned chokeholds, but this does not stop some officers from using the tactic when they perceive a threat. The New York Police Department officially bans the practice, but it receives approximately two hundred complaints a year from people who say they have been placed in chokeholds.[8] The NYPD regulations did not prevent Officer Daniel Pantaleo from tackling Eric Garner and tightly squeezing his neck for approximately twenty seconds. Pantaleo had been trying to arrest Garner, a forty-three-year-old black man, for selling cigarettes on the streets of Staten Island. Garner denied he'd been breaking the law, and when Pantaleo came at him with handcuffs, Garner moved his hands away and said, "Don't touch me please." Pantaleo jumped on Garner's back, grabbed his neck, and pushed his head facedown against the pavement. Garner said "I can't breathe" eleven times, and then lost consciousness. He was transported to a local hospital, and died an hour after arriving at the hospital. The New York City Medical Examiner's office ruled that Garner's death was a homicide, caused by "compression of neck (chokehold), compression of chest and prone positioning during physical restraint by police." Officer Pantaleo was not charged with a crime and remained a sworn officer of the NYPD.[9] As far as the district attorney of Staten Island was concerned, what Officer Pantaleo did to Eric Garner is what you call police work.

The United States Supreme Court decided a case about chokeholds that tells you everything you need to know about how criminal "justice" works for African American men. In 1976, Adolph Lyons, a twenty-four-year-old black man, was pulled over by four Los Angeles Police Department officers for driving with a broken taillight. The cops exited their squad cars with their guns drawn, ordering Lyons to spread his legs and put his hands on top of his head. After Lyons was frisked, he put his hands down, causing one cop to grab Lyons's hands and slam them against his head. Lyons had been holding his keys and he complained that he was in pain. The police officer tackled Lyons and placed him in a chokehold until he blacked out. When Lyons regained consciousness, he was lying facedown on the ground, had soiled his pants, and was spitting up blood and dirt. The cops gave him a traffic citation and sent him on his way.

Lyons sued to make the LAPD stop putting people in chokeholds. He presented evidence that in recent years sixteen people — including twelve black men—had died in LAPD custody after being placed in chokeholds. In *City of Los Angeles v. Lyons*, the

U.S. Supreme Court denied his claim, holding that because Lyons could not prove that he would be subject to a chokehold in the future, he had no "personal stake in the outcome." Dissenting from the Court's opinion, Thurgood Marshall, the first African American on the Supreme Court, wrote:

> It is undisputed that chokeholds pose a high and unpredictable risk of serious injury or death. Chokeholds are intended to bring a subject under control by causing pain and rendering him unconscious. Depending on the position of the officer's arm and the force applied, the victim's voluntary or involuntary reaction, and his state of health, an officer may inadvertently crush the victim's larynx, trachea, or hyoid. The result may be death caused by either cardiac arrest or asphyxiation. An LAPD officer described the reaction of a person to being choked as "do[ing] the chicken," in reference apparently to the reactions of a chicken when its neck is wrung.[10]

A chokehold is a process of coercing submission that is self-reinforcing. A chokehold justifies additional pressure on the body because the body does not come into compliance, but the body cannot come into compliance because of the vise grip that is on it. This is the black experience in the United States. This is how the process of law and order pushes African American men into the criminal system. This is how the system is broke on purpose.

The Chokehold is a way of understanding how American inequality is imposed. It is the process by which black lives are made vulnerable to death imposed by others and death that comes from African Americans themselves. The Chokehold works through overt state violence—such as the way communities of color are policed—and slower forms of vulnerability, such as the poison water crisis in Flint, Michigan, and the gentrification, all over the country, of inner-city neighborhoods formerly occupied by poor people of color, and the way that when a black man chooses to kill somebody, nine times out of ten it is another black person.

The Chokehold does not stem from hate of African Americans. Its anti-blackness is instrumental rather than emotional. As slaves built the White House, the Chokehold builds the wealth of white elites. Discriminatory law enforcement practices such as stop and frisk, mass incarceration, and the war on drugs are key components of the political economy of the United States. After the civil rights movement of the 1960s stigmatized overt racism, the national economy, which from the founding has been premised on a racialized form of capitalism, still required black bodies to exploit. The Chokehold evolved as a "color-blind" method of keeping African Americans down, and then blaming them for their own degradation. The rap group Public Enemy said, "It takes a nation of millions to hold us back."[11] Actually all it takes is the Chokehold. It is the invisible fist of the law.

The Chokehold means that what happens in places like Ferguson, Missouri, and Baltimore, Maryland—where the police routinely harass and discriminate against African Americans—is not a flaw in the criminal justice system. Ferguson and Baltimore are examples of how the system is *supposed* to work. The problem is not bad apple cops. The problem is police work itself. American cops are the enforcers of a criminal justice regime that targets black men and sets them up to fail.

The Chokehold is how the police get away with shooting unarmed black people. Cops are rarely prosecuted because they are, literally, doing their jobs. This is why efforts to fix "problems" such as excessive force and racial profiling are doomed to fail. If it's not broke, you can't fix it. Police violence and selective enforcement are not so much flaws in American criminal justice as they are integral features of it. The Chokehold is why, legally speaking, black lives don't matter as much as white lives.

The whole world knows that the United States faces a crisis in racial justice, but the focus on police and mass incarceration is too narrow. We might be able to fix those problems the way that we "fixed" slavery and segregation, but the Chokehold's genius is its mutability. Throughout the existence of America, there have always been legal ways to keep black people down. Slavery bled into the old Jim Crow; the old Jim Crew bled into the new Jim Crow. In order to halt this wretched cycle we must not think of reform—we must think of transformation. The United States of America must be disrupted, and made anew. This book uses the experience of African American men to explain why.

As a tool of oppression, the Chokehold does not apply only to African American men. The dynamic of blaming a victim of subordination for his or her condition, and then imposing a legal and social response that enhances the subordination, is familiar to many out-groups in the United States. This book explores the Chokehold through the lens of "policing black men," but there might be any number of other lenses.

A far from exhaustive list might include:

Chokehold: national security profiling of Muslim Americans
Chokehold: surveillance of poor women receiving government benefits
Chokehold: the appropriation of Native American land
Chokehold: exploitation and deportation of undocumented Latino workers
Chokehold: police and private violence against transgender women of color
Chokehold: sex trafficking of Asian women [12]

BLACK + MALE: AN INTERSECTIONAL APPROACH

In focusing on African American men, I want to avoid a mistake that some others have made before me. To observe that the experiences of black men are determined by their race and gender does not mean that their plight is worse than that of some other groups, particularly African American women. Intersectionality is the concept, first articulated by the legal scholar Kimberlé Crenshaw, that describes how people experience subordination differently based on their multiple identities.[13] Nobody is just male, or Asian, or bisexual; people have different group identities, and all those identities are relevant with regard to their life experiences. For example, a Latina woman and a Latino man might be subject to different kinds of stereotypes based on their race, ethnicity, and gender identity.

Intersectionality is about the difference that gender makes for race, and that race makes for gender. It helps us understand the ways that racism and sexism particularly confront women of color. In the words of a seminal text in black women's studies: "All the women are white, all the blacks are men."[14] Intersectionality explains why males are frequently perceived as standard bearers for the race in a way that females are not. Things that happen to African American men are identified as "black" problems in a way that things that happen to African American women would not be. Even if some of the same things that happen to African American men happen to African American women, men are likely to receive the most attention.

At the same time, intersectionality creates a space for black male–focused analysis. Lynching, for example, was gendered as well as raced; it was not enough to hang black men from trees, but their penises had to be cut off as well. Black women also have been terrorized, rape being one obvious example, but we should remember that black male victims too have been punished for gender as well as race. Chapter 3 makes this point about stop and frisk. It is not hard to imagine that discrimination against black men sometimes might take different forms than discrimination against black women, and that the combination of race and gender discrimination might impact African American men's educational achievement, participation in the labor market, and risk of incarceration in particular ways. The problem is that black male issues are likely to be prioritized, to the extent that any racial justice interventions are prioritized. The important #SayHerName campaign has lifted up the experiences of women of color with the police. For example, after excessive force, sexual assault is the most common complaint against the police, and African American women are the most likely victims.[15] This problem has not received the attention it deserves, which is not uncommon for issues that disproportionately impact black women. At the same time, intersectionality teaches us that gender matters for black men as well, and that ignoring gender undermines the chances of making things better. The challenge for any project that focuses on African American men—whether a black male achievement program such as former president Obama's My Brother's Keeper initiative or a book such as *Chokehold*—is to highlight the particular ways in which black men are stereotyped without marginalizing the experiences of African American women in the process. I am dedicated to that process throughout these pages.

THE CHOKEHOLD AND BLACK MEN

Let's keep it real. Many people—cops, politicians, and ordinary people—see African American men as a threat. The Chokehold is the legal and social response. It contains a constellation of tools that are used to keep them down—including a range of social practices, laws, punishments, and technologies that mark every black man as a thug or potential thug. The state—especially the police—is authorized to control them by any means necessary.

One of the consequences of the Chokehold is mass incarceration, famously described by Michelle Alexander as "the New Jim Crow."[16] The Chokehold also brings us police tactics such as stop and frisk, which are designed to humiliate African American males—to bring them into submission.[17] But the Chokehold applies to all African American men, not only the brothers who are locked up or have criminal records. It is insidious enough that it clamps down on black men even when there are no cops around. The Chokehold demands a certain kind of performance from a black man every time he leaves his home. He must affirmatively demonstrate—to the police and the public at large—that he is not a threat. Most African American men follow the script. Black men who are noncompliant suffer the consequences.

If you are the parent of a black boy, one of the most important decisions you make is when you tell them about the Chokehold. You don't want to scare them, but the Chokehold is literally a matter of life and death.

The people who carry out the Chokehold include cops, judges, and politicians. But it's not just about the government. It's also about you. People of all races and ethnicities make the most consequential and the most mundane decisions based on the Chokehold. It impacts everything from the neighborhood you choose to live in and who you marry to where you look when you get on an elevator. I like hoodies but I won't wear one, and it's not mainly because of the police. It's because when I put on a hoodie everybody turns into a neighborhood watch person. When the sight of a black man makes you walk quicker or check to see if your car door is locked, you are enforcing the Chokehold.

You are not alone. As an African American man, I'm not only the target of the Chokehold. I've also been one of its perpetrators. I've done so officially—as a prosecutor who sent a lot of black men to prison. I represented the government in criminal court and defended cops who had racially profiled or used excessive force. Many of those prosecutions I now regret. I can't turn back time, but I can expose a morally bankrupt system. That's one reason I wrote this book.

But before I get too high and mighty, you should know that I've also enforced the Chokehold outside my work as a prosecutor. I am a black man who at times is afraid of other black men. And then I get mad when people act afraid of me.

Other times I have been more disgusted or angry with some of my brothers than scared. I read the news articles about "black-on-black" homicide in places like Chicago and Los Angeles. I listen to some hip-hop music that seems to celebrate thug life. And as a kid I got bullied by other black males. Sometimes I think if brothers would just do right, we would not have to worry about people being afraid of us. I have wondered if we have brought the Chokehold on ourselves.

In order for African American men to have better outcomes, they have to learn how to navigate the system. The Chokehold is "the system" for black men. It is their government, far more than the president or the mayor. Still, most people have no idea how the Chokehold works. This book will break it all down.

Maybe you are just an ordinary person who is sometimes afraid of black men. You're not a racist, but you need to know the facts. This book is going to give you the information you need, including real talk about the kinds of crimes that African American men commit and the ways that we as a society can respond.

This book is also for people who want to understand how the criminal process really works—from an expert who has been deep in the system on all sides. In my years as a prosecutor, I learned some inside information that I am now willing to share. Some of it will blow your mind, but I don't feel bad for telling tales out of school. I was on the front lines in carrying out the Chokehold. Now I want to be on the front lines in helping to crush it.

My creds to write this book don't come just from my experience as a law enforcement officer, my legal training at Harvard, or the more than twenty years I have spent researching criminal justice. I learned as much as an African American man who got arrested for a crime I did not commit—during the time that I served as a federal prosecutor. I didn't beat my case because I was innocent, even though I was. I beat my case because I knew how to work the system. In chapter 7 I share those tips. If you have caught a case, it may be information even your own lawyer has not provided you. When the law is stacked against you—and because of the Chokehold, it is—you have to do whatever you can to fight back.

The Chokehold is perfectly legal. Like all law, it promotes the interests of the rich and powerful. In any system marked by inequality, there are winners and losers. Because the Chokehold imposes racial order, who wins and who loses is based on race.

White people are the winners. What they win is not only material, like the cash money that arresting African Americans brings to cities all over the country in fines and court costs. The criminalizing of blackness also brings psychic rewards. American criminal justice enhances the property value of whiteness.

As the Chokehold subordinates black men, it improves the status of white people. It works as an enforcement mechanism for keeping the black man in his place literally as well as figuratively. Oh the places African American men don't go because of the Chokehold. It frees up urban space for coffeehouses and beer gardens.

But it's not just the five-dollar latte crowd that wins. The Chokehold is something like an employment stimulus plan for working-class white people, who don't have to compete for jobs with all the black men who are locked up, or who are underground because they have outstanding arrest warrants, or who have criminal records that make obtaining legal employment exceedingly difficult. Poor white people are simply not locked up at rates similar to African Americans. These benefits make crushing the Chokehold more difficult because if it ends, white people lose—at least in the short term. Progressives often lambast poor white people for voting for conservative Republicans like Donald Trump, suggesting that those votes are not in their best interests. But low-income white folks might have better sense than pundits give them credit for. A vote for a conservative is an investment in the property value of one's whiteness. The criminal process makes white privilege more than just a status symbol, and more than just a partial shield from the criminal process (as compared to African Americans). By reducing competition for jobs, and by generating employment in law enforcement and corrections, especially in the mainly white rural areas where prisons are often located, the Chokehold delivers cash money to many working-class white people.

The Chokehold relegates black men to an inferior status of citizenship. We might care about that as a moral issue, or as an issue of racial justice. But honestly many people will not give a damn for those reasons. African Americans have been second-class citizens since we were allowed—after the bloodiest war in U.S. history and an amendment to the Constitution—to become citizens at all.

In the standoff between African Americans and the police, U.S. presidents have sided with the cops. For the last fifty years, every man who has been elected president has taken steps during his campaign to send a message to voters that he will be tough on black men. Richard Nixon watched one of his campaign ads warning voters about urban crime and exclaimed, "This hits it right on the nose. It's all about law and order and the damn Negro–Puerto Rican groups out there." Ronald Reagan complained about criminal fraud by "strapping young bucks" who used food stamps to buy T-bone steaks. Campaigning for president in 1976, Jimmy Carter spoke out against forced integration, saying, "The government should not take as a major purpose the intrusion of alien groups into a neighborhood just to establish their intrusion." George H.W. Bush ran a television ad featuring William Horton (Bush's campaign called him "Willie" although Horton never went by that name), a black man who raped a white woman while on a furlough from prison in Massachusetts. Bush's campaign manager, Lee Atwater, said, "By the time we're finished they're going to wonder whether Willie Horton is Dukakis' running mate."

President Bill Clinton left the campaign trail to oversee the execution of Ricky Ray Rector, a black man who was so intellectually disabled that when the correctional officer came to take him to the death chamber Rector set aside the pecan pie he had ordered for his last meal because he was "saving it for later." George W. Bush, soliciting the endorsement of the Fraternal Order of Police, complained about Justice Department investigations of police departments, saying as president he would support cops "rather than constantly second guessing local law enforcement decisions." During his first presidential campaign, Barack Obama mocked "gangbangers," saying they are so lazy they ask "Why I gotta do it? Why can't Pookie do it?" During the 2008 campaign, the Supreme Court ruled that it was unconstitutional to execute people for rape—even of a child. Obama criticized the decision, indicating that he would have voted with the conservative justices Antonin Scalia and Clarence Thomas to uphold the death penalty in such cases. As a former law professor, Obama had to know that historically African American men were virtually the only people executed for rape. Donald Trump, answering a question in a debate with Hillary Clinton about what he would do to bridge the racial divide, said, "We need law and order. If we don't have it, we're not going to have a country. . . . We have a situation where we have our inner cities—African Americans, Hispanics are living in hell because it's so dangerous. You walk down the street, you get shot."

Once in office, the presidential record has been mixed. Bill Clinton endorsed a crime bill that created federal "three-strikes" laws and allocated $16 billion to build new prisons and put thousands of police officers on the street. But George W. Bush frequently spoke of the importance of showing compassion to people returning to their communities after serving time in prison. Barack Obama went further than any president before him. He was the first sitting U.S. president to visit a prison. He commuted the sentences of more than 1,300 inmates, far more than any president before him. Obama established the "President's Task Force on 21st Century Policing" and his Justice Department investigated over twenty local police departments.

But in the main, the U.S. criminal process carried on during the Obama era was as violent and harsh as ever. The policing commission's recommendations were largely ignored by the nation's 18,000 police departments. Obama's commutations were only a fraction of the people who were potentially eligible; his first pardon attorney resigned in protest because the White House did not give her the resources to properly consider all who were eligible.

But something significant did happen during Obama's time in office. A movement rose up. A movement that has the potential to transform the United States as profoundly as the abolition of slavery and the dismantling of Jim Crow. The movement for black lives ascended as a response to an endless roll of videos of police shooting African American people. The killings themselves certainly were not new, but the widespread dissemination of the images of state-sponsored violence against American people was. The Chokehold is far from the only marker of racial inequality but for African American men it is the worst. In a few years, white people will be a minority in the United States. This certainly does not mean that white racial dominance will end, but the demographic shift will make the racial hierarchy plain, and ultimately more vulnerable.

Everyone who has a stake in the future of the United States must be concerned about the Chokehold. You could say that the Chokehold threatens our democracy, or, alternatively, you could say that the Chokehold is constitutive of our democracy. Either way it is destabilizing. While politicians worry about ISIS and al-Qaeda, legal violence by our own government poses a greater threat to the future of this country—and certainly to individual black men—than illegal violence by terrorists.

The political scientist Lisa Miller has described the United States as a "failed state" for African Americans.[18] Indeed some activists involved in the movement for black lives speak of their work as creating a "Black Spring," similar to the Arab Spring movements that attempted to bring democracy to some Middle Eastern countries.[19]

We face a crucial choice. Do we allow the Chokehold to continue to strangle our democracy and risk the rebellion that always comes to police states? Or do we transform the United States of America into the true multiracial democracy that, at our best, we aspire to be? This book is about the urgency of transformation. All of the people will be free, or none of them will. "All the way down, this time."[20]

1

Constructing the Thug

American criminal justice today is premised on controlling African American men. Many other people—including African American women, immigrants, poor white people, Muslims, and Native Americans—are caught in its snares, but they are collateral damage of a process that is designed for black men. This obviously does not blunt the pain that the system has caused people other than African American men. Collateral damage is as destructive as any other kind of damage. The point is that black men are the reason why police and prosecutors have so much power in the first place.

Fear and anxiety mark our daily interactions with African American men. Many people see them as a threat. Police, lawmakers, and judges step up to make us feel safer by controlling those men by any means necessary, including by authorizing violent forms of policing and punishment, on a massive scale. The most problematic practices of American criminal justice—excessive force by police, harsh sentencing, the erosion of civil liberties, widespread government surveillance, and mass incarceration—are best understood as measures originally intended for African American men.

The Chokehold is a way of describing law and social practices designed to respond to African American men. It is a two-step process. Part one is the social and legal construction of every black man as a criminal or potential criminal. Part two is the legal and policy response to contain the threat—to put down African American men literally and figuratively. Think of these two parts as "garbage in/garbage out." The "garbage in" is anxiety about black men that we internalize. The "garbage out" is law and policy based on this anxiety, which positions African American men as public enemy number one.

Americans of all races and genders are complicit in the Chokehold. Indeed African American men ourselves perpetrate the Chokehold even as we are its victims. Sometimes we are scared of each other, and other times we exploit the fear that people have of us. Some black men do things—such as commit violent crimes—that reinforce the stereotypes. Some cultural performances associated with black men—such as hip-hop music—also feed the fear of them. So does the fact that many of the best-known African Americans are professional athletes—men celebrated for their big black bodies. It is not so much that African American men endorse the thug construction as, accepting reality, we try to make it work for us. There are benefits, in a patriarchal society, to being perceived as hyper-masculine. But in the end, these benefits, for example "street cred" and a "bad boy" kind of sex appeal, are sorry compensation for the Chokehold's crippling burden.

This chapter explains the first step of the Chokehold—the construction of the thug, based on the presumption that every African American man is a criminal. It is important to remember that this is a rebuttable presumption: African American men can do things to communicate that we are not dangerous. It would not be an understatement to say that the vast majority of black men engage in those kinds of performances every time we step out of the house. It's also true that many people can and do treat individual African American men with respect and kindness. The Chokehold means, however, that conjuring up a criminal is part of how many Americans process encountering a black man. It's an instant reaction, a habit of mind, but one with tragic consequences.

WHAT WE SEE WHEN WE LOOK AT BLACK MEN

Some amazing new scientific research provides insight into how people perceive African American men. When people see black men they don't know, they have a physical response that is different from their response to other people. Their blood pressure goes up and they sweat more.[1] When a white person sees an unfamiliar black male face, the amygdala, the part of the brain that processes fear, activates.[2] In one experiment, white people were shown photos of either a black, white, or Latino man. They were then directed to look at a Chinese alphabet character, like 屁, which would have been unfamiliar to them, and asked what they thought about it.[3] People who had just seen a photo of a black male described the Chinese character in more negative terms than people who looked at photos of a white or Latino man. In computer exercises, people link the faces of white men with nice words like joy, love, and peace. They associate black male faces with bad words like nasty, evil, and awful.[4] If asked to pair the black male faces with the nice words, it takes them longer. In another experiment, it took drivers twice as long to stop at a crosswalk for a black man as for a white man.[5] Stanford researchers found that teachers favored harsher punishment when reviewing files for students with stereotypically black names like "Deshawn" or "Darnell" than for students with whiter-sounding names like "Jake" or "Greg."[6]

These are carefully controlled studies done by scholars trained in research. But ordinary African American men report the same kinds of experiences. The writer John Edgar Wideman wrote an op-ed in the New York Times about an informal experiment he conducted for four years. It was based on his experience taking Amtrak twice a week between Providence, Rhode Island, and New York City. On Amtrak you can sit wherever there is an open seat. Wideman noted, "Almost invariably, after I have hustled aboard early and occupied one half of a vacant double seat in the usually crowded quiet car, the empty place next to me will remain empty for the entire trip."[7] The sports journalist J.J. Adande has described a similar effect on Southwest Airlines, which also has open seating. On planes that have three-seat configurations, if black men are in the window and aisle seats, and the middle seat is vacant, no white person will sit there, unless it is the only vacant seat on the plane. Adande says African American men love Southwest because they get extra legroom.[8]

It's true that there are some benefits to the whole "menace to society" thing. I often take Amtrak between Washington, D.C., and New York City. The train cars have two seats on each side of the aisle. I like it when people don't sit next to me because I prefer having both seats to myself. When Wideman's op-ed was published, it received a lot of attention in the media, and for the next month or so, white folks on the train made a beeline to sit next to me. One time there were rows of empty seats and this white dude in a suit plopped down right next to me. Big smile on his face. I appreciated the gesture but I wanted to move to another row.

Believe it or not, that white guy provides some limited hope that we can overcome the Chokehold. Before he read the *Times* article, he probably didn't realize that he was avoiding sitting next to African American men. When he became aware of his discrimination, he checked it. He made an effort to remedy it. Like the elders say, "When you know better, you do better."

People can actually unlearn bias the same way. One experiment had people look on a computer at a photo of a black person's face that was paired with a stereotypical image like a gun or a watermelon. They had to click "no" every time they saw an image like that. After forty-five minutes of doing so, they registered less prejudice against African Americans.[9] Other studies have demonstrated that if white people are exposed to photos or stories about successful African Americans, it reduces their bias.[10]

My optimism is limited, however, because it didn't cost that white man anything to sit next to me on the train. I'm cute, for an old guy, and I smell pretty good. Remedying discrimination in criminal justice, however, might actually require white people to give up some benefits. Some folks may not be willing to bear those costs. I'll discuss this more in the next chapter. For now, let's ask a more basic question.

ARE BLACK MEN ACTUALLY DANGEROUS?

The most common explanation for fear of African American men is that they commit more crime. For young black men, this stereotype is so deeply entrenched that unless they affirmatively demonstrate they are not criminals, people assume that they are. That's why "Ban the Box" (BTB) policies, often touted as reforms designed to help formerly incarcerated people, have had the perverse consequence of hurting black men. BTB policies prohibit employers from conducting criminal background checks until late in the application process. The hope was this would give people coming home from prison a better chance at landing an interview, but studies have shown that BTB policies have actually done more harm than good for black men. When employers don't have actual information about whether people have a criminal background, they tend to assume that young African American men do.[11] One estimate found that BTB policies reduced employment for young black men without a high school diploma or GED by 15 percent.[12] Another study from New York and New Jersey found that before BTB, white applicants were called back slightly more often than black applicants. After BTB, however, the gap became six times larger.[13]

So clearly there is a pervasive stereotype that African American men are prone to crime. But stereotypes don't come out of nowhere. Why do so many people think this about black men? Is it based on data about who commits crime?

As Table 1 demonstrates, African Americans commit more than their share of violent offenses (and about 90 percent of all violent offenders are male).[14] Chapter 4 is about why this is,

**TABLE 1: VICTIMS AND OFFENDERS IN THE 75 LARGEST
COUNTIES, BY DEMOGRAPHIC GROUP, 1980–2008**

	Percent of—			Rate per 100,000	
	Victims	Offenders	Population	Victims	Offenders
Total	100%	100%	100%	7.4	8.3
Race					
White	50.30%	45.30%	82.90%	4.5	4.5
Black	47.4	52.5	12.6	27.8	34.4
Other*	2.3	2.2	4.4	3.8	4.1

*Other race includes American Indians, Native Alaskans, Native Hawaiians, and other Pacific Islanders.

In America's seventy-five largest counties, a plurality of people charged with violent crimes are black.

Note: Latinos were not broken out as a separate group in the data on which this table is based.

Source: Alexa Cooper and Erica L. Smith, United States Department of Justice, Bureau of Justice Statistics, "Homicide Trends in the United States, 1980–2008," November 2011, 3, https://www.bjs.gov/content/pub/pdf/htus8008.pdf.

and how we as a society should respond. For now, let's focus on whether statistics like this justify the anxiety about black men and the harsh police response that follows. How should you use the information that black men are responsible for a larger proportion of certain kinds of crimes than other men? How should knowing that impact the way you live your life?

Here's one way: If the only thing you know about someone is that he is black and male, and the only thing you care about is avoiding being the victim of a crime, then you should be wary of African American men. If one is walking behind you, you should cross to the other side of the street. If you are in an elevator with one, you should clutch your pearls. If you are a police officer, when you approach a car to give an African American man a ticket for speeding, you should put your hand on your gun. Shoot him if he seems like he might be a threat. If you are a Supreme Court justice, you should provide the police with the power to stop black men at will.

This is, in fact, the African American male experience. Almost everywhere we go we have to engage in some performance that pushes back against the presumption that we are violent criminals. The truth is that the vast majority of black men have never committed a violent crime. It's a stereotype that, like other stereotypes, can be supported by a selective view of the evidence.

My sister was a flight attendant for an airline that specialized in international charter flights—taking tourists or soldiers from one country to another country. She says her colleagues made group-based assumptions about different ethnicities and religions all the time.

People on flights from Ireland were strictly limited to two drinks. When there were a lot of French passengers, the flight attendants put cans of deodorant in the bathroom. On flights to Israel they said no to everyone who wanted the full can of soda because if you gave it to one, you would have to give it to everyone. I still don't get what would be so bad about that, but apparently it is absolute flight attendant hell.

Sociologists explain that stereotypes are based on selective perceptions that become self-reinforcing.[15] What this means is that even if most Irish people remained sober, and most French people did not have body odor, the people who don't conform to the stereotype would not have registered with my sister's crew. At the same time, the Irish lush and the French guy with the smelly underarms make an impact, which leads to an overgeneralization.

Stereotypes have even more salience when we have less exposure to the group, and when the stereotypes implicate our personal safety and well-being. Here is an amazing fact that goes a long way toward explaining the construction of the thug: Most white people have only one black friend.[16] If the primary way you get to know African American men is the local evening news, I don't blame you for being scared of us. Several studies have demonstrated that news programs overrepresent African American men as criminals and white people as victims.[17] This is also true on other television programs.[18] So it's no wonder that, in an extensive survey by the

Associated Press, 66 percent of white people said that the word "violent" was a good description of most blacks.[19]

But don't the crime statistics prove that black men really are violent? Some people say that being suspicious of African American men is "rational discrimination." Here are two reasons why they are wrong. First, the vast majority of African American men have never been convicted of a violent crime. Second, while it is true that black men do disproportionately commit some violent crimes, they are only about 6.5 percent of the population. White men commit violent crimes, as well, and they are 31 percent of the population.[20] Even though a larger proportion of black men commit violent crimes, there are so many more white men in the population that white male violence is a bigger problem. In fact, white men commit the majority of violent crime in the United States.[21] In any event, the turn to metrics about victimization to explain our treatment of African American men seems dubious when we consider how we employ statistics in other areas of our lives, including our chances of being victimized by a criminal.

A white person's lifetime chance of being the victim of homicide, assault, or robbery by a black person: 1 in 480.[22]

A black person's lifetime chance of being the victim of homicide, assault, or robbery by a black person: 1 in 115.[23]

A woman's lifetime chance of being raped by a man: 1 in 5.[24]

IRRATIONAL DISCRIMINATION

The bottom line is that it is not crazy or racist for a person to think she is more likely to be the victim of a street crime perpetrated by an African American man than a man of another race. It is just that it is unlikely that either event will occur. The person who is at most risk from a black man is another black man, and even this risk is relatively low. For the most serious crimes—homicide and rape—whites are much more likely to be victimized by white people they know than by black strangers.

Keep two thoughts in mind. First, a very small group of black men is responsible for a significant amount of street crime. Their most likely victims are other African American men. Second, if you see a black man behind you in the street, your rational, evidence-based assumption should be that he presents no threat. He is literally hundreds of times more likely to be on his way to work, school, or the movies than he is to rob, rape, or murder you.

In the end, it is not smart to treat African American men differently because you think one of us is going to harm you. It's true that people act irrationally in many areas of life. We buy lottery tickets in spite of prohibitive mathematical odds.[25] We wear lucky shirts on game day even though it has no effect on whether our favorite team wins or loses. We buy things that we don't need because we think we're getting a good deal.[26] But this kind of response to black men has wretched consequences for them and for our democracy.

In any event, when people choose not to sit next to an African American man on a train or airplane, it is probably not because they think they are going to be robbed or raped. The stigmatization of black men cannot be explained simply as fear of crime.

THE APE THESIS

In fact the anxiety about African American men has origins more sinister than data about victimization. A surprisingly large number of Americans don't actually think of blacks as human beings. They think of us as apes, to be exact. Psychologists call this "the dehumanization thesis."

Stanford psychologist Jennifer Eberhardt received a MacArthur genius award for her groundbreaking work in this area. She, along with several other researchers, has consistently found that people unconsciously associate blacks with apes. In one experiment subjects were quicker to recognize an ape if they had been exposed to a black face than a white face. In another experiment people were asked to categorize names as stereotypically black or white, and to categorize species of animals as either "great apes" or "big cats."

People were faster to recognize words like "monkey," "gorilla," and "chimpanzee" as "great apes" if the word were paired with a stereotypically black name. It took them longer to categorize if black names appeared with "big cat" words like "lion," "tiger," or "cheetah."[27]

Phillip Atiba Goff, a professor at John Jay College of Criminal Justice, looked at media coverage of capital cases in a Philadelphia newspaper from 1977 to 1999. He found that phrases like "urban jungle" or "aping the suspect's behavior" were more likely to be used for African American than white defendants, and that blacks who were described as apelike were more likely to be executed. In another study, Goff primed subjects to think about apes and then showed them videos of police using force against blacks and whites. People exposed to images of apes were more likely to think the police were justified in using force against blacks, but not whites.

Sometimes the association between black men and primates is explicit. Los Angeles police officers referred to cases of "black-on-black" crime as "N.H.I."—no human involved.[28] Along the same lines, Officer Darren Wilson, the police officer who killed Michael Brown in Ferguson, Missouri, described Brown in non-human terms. Testifying before the grand jury, Wilson called Brown "it," saying, "The only way I can describe it, it looks like a demon, that's how angry he looked." Of his physical altercation with Brown, Wilson said, "I felt like a five-year-old holding on to Hulk Hogan."[29] Officer Wilson is six foot four, which was also the height of Michael Brown. Though Brown weighed eighty pounds more than Wilson, the police officer's description of himself as "like a five-year-old" seems hyperbolic. It conveys Wilson's perception of Brown as having brute-like strength.

This imagery is even more pronounced when Wilson described firing his gun at Brown. He told the grand jury, "At this point it looked like he was almost *bulking up to run through the shots*, like it was making him mad that I'm shooting at him. And the face that he had was looking through me, like I wasn't even there, I wasn't even anything in his way."

Even the most respected or popular African Americans are depicted as apelike. Former president Obama and first lady Michelle Obama have frequently been caricatured as apes. The basketball

FIGURE 1: LEBRON JAMES DEPICTED BY *VOGUE* MAGAZINE

The image of professional basketball player LeBron James clutching the model Gisele Bündchen invites comparison to King Kong.

Source: Vogue magazine.

player LeBron James appeared on the cover of *Vogue* magazine clutching a blonde white model in a manner that invited comparison to King Kong, as shown in Figure 1.

The Chokehold's construction of the black man as a thug didn't come out of nowhere. The association of African American men with criminality was calculated as a way to preserve white privilege after slavery ended. In *The Condemnation of Blackness: Race, Crime, and the Making of Modern Urban America*, the Harvard historian Khalil Gibran Muhammad examined the anxiety that many white people felt after emancipation about how to handle the "Negro problem." New social scientist "experts" about race used data about arrest rates to make the case that the recently freed blacks were, essentially, a criminal class. Other groups, including Irish and Italian immigrants, also had high levels of arrests but, different from African Americans, this was seen as a sign of poverty. The response was to deliver social services to the white ethnic groups to lift them from poverty. African Americans, on the other hand, were thought to be inherently inferior, with the criminal process and private violence being the necessary ways to regulate them.[30] The twisted logic was, in the words of the historian David Levering Lewis, "whites commit crimes, but black males are criminals."[31]

DO BLACK MEN CHOKEHOLD EACH OTHER?

A great sketch by the comics Key and Peele demonstrates how insidious the Chokehold is. Two black men, strangers to each other, are on a corner, waiting for a streetlight to change. Each is talking on his cell phone, aware that the other man is listening to him. Key and Peele stare each other down and, as they talk on the phone, make their voices deeper and use hip-hop slang, which they hadn't been doing before. Key had been surprising his wife with theater tickets for her birthday "because you're my wife and I love you." He'd said there were no tickets available in the orchestra section but they could sit in the dress circle. When Peele walks up, Key's tone abruptly changes and he says to his wife, "All the seats are good, and I'm going to pick your ass up at 6:30." Peele says to his friend on the phone, "Dog, I'm five minutes away." When the light changes, Peele walks quickly away. When he is out of earshot of Key, Peele says to his friend on the phone, "Oh my God, I almost totally just got mugged right now."

Recall the studies of bias that I mentioned earlier, in which people associate negative words with blacks and positive words with whites. Black people do that too—not to the same extent as whites, but a large number of African Americans still unconsciously believe that white people are in some fundamental sense better than black people. On the one hand, African American men should know better. On the other hand, we actually have more cause to be afraid because we are our most likely victims. This double consciousness may explain a weird effect in polls of black men. We tend to think highly of ourselves as individuals but negatively of ourselves as a group.[32] Who would you expect to be more critical of African American men—white men or African American men? The answer will be surprising to many. We black men can be our biggest haters. Here are the results of a survey of black and white men, conducted by the Opportunity Agenda, a public interest research organization.[33]

Black men put too little emphasis on:

- Education—white men (56 percent); black men (69 percent)
- Their health—white men (43 percent); black men (66 percent)
- Their families—white men (37 percent); black men (48 percent)
- Getting ahead at work—white men (29 percent); black men (43 percent)

Black men put too much emphasis on:

- Maintaining a tough image—white men (43 percent); black men (41 percent)
- Sex—white men (34 percent); black men (54 percent)
- Sports—white men (47 percent); black men (49 percent)

At the same time, African American men were more optimistic about the future than white men.[34]

- Optimistic about future—white men (72 percent); black men (85 percent)
- My child's standard of living will be better than mine—white men (36 percent); black men (60 percent)

We have a perfect storm. The Chokehold constructs African American men as thugs, and, in some ways, African American men concur—except not as applied to our individual selves. And then we pay for the price for our concurrence. I know because it happened to me. All of it.

BLACK-ON-BLACK-ON-BLACK: DIDDY AND ME

Sean "P Diddy" Combs, the hip-hop mogul, is among several prominent African American men who have castigated other black men for being prone to violence. After a New York rapper named Lionel "Chinx Drugz" Pickens was killed in a drive-by shooting, Combs posted this on Instagram:

> We are committing genocide on ourselves. We are always looking for scapegoats. We as a people hurt ourselves more than anyone has ever hurt us. That makes no sense. We as a people including myself have to take accountability and do whatever we can do individually or together to stop the madness and realize that we are kings and queens and must love ourselves and each other.

Two months after making this statement, Combs was arrested for three counts of assault with a deadly weapon, one count of making terrorist threats, and one count of battery.[35] All of this was based on an altercation between Diddy and the coach of his son's football team. The "deadly weapon" was a kettlebell, since the incident occurred in a gym. Nobody was injured, and the coach, a white guy, was not charged. It's unlikely that a white dad, angry that the coach was not treating his son right, would pick up those serious felony charges for what was essentially a schoolyard fight. Many studies have shown that black men receive harsher charges, especially when the victim is white.[36] I wonder if Diddy would consider it "looking for scapegoats" to acknowledge that he probably got treated worse by the prosecutor because he is black. And he is a multimillionaire celebrity. Imagine what it's like for the average brother. Here's the difference: Combs retained a high-priced lawyer and the charges were dropped.

Here's the way it would work for a regular brother. I know because throwing the book at regular brothers used to be my nine-to-five job. Let's say the brother, like Diddy, had a felony conviction record at the time he picked up these new charges. I, the prosecutor, give his defense attorney this little speech:

> Your client is staring at five felony charges. Here is what we are going to do. Dude will plead guilty to one count of assault with a deadly weapon and one count of making terrorist threats, and then I'll drop the other charges. I'll recommend the judge lock him up for a year. If your client doesn't take the deal, we're going to trial. If he is found guilty, and he will be, I am going to ask the judge to give him ten years.

What would you do? Exactly. That's why more than 95 percent of prosecutions end up with plea bargains, not trials. So then the regular brother does his year and comes home. You see him hanging out on the corner in the middle of the day and you shake your head and ask, why doesn't he at least get a job at McDonald's?

Ask yourself this instead: If you are the manager at McDonald's are you really going to take a chance on a dude with a resume that includes prison time for assault with a deadly weapon and making terrorist threats?

Even if McDonald's hires people with criminal records, there is a lot of competition for the job. Each year there are somewhere around 100,000 job openings in the fast food industry. And every year about 600,000 people come home from prison.[37] This guy's life is basically screwed — over a stupid fight with his kid's coach.

That's some of the work I did as a prosecutor, and I freakin' loved it. Maybe I saw my work as vindication against the black boys who had bullied me when I was a kid. Maybe I liked holding myself out to the world as one of the good black guys. Every time I stepped into court and sat at the prosecutor's table I sent the message that not every African American man was like the bad dude I was prosecuting. My work was the lawyer's version of Chris Rock's old joke about "black people versus niggas."

But it turned out that Diddy isn't the only brother whose critique of other black men bounced right back in his face. During my time as a prosecutor in D.C., all of my defendants were African American or Latino. If you were to go to criminal court in D.C. you would think that white people, who make up almost half the city, don't commit any crimes. The next chapter explains how the U.S. Supreme Court makes that fantasy possible, by giving police what amount to super powers to focus on African American men.

There were lots of cases in which defendants claimed that the police lied. As a prosecutor, I would have a great time cross-examining the perp, probing him on why he thought the police had nothing better to do than make up stories about him. I'd point to the police officer on the stand; I always made sure my cops wore their uniforms to court and looked buttoned down and professional, which the defendants rarely did. Then I would ask the jurors who they believed: the impressive public servant or the low-life who'd been busted for selling crack. I won almost all my cases.

Then I got arrested for a crime I did not commit. And when

my trial came, the cop who locked me up got on the stand and lied his ass off. But he picked the wrong black man to do that to. While I didn't have P Diddy's fame and fortune, I had enough resources to hire the best lawyer in the city to defend me. In her cross-examination, my defense attorney destroyed the mendacious cop, and the jurors found me not guilty after deliberating for less than ten minutes.

But after that experience I didn't want to be a prosecutor any more. I don't think every cop lies in court but I know for sure that one did. I've said that the whole experience made a man out of me. A black man. After that I wanted my life's work to be something other than putting other black men in jail. I understand how seductive it is for an African American man to want to disassociate himself from the group. In many ways black men have a bad reputation, and it's easier to demonstrate you're different than that the group's bad reputation is undeserved. But as both Diddy and I found out, the Chokehold does not distinguish between its African American men as carefully as we did. Every black man is suspect.

WHY BLACK MEN SHOULD PREFER WHITE COPS

The low group esteem of African American men has especially troubling ramifications when it comes to the police. Although much attention has been focused on white police officers who shoot unarmed African Americans, studies have revealed that a black cop is more likely to shoot a black person than a white cop is.

ProPublica, the public interest news organization, looked at federal data on fatal police shootings from 2010 to 2012.[38] Seventy-eight percent of the people African American officers shot were black, compared to 46 percent of the people killed by white officers.[39]

A U.S. Justice Department report confirms that African American men are more likely to be killed by black than white cops.

One study, done in 1998, found that the black-officer-kills-black-suspect rate was 32 per 100,000 black officers and the white-officer-kills-black-suspect rate was 14 per 100,000 white officers.[40] An officer of the same race as the suspect committed some 65 percent of the justifiable homicides.[41]

There isn't enough data in these reports to know whether black cops have higher kill rates with black suspects because African American cops are quicker on the draw or, alternatively, because black officers are deployed in areas where they have fewer interactions with white suspects. It's also important to note that because there are many more white officers than black ones, white cops still kill more African Americans overall than black cops do.

But another investigation by the U.S. Department of Justice of the Philadelphia Police Department raises serious concerns about police officers of color. Among other things, the Justice Department investigated "threat-perception failure," which means that the officer mistakenly believed that an unarmed suspect had a weapon.[42] The threat-perception failure for white officers and black suspects was 6.8 percent. For black officers and black suspects, the threat-perception failure rate was 11.4 percent. For Hispanic officers and black suspects, the threat-perception failure rate was 16.7 percent. Hispanic officers were most likely to mistakenly think a black suspect was armed, followed by African American officers. White officers were actually the least likely to shoot an unarmed black person. This data may not come as a surprise to many African American men. Hip-hop artists have expressed strong critiques of black police officers. In its notorious song "Fuck tha Police" the group NWA describes black officers as being tougher on black men to "show off for the white cop."

The fact that black men absorb stereotypes about other black men does not mean the stereotypes are accurate. It mainly means that African American men consume the same media and are subject to the same cultural cues as everybody else.

WAIT A MINUTE. BLACK MEN ARE
THE STARS OF POP CULTURE

Some of the most popular people in the United States are African American men.

In addition to being disproportionately arrested and incarcerated, black men have an outsize influence on American culture. Black men, about 6.5 percent of the population, are 12 percent of the people with the most Twitter followers and 14 percent of those with the most Facebook likes.

The Most Popular People in America in 2015
By Twitter followers (in the top 100) [43]
3. Barack Obama
25. Drake
28. Lil Wayne
29. LeBron James
36. Kevin Hart
39. Wiz Khalifa
45. Neymar Jr.
70. Chris Brown
74. Kanye West
84. Will.I.Am
90. Snoop Dogg
94. Ronaldinho Gaucho

By Facebook likes (in the top 100) [44]
13. Michael Jackson
14. Will Smith
15. Bob Marley
38. Neymar Jr.
41. Akon
44. Lil Wayne
46. Dwayne Johnson

52. Usher
59. Barack Obama
70. Chris Brown
75. Curtis Jackson (50 Cent)
76. Wiz Khalifa
87. Snoop Dogg
92. Drake

With the exception of Barack Obama, all of these men are enter-
tainers or athletes. It should not slight their considerable achieve-
ments, talent, and hard work to observe that the Chokehold might
actually enhance their appeal. Athletes like LeBron James and the
soccer players Neymar Jr. and Ronaldinho Gaucho are celebrated
for their physicality. Hip-hop artists like Lil Wayne, 50 Cent, and
Chris Brown all have had well-known run-ins with the law, which
seems to have made them even more popular.

Bad guys are sexy. Americans have always had a thing for the
outlaw. The Chokehold concedes some traditional attributes of
masculinity to African American men. Black men are allowed ath-
letic prowess and virility. In our culture, violence is gendered—to
the extent that black men are perceived as more violent, that also
makes them more male.[45]

But, at the same time, race discrimination prevents many African American men from serving the traditional male role as family provider. They, along with black women, encounter rank bias
in the economic marketplace. Black men are more likely to be
unemployed than black women, or white men or women. In that
way, they are not allowed to be as masculine as white men.

One response is to blame African American women. Some
people have suggested that they de-masculinize black men. This
bizarre idea became the basis of official government policy after
publication of the Moynihan Report in 1965. This influential
government study, which played a huge role in shaping urban
policy, criticized the black family as "matriarchal" in ways that
undermine black progress. Senator Moynihan made the case for

African American patriarchy with a graphic image: "The very essence of the male animal from the bantam rooster to the four-star general is to strut."

Fifty years later, African American men are now allowed to strut—but not in the way that Moynihan meant. In pop culture, black men strut through scoring touchdowns, boasting about guns and sex in rap music, and romancing the Kardashian women. But they do not, the public imaginary goes, strut by taking care of their children. Indeed, the black family has gotten more matriarchal since the Moynihan Report was written. In 1965, about 25 percent of black children grew up in homes without their father. Now the number is close to 70 percent.

I do not endorse the Moynihan's Report analysis, which is sexist and ahistorical. I'll have more to say about it later, when we think about government programs, such as President Obama's My Brother's Keeper initiative, designed to "fix" African American men, that is, repair their masculinity. The Moynihan Report does, however, describe an influential cultural construct of masculinity, and one that most black men fail to meet.

The point here is that white supremacy's insult to masculinity is raced in particular ways. Asian American men provide an interesting counterpoint to African American men. By many indicia of achievement, they not only outperform black men, but they also outperform white men. They have higher employment rates and earn more money. But Asian American men are frequently stereotyped as effete, nerdy, and sexually deficient. Thus they also don't get to be masculine, but for different reasons than African American men.

So yes, black men have a huge impact on pop culture. The nature of the influence, however, reinforces the Chokehold more than it negates it. There is the potential, however, for this power to be deployed in a more productive way. In the final chapter, I will propose ways that African American men might use their prominence in entertainment and athletics to help crush the Chokehold.

HIP-HOP'S THUG LOVE:
STEREOTYPE VULNERABILITY?

There's a perception that hip-hop culture, closely associated with young black men, glorifies crime and violence. Some of it certainly does, whether it's the gangsta rap that was popular in the 1990s or contemporary artists such as Rick Ross, who boasts about his fictional criminal past. Ironically, before he became a rap star, Ross was actually a prison guard.

Sometimes the artists say that when they rap about violence they are just reflecting their own experience. Some hip-hop stars have been victims, and others have been perpetrators.

The best-selling artist Drake contests the authenticity of some of those claims. In his autobiographical song "You and the 6," Drake says, "I used to get teased for being black and now I'm here and I'm not black enough/cause I'm not acting tough or making up stories about where I'm from."

Jay-Z's theory is that some artists focus on guns, violence, and lawbreaking because that's what sells. In "Moment of Clarity" he regrets that he doesn't make songs like "conscious" artists Talib Kweli and Common but says, in his own defense:

> I dumb down for my audience
> And double my dollars
> They criticize me for it
> Yet they all yell "Holla"
> If skills sold
> Truth be told
> I'd probably be
> Lyrically
> Talib Kweli
> Truthfully
> I wanna rhyme like Common Sense
> (But I did five Mil)
> I ain't been rhyming like Common since

Most hip-hop songs are about the same subjects as other pop music—partying and having fun, followed by romantic or sexual relationships. By my reckoning, however, the third most common subject of hip-hop music is issues relating to criminal justice. Much of this music is extraordinarily insightful—ground level reporting about the effects of crime and punishment from "the Black CNN."[46] But some hip-hop music presents an almost gleeful version of gun violence and retaliatory killings. It is true that the same can be said of the films of Quentin Tarantino or the novels of Cormac McCarthy.[47] But those artists are not burdened with the obligation of representing their race, as black people in public spaces are expected to do.

As we have seen, the stereotype that African American men are violent and lawbreaking existed long before 1986, when Ice-T made "6 in the Morning," considered to be the first gangsta rap song. If no rapper ever spit another lyric about drugs, gangs, or guns, African American men would still be stigmatized as criminals. Still, if image matters, or what the Harvard law professor Randall Kennedy calls "racial reputation," some hip-hop artists do not help the cause. This is mainly because of the audience for these hyper-violent images of African American men. Here is a revealing statistic: 70 percent of the people who buy hip-hop music are white.[48] For these consumers, hip-hop artists bragging about busting caps are performing a twenty-first-century coon show.

That fact hit home to me one evening in 2008 when I attended a concert with a superstar double bill: the best-selling artists Eminem and Jay-Z. It was the first hip-hop concert ever at Yankee Stadium, and Kanye West, Drake, and Rihanna all made cameo appearances. My seat was in the bleachers, and I was literally surrounded by white people, mainly young white men. I was the only African American on my row or the row in front of me, although there were other blacks within sight. There were also many Latinos and Asian Americans in the audience.

Eminem opened and did a great set, but it was clear that most people, like me, were there mainly to see Jay-Z. Indeed, after

Eminem had been on stage for a while, the audience started chanting, "Hova, Hova, Hova." Hova is one of Jay-Z's nicknames.

When Jay-Z finally appeared, the audience stood up and remained standing for his entire performance. Most people seemed to know all the words to every song.

Then came the familiar hook to a song called "Jigga My Nigga." Jigga is another of Jay-Z's nicknames. In the refrain, Jay-Z asks "what's my mothafuckin name?" and the response is "Jigga." Then Jay-Z asks "and who am I rolling with huh?" and the response is "my niggaz." Then there is an interlude in which the chorus repeats, over and over in a singsong fashion, "Jigga you're my nigga."

I stopped listening to Jay-Z and started watching the people in the rows around me. I thought, *I know these white boys are not going to start shouting "nigga" right in front of me.* And then I wondered what I would do if they did. There were too many of them for me to start ass kicking, which would have been my first inclination. The best that I could think to do was to record them. I took my phone out like a gun.

Several of the white folks sitting around me suddenly seemed to notice me as well. What happened next is that the white folks around me shouted "Jigga, you're my . . ." and then they stopped. Jay-Z continued, very loudly, "nigga," and then the audience members would pick up the chorus again with "Jigga, you're my . . ." I observed the whole thing with a stern expression on my face. In this fashion, fifty thousand mainly white people at Yankee Stadium and I worked our way through "Jigga My Nigga."

I know they wanted to say it. I know they felt like they had permission from Jay-Z to say it. That they did not say it, in front of me, was probably due to some combination of courtesy, political correctness, and a quite reasonable fear of winding up on YouTube saying the "n" word for the whole world to see.

I love rap music, but some of it borders on minstrelsy. Some people have always been entertained by hyper-violent and hyper-sexual depictions of black people. Some hip-hop artists literally play into the stereotypes. They don't only give white people permission to say "nigga"; they also give them permission to be amused by images of black men as gun-toting thugs. If, as this chapter demonstrates, African American men are perceived as criminals, some hip-hop music provides the soundtrack to this warped racial fantasy.

But, at the same time, the negative images in hip-hop are not the cause of the Chokehold. The racial reputation of African Americans is largely outside of their control. Black men were constructed as criminals decades before gangsta rap, and they have retained that construct in the many years since gangsta rap faded from popularity. I'm not saying that music that condones violence is constructive, any more than African American teenagers wearing pants that sag off their behinds, or black men calling each other "nigga" help the cause. I'll have more to say about those kinds of black male cultural performances in chapter 4. My point here is only that these practices are more a *response* to the Chokehold than the cause of it.

I'm also not trying to get on a high horse. Maybe you have seen me in my car, on a beautiful summer day, radio turned up too loud, bass thumping. I'm spitting the lyrics to "Blowin' Money Fast," Rick Ross's tribute to two big-time cocaine dealers. It's a bombastic anthem, and rapping along to it makes me feel rebellious and badass. There's a reason that catchy refrains are called "hooks." The most seductive of those songs—even with objectionable lyrics—create an emotional release that bypasses the ego and goes directly to the id. But I understand the disapproving stares, which most often come from other African Americans. Grown-ass man like me should know better. Indeed.

WHAT IT FEELS LIKE TO BE SCARY

Y'all gone make me lose my mind.

—DMX, "Party Up"[49]

It's okay sometimes. I have yet to meet the white dude whose ass I didn't think I could kick. Fortunately, the proposition has not been tested. I think I can fight because I'm black. I know that's silly. My friends say that being black hasn't improved my dancing any. Still, if the fear factor gives a middle-aged professor like me some street cred and some cool, I can make it work.

Most of the time, however, people being afraid of you is aggravating, embarrassing, and dispiriting. You take steps to allay the fear. You look down on the elevator. You wear your college T-shirt, and conspicuously display your work ID. You love the Dodge Charger, but if you buy the Mini Cooper you won't get pulled over as much.

You try not to care. But it comes to feel like you are apologizing for your existence. It eats you up inside because it is relentless. Every time you leave your home, you are the star of a bizarre security theater.

Still I want to suggest, strange as it may seem, that there is a joy in this identity as well. African American men invented cool. The swag in Barack Obama's walk, the muted ache in Coltrane's saxophone, the half smile/half smirk on LeBron's face when he dunks the ball, the wordplay tossed from W.E.B. DuBois to Langston Hughes to James Baldwin to Martin Luther King to Malcolm X to Ta-Nehisi Coates to Kendrick Lamar—all of that binds us together. We see each other. That our gaze is often critical does not mean that it is not loving. The word we call each other, "brothers," was never meant to imply an uncomplicated relationship. We are brothers born to a hostile world that mainly blames us for the hostility. We have to hold each other up to survive, and, imperfectly, that is what most of us try to do.

THE CHOKEHOLD CRADLE TO GRAVE

The Chokehold starts really young.

There is an urban myth that the criminal justice system uses the reading scores of black boys in the third grade to project the need for prison beds when those boys become young men. This is not true, in part because there is not one "criminal justice system." Instead we have several different systems. The participants in these systems include police, prosecutors, judges, lawmakers, and jailers. There is not much coordination between these different actors. So, for example, the people who make criminal laws and the people who enforce those laws don't talk to the people who run the prisons. That is one reason why many prisons are overcrowded.

Still the urban myth contains the essence of truth. Black boys are viewed as more threatening pretty much from the time we start walking. About half the children suspended from preschool are black, even though they are only about 18 percent of kids enrolled in preschool. We're talking about four-year-olds.

African American boys are perceived to be older than they actually are. The psychologist Phillip Attiba Goff showed several people, including police officers, photos of African American, Latino, and white boys and asked them to guess how old the children were. The black boys were estimated to be more than four years older than they actually were.[50] Tamir Rice was twelve years old, and playing with a toy gun in a Cleveland public park, when a police car rolled up, Officer Timothy Loehmann jumped out, and, two seconds later, he shot Tamir dead. To state the obvious, this was extraordinarily bad policing. Every cop learns in the police academy that if you think someone has a gun, you take cover and try to communicate with the suspect. You don't unnecessarily expose yourself and then use that as an excuse to kill the suspect, which is what Officer Loehmann did.

Goff's research suggests that another problem is that the cop may not have seen a twelve-year-old boy when he looked at Tamir. If Officer Loehmann is like many other white folks, he would have perceived a sixteen-year-old teenager, and maybe that is why he did not notice that Tamir's gun was a toy. We'll never find out because Officer Loehmann has not been charged with a crime.

Professor Goff, in another study, found that black boys get to be children until they are ten. He asked a group of people to look at photos and to say whether the people in the photos looked innocent or guilty. Until the age of ten, the African American kids were thought to be as innocent as the other kids. After age ten, black boys were seen as guiltier than white children.[51] The lack of innocence has major consequences when African American children act out. They are treated not like misbehaving kids but rather like juvenile delinquents. Sixteen percent of black kids are suspended from school every year. Many public schools have "school safety officers," that is, police. In a situation in which a teacher sends a white boy to the principal's office, she calls the cops on an African American boy. In fact, 70 percent of school discipline cases referred to the police are African American or Latino kids.[52]

The Chokehold also ends late. Black men die sooner than other Americans, as shown in Table 2.

TABLE 2: LIFE EXPECTANCY BY RACE AND GENDER

	Men	Women
Hispanic	78.8	83.7
White	76.6	81.3
Black	72.2	78.2

On average, black men die younger than white and Hispanic men.

Sources: National Center for Health Statistics, "QuickStats: Life Expectancy at Birth, by Sex and Race—US, 2011," Center for Disease Control and Prevention, 2011, www.cdc.gov /mmwr/preview/mmwrhtml/mm6335a8.htm; National Vital Statistics Reports, "Deaths: Final Data for 2011," Center for Disease Control and Prevention, www.cdc.gov/nchs /data/nvsr/nvsr63/ nvsr63_03.pdf; Kelly Blake, "Racism May Accelerate Aging in African American Men," UMD Right Now, January 7, 2014, www.umdrightnow.umd.edu/news /racism-may-accelerate-aging-african-american-men.

For many African American men, between their brief boy-hoods and their early deaths, there is arrest and incarceration. Of black men born in 2001, one in three will serve time. The rate for Latino men is one in six, and for white men, one in seventeen.[53] And for the same crime, black men will get the longest sentences.[54]

Perhaps the most revealing emblem of the Chokehold is this: the blacker you look, the more time you get.

FIGURE 2: PERCEPTIONS OF STEREOTYPICALLY BLACK FEATURES HAVE BEEN LINKED TO HARSHER SENTENCING OUTCOMES

These images are the faces of people with no criminal history and are shown here for illustration purposes only. The face on the right would be considered more stereotypically black than the face on the left.

Source: Jennifer L. Eberhardt, Paul G. Davies, Valerie J. Purdie Vaugns, and Sheri Lynn Johnson, "Looking Deathworthy: Perceived Stereotypicality of Black Defendants Predicts Capital-Sentencing Outcomes," *Psychological Science* 17:5 (May 2006): 383–86.

Studies have demonstrated that black men with more Afro-centric features are more likely to be executed and, in non-death cases, receive longer sentences than black men with less Afro-centric features.[55] So, in Figure 2, the man on the right would be punished more than the man on the left for the same crime.

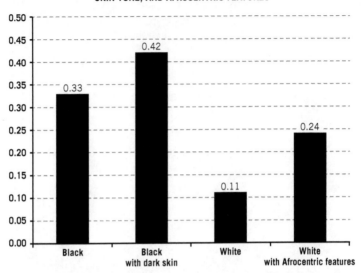

FIGURE 3: PREDICTED PROBABILITY OF PRISON BY RACE, SKIN TONE, AND AFROCENTRIC FEATURES

The race effect is so strong that it even extends to white men with Afrocentric features, making them more likely to receive criminal punishment than white men without Afrocentric features.

Source: Ryan D. King and Brian D. Johnson, "A Punishing Look: Skin Tone and Afrocentric Features in the Halls of Justice," *American Journal of Sociology* 122:1 (July 2016).

He receives more punishment because he is perceived as more black.

The race effect is so strong that it even extends to white men with Afrocentric features, as shown in Figure 3. A study published in the *American Journal of Sociology* in 2016 examined 850 photos of black and white men who were arrested in Minnesota. It found that having dark skin increased the chances that an African American would be sent to prison, rather than receive probation or have his charges reduced. Likewise, white men with Afrocentric features like larger lips or fuller noses were more likely to be punished than other white men.[56]

Blackness, we have seen, is the Chokehold's mark of the thug.

2

Controlling the Thug

The city of Ferguson, Missouri, has approximately 21,000 people. In 2013, the city's police officers obtained arrest warrants for 32,975 criminal offenses.[1] In other words, Ferguson had more crimes than it had citizens. But Ferguson was not an especially dangerous place. The majority of the arrest warrants were for people who had not paid traffic tickets. Other offenses included "manner of walking in the roadway" and "high grass and weeds."

Ferguson police charged a man named "Michael" with "making a false declaration" because he told them his name was "Mike." Michael had been playing basketball in a public park and went to his car to cool off. The police approached him and, for no apparent reason, accused him of being a pedophile. They requested his consent to search his car and Michael, citing his constitutional rights, declined. At that point Michael was arrested, at gunpoint. In addition to "making a false declaration," the police charged Michael with seven other minor offenses, including not wearing a seat belt. Michael had been sitting in a parked car.[2]

A woman called the Ferguson police to report that her boyfriend was assaulting her. By the time the officers arrived, the man was gone. Looking around the house, the police determined that the boyfriend lived there and the woman admitted that he was not listed on the home's "occupancy permit." The police arrested the woman for "permit violation" and took her to jail.[3]

African Americans are approximately 67 percent of Ferguson's population, but they constituted the vast majority of arrests, especially for minor offenses. They made up 94 percent of arrests for "failure to comply," 92 percent for "resisting arrest," 92 percent for "disturbing the peace," and 89 percent for "failure to obey."[4]

Ferguson is America. A few miles away lies St. Louis, which has approximately 320,000 citizens and approximately 300,000 outstanding arrests warrants. In Houston, the police also have a backlog of 300,000 warrants. In Chicago, the number is around 120,000. In New York City, the police are much busier. There are 1.2 million arrest warrants waiting for the police to serve.[5]

The second step of the Chokehold is the transformation of anxiety about black men into law and policy intended to contain and control them. The Chokehold is the reason that the United States has the largest and one of the most punitive criminal justice systems in the history of the world. Our methods of defining, investigating, and punishing crime are centered on African American men.

THE HARD STARE

In the contemporary USA the Black man is he who must be seen.

—John Fiske, media studies scholar

African American men and boys are constantly under watch. Police, security guards, school safety officers, basically anybody with a badge and a gun has a mandate to focus on blacks. In the words of FBI director James Comey, police officers "work in environments where a hugely disproportionate percentage of street crime is committed by young men of color. Something happens to people of good will working in that environment. After years of police work, officers often can't help but be influenced by the cynicism they feel." Cops are likely to pay more attention to two African American men than to two white men, the FBI director said, because the black men "look like so many others the officer has locked up." The focus on black men is not racist, according to Comey, but a "mental shortcut" that is "almost irresistible and maybe even rational" and that "complicates the relationship between police and the communities they serve."[6]

The problem is so extreme that police are actually more likely to pursue vehicles when they can see that the driver is black. The newspaper USA Today looked at data from the National Highway Traffic Safety Administration. When it's dark outside and the police can't see the race of the driver, more white drivers get pursued. When police can see the race of the driver—because it's daylight or it's a lit area—then black drivers are more likely to be chased. The study also demonstrated that African American drivers were more likely to be pursued for reasons not related to safety, like having expired registration or being in a stolen vehicle. White drivers tended to be chased for more serious reasons, like reckless driving or having recently committed a serious felony.[7]

THE BEAT DOWN

Frequently the Chokehold ends with violence. This violence can take any number of forms. Sometimes, when things are done to black men, we don't think of them as violent in the way that we would if these things were done to anyone else. The next chapter explains how this is true about the police tactic called stop and frisk.

But often the violence the Chokehold authorizes is the old-fashioned kind: beating and killing. Most urban police departments use some version of "use-of-force continuums." Police are supposed to start at the top and work their way down until they get the subject to comply.

Here are federal guidelines provided by the National Institute of Justice, which is the research agency of the U.S. Department of Justice. These guidelines are recommendations to local police departments, but they are not required to be followed:

Officer Presence—No force is used. Considered the best way to resolve a situation.

- The mere presence of a law enforcement officer works to deter crime or diffuse a situation.
- Officers' attitudes are professional and nonthreatening.

Verbalization—Force is not physical.

- Officers issue calm, nonthreatening commands, such as "Let me see your identification and registration."
- Officers may increase their volume and shorten commands in an attempt to gain compliance. Short commands might include "Stop," or "Don't move."

Empty-Hand Control—Officers use bodily force to gain control of a situation.

- *Soft technique.* Officers use grabs, holds, and joint locks to restrain an individual.
- *Hard techniques.* Officers use punches and kicks to restrain an individual.

Less-Lethal Methods—Officers use less-lethal technologies to gain control of a situation.

- *Blunt impact.* Officers may use a baton or projectile to immobilize a combative person.
- *Chemical.* Officers may use chemical sprays or projectiles embedded with chemicals to restrain an individual (e.g., pepper spray).
- *Conducted energy devices (CEDs).* Officers may use CEDs to immobilize an individual. CEDs discharge a high-voltage, low-amperage jolt of electricity at a distance.

Lethal Force—Officers use lethal weapons to gain control of a situation. Should only be used if a suspect poses a serious threat to the officer or another individual.

- Officers use deadly weapons such as firearms to stop an individual's actions.

Many police departments use versions of these procedures. Here is a representative sample:

Charlotte-Mecklenburg, North Carolina
Officer Presence
Verbal Direction
Soft Empty Hand
Oleoresin Capsicum (pepper spray)
Hard Empty Hand
Intermediate Weapons
Lethal Force

St. Petersburg, Florida
Officer Presence
Verbal Direction
Restraint Devices
Transporter
Takedown
Pain Compliance
Countermoves
Intermediate Weapons
Lethal Force

Dallas, Texas
Officer Presence
Verbal Control
Empty-Hand Control
Intermediate Weapons
Lethal Force

San Diego, California
Deputy Presence
Verbal Direction

Soft-Hand Control
Chemical Agents
Hard-Hand Control
Intermediate Weapons
Lethal Force[8]

We know, based on the stories of African American men, that police use these methods all the time. We know from the data that most of these methods are *more likely* to be used against black men. We even have specific information from the relatively few cities including Houston and New York that collect and release this information to the public, as shown in Figures 4 and 5:

FIGURE 4: USE OF FORCE IN ALL TYPES OF POLICE ENCOUNTERS, ACCORDING TO CIVILIANS

Based on data from Houston, Austin, and Dallas, Texas; Los Angeles, California; and Orlando and Jacksonville, Florida . . .

Blacks are more than	**87%*** As likely as whites	To be **kicked, pepper sprayed, or shot with a "stun gun"**
Blacks are more than	**170%** As likely as whites	To be **grabbed** by police
Blacks are more than	**217%** As likely as whites	To be **handcuffed**
Blacks are more than	**305%** As likely as whites	To have a **gun pointed at them** by police

*95% confidence interval for this specific 87% figure

Blacks are more likely than whites to be the target of non-deadly force by police.

Source: Roland G. Fryer Jr., "An Empirical Analysis of Racial Differences in Police Use of Force," National Bureau of Economic Research Working Paper No. 22399 (July 2016).

**FIGURE 5: FOR EVERY 10,000 STOPS THEY MAKE,
POLICE OFFICERS IN NEW YORK . . .**

Place their hands on **blacks 2,165** times	Place their hands on **whites 1,845** times	**17% more likely for blacks**
Push **blacks** into walls **623** times	Push **whites** into walls **529** times	**18% more likely for blacks**
Handcuff **blacks 310** times without arresting	Handcuff **whites 266** times without arresting	**16% more likely for blacks**
Draw their weapons on **blacks 155** times	Draw their weapons on **whites 129** times	**19% more likely for blacks**
Push **blacks** to the ground **136** times	Push **whites** to the ground **114** times	**18% more likely for blacks**
Point their weapons at **blacks 54** times	Point their weapons at **whites 43** times	**24% more likely for blacks**
Use baton or pepper spray on **blacks 5** times	Use baton or pepper spray on **whites 4** times	**25% more likely for blacks**

New York police officers use coercive tactics against blacks more than whites.

Source: New York Police Department, "Stop, Question and Frisk Report Database," www
.nyc.gov/html/nypd/html/analysis_and_planning/stop_question_and_frisk_report.shtml.

But exactly how often, on a national basis, we don't know, even for the most severe use of force—police shootings.

The information about itself that a society collects—and does not collect—is always revealing about the values of that society. We know, as we should, exactly how many police officers are killed in the line of duty. But we do not know, as we should, exactly how many civilians are killed by the police.

- Number of police officers killed in the line of duty in 2015: 94[9]

- Number of civilians killed by police officers in 2015: ? Estimates include 991 (*Washington Post*[10]) and 1,146 (*The Guardian*[11])

The *Washington Post* estimates that African Americans are 2.5 times more likely to be killed by police than whites.[12] The reason that we don't have firm numbers on the number of people U.S. police departments kill is because that information is not required to be made public. Of course police departments themselves know exactly how many people their officers have killed. It's just that most departments do not have to tell anybody else.

Police departments could be forced to share this information. The president, Congress, state lawmakers, and city mayors all have ways of requiring data about police shootings to be made transparent.[13] But in general government officials do not seem to think the public needs to know how many people our law enforcement officers—public servants paid by tax dollars—kill every year.

Fortunately, some police departments have voluntarily provided information about use of force, and others have been ordered to do so by courts, usually after those police departments have been sued for excessive force. Here's data from some cities:

Philadelphia 2007–2013:
Total Officer-Involved Shootings: 364
Black Suspects: 291 (80 percent)
White Suspects: 33 (9 percent)
Hispanic Suspects: 36 (10 percent)
Asian Suspects: 4 (1 percent)[14]

New York City 2009–2013
Total Officer-Involved Shootings Resulting in Death: 53
Black Suspects: 28 (53 percent)
White Suspects: 8 (15 percent)
Hispanic Suspects: 15 (28 percent)
Asian Suspects: 2 (4 percent)[15]

Los Angeles 2010–2012 (includes ALL use-of-force incidents)
Total Use-of-Force Incidents by Police: 6,062
Black Suspects: 2,074 (34 percent)
White Suspects: 1,077 (18 percent)
Hispanic Suspects: 2,837 (46 percent)
Asian Suspects: 74 (1 percent)[16]

Police brutality is so widespread, and so predictable, that many small and medium-size cities actually purchase insurance policies to pay money to people who have been subject to police abuse.[17] Big cities, however, self-insure, which means they set aside a certain amount of money to be used for this purpose. This raises an issue scholars call moral hazard, since police departments might be less likely to encourage their officers to act responsibly because paying for brutality is already included in the budget. John Rappaport, a law professor at the University of Chicago, has suggested that insurers could play a valuable role in reducing police violence. Insurers make money when they don't have to pay out misconduct claims, and this provides them with an incentive to keep cops on the straight and narrow. Some insurers have encouraged police to adopt use-of-force continuums and provided written and video materials for officers to learn about appropriate uses of force.[18] Some insurers have even conducted psychological testing to ensure that officers are capable of adequate self-control.[19] In California, local cops were forced to implement a series of reforms after an insurer threatened to revoke coverage.[20] Still, the prevalence of misconduct insurance suggests police are well aware of systemic deficiencies and would rather pay their costs than address them head on.

It doesn't have to be this way. Other countries enforce their laws and are just as safe as the United States, but their police officers kill far fewer people, as shown in Table 3.

TABLE 3: COMPARING FATAL POLICE SHOOTINGS IN THE U.S. AND OTHER COUNTRIES

Other countries (population)	United States (316.1 million)
England and Wales (56.9 million): 55 in 24 years	59 in the first 24 days of 2015
Germany (80.7 million): 15 in 2 years (any race)	19 unarmed black men
Australia (23.1 million): 94 in 19 years	97 in March 2015
Canada (35.2 million): 25 in 1 year	California (38.8 million): 72 in 1 year

Police officers in the United States kill more people in a matter of days than do police officers in other countries over the course of a year.

Source: Jamiles Lartey, "By the Numbers: US Police Kill More in Days than Other Countries Do In Years," *The Guardian*, June 9, 2015.

THE SUPER POWERS OF THE AMERICAN COP

What's the difference? The widespread availability of guns is a major factor. U.S. cops are allowed to shoot to kill if they reasonably believe that someone is about to shoot them, and police in the United States probably face deadly force more than cops in some other countries. But that is not the whole, or perhaps the most important, explanation. Many Canadian citizens own guns—in Canada, there are about thirty guns for every one hundred people (versus eighty-eight for every one hundred people in the United States), yet more people die from police violence in one week in the States than in one year in Canada.[21]

Another important difference is that U.S. police officers have super powers that cops in those other countries do not. The Chokehold authorizes them to take out their guns a lot more. The police have been granted these powers in a series of court rulings from the United States Supreme Court, including *Scott v. Harris*, *Atwater v. Lago Vista*, and *Whren v. United States*. With its decisions in these cases, the Court has created the legal platform for black lives not to matter to the police.

These cases are not the first time the Supreme Court has used its power over the criminal justice system to make a point about race. Michael Klarman, a professor at Harvard Law School, wrote a famous law journal article about how, in the early twentieth century, the Court granted criminal defendants new rights because it was concerned that African Americans were being discriminated against in the South. For example, in a case involving the Scottsboro "boys"—nine African American men who were falsely accused of raping two white women—the Court ruled that people who are charged with capital crimes have a right to an attorney. Professor Klarman argues that the Court was using criminal justice to try to install a new racial order in the South. He also states that, in doing so, the Court was not really going out on a limb. It was just reflecting the views of most Americans that southern prejudice against blacks was too extreme.

The Supreme Court is still using the criminal justice system to do race work, except that now it is imposing a different racial order. In a series of cases, the conservatives on the Court have given the police unprecedented power, with everybody understanding that these powers will mainly be used against African Americans and Latinos. Once again, the Court is just reflecting the will of the (white) majority. Many people are afraid of African American men, and the Court has authorized police procedures to contain the perceived threat. Three recent cases are instructive.

SCOTT V. HARRIS: SUPER POWER TO KILL

Victor Harris was nineteen years old when the police tried to pull over his car in Atlanta, Georgia, for speeding. He was going 73 mph in a 55 mph zone. Harris should have stopped but instead he sped away. The officers gave chase and pursued Harris down a two-lane highway for several minutes. Finally one of the cops used his car to deliberately ram Harris's car off the road. It crashed down a steep ravine and burst into flames. Harris survived, but he was rendered a quadriplegic.

Are the police allowed to use deadly force simply to enforce a traffic law? If they have to choose between letting somebody get away with speeding or killing or maiming him to make sure he doesn't get away, are they really supposed to kill or maim him? Those questions made it all the way up to the United States Supreme Court, which answered "yes." The police could have ended the danger simply by stopping the chase. They already had Harris's license plate number, so they could identify and find him. Yet the Court ruled that the police had acted reasonably because Harris's evasion of the police created a danger to other drivers.

The police originally tried to stop Victor Harris for speeding, a traffic infraction. We don't know whether they were going to give him a ticket or arrest him — in many cities, the police have either option. Why are the police even allowed to arrest someone for a traffic infraction — as opposed to giving him or her a ticket?

ATWATER V. LAGO VISTA:
SUPER POWER TO ARREST

Gail Atwater found out the answer to that question the hard way. She was driving her pickup truck in Lago Vista, Texas. Her two kids were in the backseat and nobody was wearing a seat belt. Texas has a mandatory seat belt law, and Officer Bart Turek pulled her over, jabbed his finger at her face, and told her she was going to jail. The officer put handcuffs on Atwater, placed her in the back of his squad car (the cop didn't put a seat belt on Ms. Atwater!), and took her to jail. At the station she was searched, had her mug shot taken, and then was locked up for an hour until she made bail.

Here's the kicker: in Texas, under the law, this is not an offense punishable by being sent to prison. If you are guilty of driving without a seat belt, the maximum punishment is a fifty-dollar fine. Atwater thought, not unreasonably, you should not be able to be arrested and put in jail for an offense for which you could not be locked up when you are found guilty of it. But the Supreme

Court did not agree. It said that the police can take you to jail in the course of processing you for any crime—no matter how minor and even if punishment for being found guilty of the crime does not include any prison time.

WHREN V. UNITED STATES: SUPER POWER TO RACIALLY PROFILE

Did you know the cops can stop you for waiting too long at a stop sign? That's one of the reasons they stopped Michael Whren, a young black man driving a car in Washington, D.C. The car stayed at the stop sign for about twenty seconds and then made a quick right turn without signaling. At that point police officers in an unmarked car pursued Mr. Whren's vehicle and pulled him over.

There was no serious claim that the officers were concerned about the traffic violations. They just wanted an excuse to stop the car to see what was going on with Mr. Whren and his passenger. That's called a pretextual stop—the pretext is the traffic violation, but it's not the real reason why the cops are stopping you.

In Whren v. United States, the Supreme Court blessed this kind of police activity. As long as the cops have a legitimate reason, like a traffic violation, to make the stop, it's all good. The actual motive of the cop, what the Court called his or her "subjective state of mind," does not matter.

A cop friend of mine invented a game that tells you everything you need to know about the extraordinary consequences of Whren. The cop takes my law students on ride-alongs in his squad car so they can see what it's like to be a police officer. The game is called Pick a Car. My friend tells the students to pick any car they see on the street and he will legally stop it. He says that he can follow any driver and within a few blocks he or she will commit some traffic infraction. Then he turns on his siren and flashing lights. He can order the driver and passenger to exit their vehicle. He can pat them down if he feels like his safety is threatened.

This gives him an enormous amount of power. As a practical matter, if you are driving a car, he can stop you at will.

This is exactly what the police do to African Americans and Hispanics. Study after study has found that there is a lower threshold for minorities than white people when it comes to traffic stops. Stanford University researchers looked at 4.5 million traffic stops in North Carolina and found that, though they are searched at higher rates than whites, African Americans and Hispanics possess contraband at lower rates than whites do.[22] To put this gap in perspective, had black drivers been searched at the same rate as white drivers, thirty thousand searches, or a third of all searches of black drivers over a six-year period, would not have occurred.[23] Similarly, had Hispanic drivers been searched at the same rate as white drivers, more than half of the total searches of Hispanic drivers would not have taken place.[24]

Because of these super powers, New York City police officers were able to arrest Eric Garner in Staten Island, New York, for selling a "loosie" cigarette, a minor infraction akin to not wearing a seat belt. Then the police could use deadly force when Garner resisted arrest, if they reasonably believed he posed a threat to them or others. They put him in a chokehold, which killed him. The chokehold was against NYPD regulations but not against the U.S. Constitution. After all, in *Scott v. Harris* the police were permitted to deliberately ram a car down a steep ravine to enforce the law against speeding. These super powers enabled the Ferguson, Missouri, police to stop Michael Brown for "manner of walking in the roadway." If, in making the arrest, Officer Wilson reasonably feared for his life, he was allowed to shoot Brown dead, which is what Officer Wilson did.

The super powers allowed the Ferguson police to arrest another man named Michael simply because he told them his name was "Mike." And when a woman called the police because her boyfriend had assaulted her, these super powers allowed the police to arrest the woman for "permit violation." It's all legal. When the police treat black people like this, they are just doing their jobs. U.S. Supreme Court Justice Sonia Sotomayor, dissenting in another pro–police power case, wrote that the majority opinion told "everyone, white and black, guilty and innocent, that an officer can verify your legal status at any time. It says that your body is subject to invasion while courts excuse the violation of your rights. It implies that you are not a citizen of a democracy but the subject of a carceral state, just waiting to be cataloged." [25]

WHY ARRESTS ARE A BIGGER PROBLEM THAN INCARCERATION

Thanks to the powerful analysis in Michelle Alexander's groundbreaking book *The New Jim Crow*, there's been a lot of focus on incarceration as a form of social control of African Americans. But it turns out arrests, which *precede* incarceration, are an even bigger deal. That's because for most kinds of arrests—for low-level crimes called misdemeanors—police and prosecutors don't care

TABLE 4: ARRESTS IN 2012 BY RACE

Race	Arrested by age 18	Arrested by age 23
Black	30%	49%
Hispanic	26%	44%
White	22%	38%

Blacks are arrested disproportionately more than other racial and ethnic groups in the United States.

Sources: Arrest Data Analysis Tool, BoJ (available at www.bjs.gov/index. cfm?ty=datool&surl =/arrests/index.cfm#); Brame, Bushway, Paternoster, and Turner, "Demographic Patterns of Cumulative Arrest Prevalence by Ages 18 and 23," *Crime & Delinquency* 60, no. 3 (January 6, 2014), cad.sagepub.com/content/60/3/471.

really whether you are guilty. That's not the point of the arrest. African American men are arrested mainly so that they can be officially placed under government surveillance. Table 4 shows these arrests broken down by race.

You may be thinking the fact that so many black men get arrested is proof that they are more dangerous. Here's why that's wrong. The vast majority of arrests are for misdemeanors—minor crimes for which the punishment is less than one year in prison. Only one out of twenty-four arrests in the United States is for a violent crime. In an article in the *Georgetown Law Journal*, law professor Devon Carbado listed some of the conduct that states punish as misdemeanors:

- Spitting in public places;
- Possession of spoons, bowls, and blenders (as indicative of drug paraphernalia);
- Loitering for illicit purposes;
- Selling alcohol to a "common drunkard";
- Public intoxication;
- Sleeping in a public place;
- Sitting or lying down in particular public places;
- Camping or lodging in a public place;
- Panhandling anywhere in the city;
- Storing personal property in a public place without a permit;
- Drinking in public;
- Jaywalking;
- Riding bicycles on the sidewalk;
- Removing trash from a bin;
- Urinating or defecating in public.[26]

The hard stare is the main reason why more African American men get locked up for those crimes. If the police spent as much time staring at any other group as they do at black men, that group would be under arrest just as much as black men are. Imagine if you had your own personal cop, watching you every time you left the house, from the time you were ten years old. What if you were subject to intense government surveillance any time you jaywalked, littered, got into a fistfight, smoked a joint, or committed a traffic infraction? The National Longitudinal Survey of Youth surveyed people who turned eighteen years old in 1980 and then looked at the same age group in 2000. The survey asked the youth questions about contacts with the criminal justice system, and also about actual involvement in criminal activity. In 1980, African Americans and whites who reported that they broke the law were arrested at around the same rates. And blacks and whites who reported that they obeyed the law were not arrested at roughly equivalent rates.

But twenty years later, in 2000, as the Chokehold came into full effect, everything changed. The survey looked at the same cohort, and now guilty white people were *less* likely to be arrested, and innocent black people were *more* likely to be arrested.[27]

KIDS, DON'T COMMIT YOUR MISDEMEANORS ON WEDNESDAYS!

I'm not saying black men don't disproportionately commit some kinds of crime. They do, and why that is and how the government and ordinary people should respond is the subject of chapter 4. The point here is that most of the crimes that African American men get arrested for—misdemeanors such as marijuana possession, fistfights, public drinking, and traffic infractions—are because the police are basically hunting them down and not because someone has called 911 about some real public safety emergency.

One revealing example of this phenomenon is that in New York City more people get arrested for misdemeanors on Wednesday than any other day. Is that because more crime happens on Wednesday? No. That's just the day when police staffing is highest.[28]

So arrest rates don't prove that African American men are more dangerous, because the vast majority of arrests are for minor offenses, and enforcement of those offenses is focused on black men.

I know from arrests. In my book *Let's Get Free: A Hip-Hop*

Theory of Justice I tell the story of how I was arrested for a crime I didn't commit. I'm still dealing with the psychological ramifications, but I'm lucky. It's one thing to be arrested when you are a prosecutor, with sufficient legal and financial resources, and social capital, to fight the case. It's another thing to be arrested when you are young and poor and don't have much of a choice in who your lawyer is, and you look like the perp featured on the evening news every night. Chapter 7 features some real talk for brothers who face that dilemma.

WHEN ACTUAL INNOCENCE OR GUILT ISN'T A BIG DEAL

When I got arrested, I thought it would matter that I was innocent. It turns out, however, for misdemeanor arrests, whether you are innocent or guilty is not the most important thing.

I got my first clue when I was in training to be a prosecutor. My supervisor encouraged us rookies to try different styles of presenting evidence to judges and juries. New prosecutors treat misdemeanor court like an advanced law school classroom—it's where they practice to become better courtroom advocates. "Don't worry if you win or lose the case," my supervisor told us. "It's only a misdemeanor—if the defendant is that bad, he'll be back."

It turns out that was not just a joke. It's criminal justice policy in the twenty-first century. African American men are not arrested to determine whether they have committed a crime. Rather it's because of all the control the government has over its arrestees.

When you get locked up, the police can do a full body search of you. They can look for whatever they want; the search does not have to be related to the offense for which you have been arrested. If you are arrested in your home, they can search the room where you are arrested, ostensibly to see if there is a weapon or evidence of the crime for which you are being arrested. The same rule applies to car searches when people get arrested in their vehicles. Anything the police come across as they conduct the search is fair game for the prosecution.

This extraordinary power, called "search incident to arrest," is one of the primary tools of an influential school of policing called "order maintenance" or "broken windows." The idea is for the police to arrest people for low-level offenses like drinking in public, jaywalking, and riding a bike on the sidewalk—not because they really care about those "crimes" but because then they can search you to see if you have a gun or drugs.

Order maintenance policing is almost exclusively directed at African American and Latino men. Brothers in New York know what it means if you are walking on the street drinking from a cup or plastic bottle and a cop approaches you. You are supposed to hand the cup or bottle to the cop so he or she can smell it to see if it contains alcohol. The purpose of this humiliation is that the cops are looking for an excuse to arrest you. The effect of this humiliation is to make you hate the police.

In addition to giving cops the power to search, misdemeanor arrests serve to formally enroll black men in the criminal justice system. Arrests enable a set of surveillance practices. The police are allowed to take your photo, fingerprints, and blood, to look at everything in your pockets, to do a body cavity search if they are taking you to jail, to inventory the contents of your wallet, briefcase, and backpack, and to lie to you about evidence they have against you to try to make you talk. In New York City, they stick a camera in your eye to take an image of your iris. The point is to find out, in the words of Michael Jackson, "who's bad." The criminal justice system wants the DNA of black men, literally and figuratively, and, through arrests, it gets it—literally and figuratively.[29]

Issa Kohler-Hausmann, a Yale law professor, spent years observing misdemeanor court in New York City and talking to judges, prosecutors, defense attorneys, and defendants. She found that prosecutors dismissed some cases when they had plenty of evidence that the defendants were guilty. Other times, they zealously went after defendants who were probably innocent. What made the difference is the number of contacts people had with the system. People who had misdemeanor convictions were more likely to get convicted again—even if the evidence against them was weak. By contrast, people who had fewer contacts frequently got their charges dismissed—even if the state had a good case. This effect was not seen in serious felony crimes, where evidence about actual guilt or innocence was more meaningful. In those cases, your record made a difference with regard to sentencing but not with regard to whether you got convicted.

Kohler-Hausmann theorized that, with misdemeanor arrests, a kind of sorting process is going on. The state is trying to categorize African American and Latino men to see which ones need the closest watch. Contacts with the police are how prosecutors try to figure that out.

The good news is that Kohler-Hausmann's study debunks the conventional wisdom in the hood that prosecutors are trying to lock up every black man they can. It turns out they are actually trying to devise an efficient way to determine which ones, in their worldview, should be locked up. The bad news is that, in places like New York, whether or not you are guilty of a misdemeanor is not the most important criteria for whether you get punished for one. The system then becomes self-perpetuating. If you have one conviction you are more likely to get another, whether you are guilty or not. And even more likely the time after that.

WHAT'S RACE GOT TO DO WITH IT?

Imagine what we would feel and what we would do if white drivers were three times as likely to be searched by police during a traffic stop as black drivers instead of the other way around. If white offenders received prison sentences ten percent longer than black offenders for the same crimes. If a third of all white men went to prison during their lifetime. Imagine that.

—Hillary Clinton

Sometimes racism in the law is so obvious that it spits in your face. In some states the law allows African Americans to be given extra points on IQ tests, just so that they can be executed. In *Adkins v. Virginia*, the United States Supreme Court ruled that it was unconstitutional to execute people with intellectual disabilities. Prosecutors have devised a way to circumvent this requirement for developmentally disabled African Americans. They ask judges to add 5 to 15 points to the IQ scores of minorities under the guise that traditional IQ tests underestimate minority intelligence.[30] This bumps up the IQ of black inmates enough for them to be executed. This isn't just a crazy technique that was used once in a rural courtroom. It's actually the law in a growing number of states, including Florida, Pennsylvania, Missouri, and Alabama.[31]

But usually the white supremacy in criminal law is not so blatant. Most police and prosecutorial practices are formally color-blind but in reality are designed to target African American men. There is one system of justice in this country for them and other systems for other groups of people. In the most comprehensive study ever done of how state judges sentence people, journalists at the *Sarasota Herald Tribune* looked at millions of records from every trial judge in Florida. Their report, published in 2016, found that when black defendants have committed the same crime under the same circumstance as white defendants, they get significantly more time. In half of the counties in Florida, African

Americans get twice as much time as white people for identical offenses.

The *Herald Tribune* article describes the case of Allen Christopher Peters, a seventeen-year-old white man, who used a gun to rob a gas station of about $640. The sentencing guidelines called for a minimum of four years, but Peters was sentenced to probation with no jail time. Jaquavais Sturgis, an African American teenager, appeared before the same judge. He was charged with armed robbery of a convenience store, netting about $300. Sturgis was charged with the same crime—armed robbery with a deadly weapon—as Peters, and had the same criminal background— three offense committed as a juvenile. Sturgis was sentenced to four years in prison.[32]

The claim that the law places people in categories from which flow a certain set of practices is hardly unique to African American men. The law does or has done the same thing to women, immigrants, LGBT people, and Muslims, among others. And of course all of these categories intersect—some people are African American and female and foreign born and lesbian. The Chokehold is at the intersection of blackness and maleness, and it is about the social and legal response to that specific identity. This response is mainly horrific, but the violence of the law is not limited to black men. African American women aren't doing any better overall, but criminal justice is not the primary instrument of their subordination.

So the Chokehold is not a ranking of oppression or a race to the bottom. It is, though, a reckoning of how anxiety about African American men has created one of the harshest punishment regimes in the history of the world.

As Figure 6 shows, the sweet spot is around one hundred people per 100,000 population. If there is a "natural" rate of incarceration, it seems to be there. That is where the United States has been most of its history, until the 1970s.

By contrast, today white and Latino men in the United States experience extreme levels of incarceration, and the numbers

FIGURE 6: INCARCERATION RATES PER 100,000

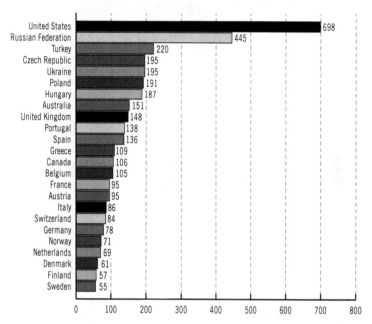

The United States has the highest incarceration rate of any country in the world.

Source: Roy Walmsley, "World Prison Population List, Eleventh Edition," World Prison Brief, Institute for Criminal Policy Research, October 2015, www.prisonstudies.org/sites/de fault/files/resources/downloads/world_prison_population_list_11th_edition.pdf.

for African American men are almost off the chart, as shown in Figure 7.

What happened? Did something in the water starting in the 1970s make people in the United States suddenly take a turn toward degeneracy? Hardly. What happened was that the United States began to use policing and punishment as a fundamental way to control the urban poor—especially black men. The same law that creates the Chokehold makes it very difficult to "prove" racial bias in criminal justice. To make a case requires extraordinary resources, and even then success is not guaranteed. For example, in order to document discrimination against African Americans by the Ferguson police department, the U.S. Justice

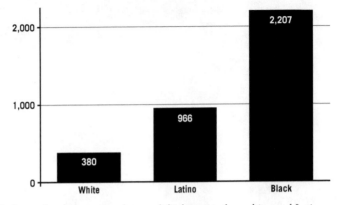

FIGURE 7: U.S. INCARCERATION RATES BY RACE AND ETHNICITY, 2010 (NUMBER OF PEOPLE INCARCERATED PER 100,000 IN THAT GROUP)

Black people are incarcerated at much higher rates than whites and Latinos.

Source: Leah Sakala, "Breaking Down Mass Incarceration in the 2010 Census: State-by-State Incarceration Rates by Race/Ethnicity," Prison Policy Initiative, May 28, 2014, www .prisonpolicy.org/reports/rates.html.

Department investigation, in 2014–2015, included "100 person days on site in Ferguson," and review of "35,000 pages of police records as well as thousands of emails."[33] An average citizen or even a community does not have the resources to do this kind of research and documentation, making it very difficult for a victim of bias to substantiate that kind of claim.

Likewise, persuading a federal district judge in New York that the NYPD's stop-and-frisk program intentionally discriminated against African American and Latino men took a two-month trial, an endeavor far beyond the resources of most individuals who may feel they have been discriminated against. So the claim that American criminal justice is all about black men is like a lot of claims about racial subordination—at once obvious and hard to prove in a court of law. Here is what we know: whenever a harsh new criminal justice policy is implemented, researchers and activists predict that the practice will have an adverse impact on African Americans. Then that prediction comes true. Then the practice is continued, in spite of this problem.

Former president Bill Clinton has suggested that if our criminal policies had the same adverse impact on white people that they have on black men we would change the policies. This is exactly what is happening with the emerging heroin and opioid epidemics. According to the American Medical Association, 90 percent of the people who have tried heroin for the first time in recent years are white.[34] The problem has been especially severe in New England, in places like New Hampshire and Massachusetts. In contrast with the crack epidemic in the 1990s, which had a black face and led to harsh sentencing laws and harsher rhetoric about crackheads and "crack babies," the new focus on heroin users is on getting heroin addicts medical care.

The difference is so stark it recalls the classic *Saturday Night Live* sketch in which Eddie Murphy turns white and people give him stuff for free. In Gloucester, Massachusetts, you can walk into the police station carrying heroin and the cops don't arrest you, they refer you to treatment. This is true of thirty-six other police departments as well.[35]

Eric Adams, a police officer in Laconia, New Hampshire, is deployed to reach out to people who have overdosed on heroin and get them into a program. He used to be an undercover narcotics detective. He told the *New York Times*, "The way that I look at addiction now is completely different. I can't tell what changed inside of me, but these are people and they have a purpose in life and we as law enforcement can't look at them any other way."[36] Thirty-two states have passed "Good Samaritan" laws that prohibit prosecution of people who call the police to report overdoses.

When crime has a black face, the reaction is quite different.

In general, white people support harsher criminal justice policies than African Americans do, as Figures 8 and 9 show. Remarkably, if white people are informed that a policy has an adverse impact on blacks, it actually increases their support for it. So, for example, if white people are asked about their support for practices such as three-strike laws or trying children as adults and not cued about race, they provide one set of responses. If, however,

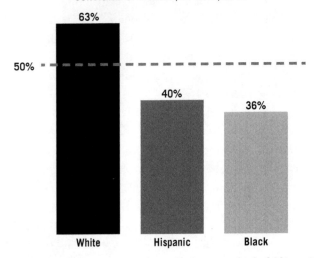

**FIGURE 8: SUPPORT FOR DEATH PENALTY FOR PERSONS
CONVICTED OF MURDER, BY RACE, 2013**

A large majority of whites, compared to only about one-third of African Americans, support the death penalty.

Source: Pew Research Center, "Shrinking Majority of Americans Support Death Penalty," Washington, D.C., March 2014, www.pewforum.org/2014/03/28/shrinking-majority-of-americans-support-death-penalty.

they are asked about these practices and informed that the policies will have a disproportionate impact on blacks, it makes white people support the practices more. Studies have shown that whites who associate crime with people of color are more likely to support punitive criminal justice policies.[37] For example, a 2002 survey found that white respondents who linked high crime rates to blacks were more likely to support lengthier sentences, harsh treatment of prisoners, and the death penalty. Similarly, another study revealed that whites' support for "getting tough with juvenile offenders is in part tied to racialized views of youth crime."[38] This should not surprise us when we recall that 66 percent of whites told the Associated Press that "violent" is a good or excellent way to describe African Americans. The Chokehold is a function of

FIGURE 9: SUPPORT FOR VARIOUS PUNITIVE MEASURES, BY RACE, 2000–2001

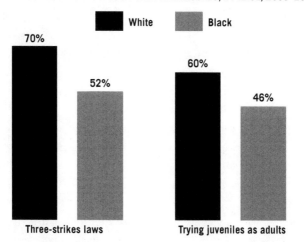

Whites are more likely than African Americans to support three-strike sentencing laws and the prosecution of minors under rules typically reserved for adults.

Source: Mark Peffley and Jon Hurwitz, *Justice in America: The Separate Realities of Blacks and Whites* (New York: Cambridge University Press, 2010), 152–53.

the will of the people. It is the tyranny of the majority, and it has been remarkably effective at putting down black men.

RYAN AND THE JUMP OUTS: HOW THE CHOKEHOLD PRODUCES THE STARBUCKS NEAR YOU

The Chokehold is how the system is supposed to work. When police who shoot unarmed black people go free, or when Michael gets locked up for telling the police his name is "Mike," those are not faults in the process. That's called criminal justice. Those are features integral to the system.

Our "justice" system actually serves interests that are often obscured from view. This includes maintaining relationships of racial subordination and white privilege that are different from the system's stated purpose of deterring crime and punishing wrongdoers. Ryan got a close-up view of this when he was a law student at Georgetown. He spent the summer interning at the local D.C. prosecutor's office. Ryan was invited, by cops he worked with, to ride with the "jump out" squad. That is a team of plainclothes cops who roll up on a street in an unmarked van and suddenly jump out of the van to make arrests or interrogate suspects. If you don't know what is going on, you just see a bunch of men in street clothes leave a vehicle and tackle somebody. It's very rough policing, about which African American residents of D.C. have long complained.

Ryan observed that the jump outs were focused in the many neighborhoods in the District of Columbia that are gentrifying. The police were engaged in a practice that made African Americans feel less welcome in neighborhoods that had been their home for decades.

In the 1980s, longtime African American residents of the city often discussed "The Plan." The Plan was a speculation that, at some point in the not too distant future, white people were going to realize low-income black people lived in the most desirable neighborhoods of the city with the best housing stock. The white people would then force out the longtime residents of these communities.

When I first heard about the Plan, back in the 1990s, I thought it was a silly conspiracy theory. It was true that those neighborhoods were close to downtown, but they were marked by open-air drug markets and sex workers. And the homes might have looked good back in the day, but now they were broken down and rodent infested. That's why poor people lived there; anyone who had a choice would prefer the tonier, mainly white communities like Georgetown and Cleveland Park, even if they were a farther commute to work and nightlife.

Today the Plan is in full effect. Middle-class, mainly white people have pushed African Americans out of much of what used to be called "the inner city." The police advanced this takeover by ratcheting up law enforcement against African American and Latino folks in a way that made white people feel safe.

It's not just a D.C. thing. One study looked at cities that are trying to attract a "creative class" to offset the decline of long-gone manufacturing jobs. In those cities, "order maintenance" arrests increase significantly.[39] As neighborhoods in San Francisco became wealthier and whiter, calls to police for non-emergency reasons like reporting loitering increased almost 300 percent.[40] The city actually created an app, Open311, that allowed the new residents to report public disorder by sending a photo and a map-based location.[41] Gentrification has other criminal justice impacts as well, including what is known in Brooklyn as the "Williamsburg Effect." As wealthier, educated people enter the city, they begin sitting on juries. When these individuals are on juries, they tend to trust the police more and the defendant less, which results in more convictions.

The story of Ryan and the Jump Outs is one example of how the Chokehold advantages white people. The police help gentrifiers take over African American spaces. And to reinforce the point that black cops don't necessarily make things better, it is interesting to note that in D.C., African Americans are actually *overrepresented* on the police force. For a long time, they made up about 70 percent of the Metropolitan Police Department officers, even though blacks are only about 50 percent of the population of the city. What Ryan, the Georgetown law student, observed was mainly young black men chasing other young black men out of neighborhoods to make the neighborhoods seem safe for white people.

If you are white, this is an example of the kind of benefit you receive from the Chokehold. One of its functions is to enhance the property value of being white. Part of the return is psychic, but part of it has to do with cash money.

Let's look at some data:

For every one hundred white women ages twenty-five to fifty-four, there are ninety-nine white men.
For every one hundred black women ages twenty-five to fifty-four, there are eighty-three black men.[42]

This amounts to 1.5 million missing African American men. They are missing primarily because of incarceration and early death. This means that one in every six African American men is absent from the economy during his prime earning years.[43] The Chokehold reduces competition for jobs by removing hundreds of thousands of black men from the labor market.

And it is not just the black men who are currently locked up, or those who have previously been locked up and now have criminal records. The Chokehold reduces the competition from virtually every black man. Devah Pager, a sociologist at Harvard, conducted studies in Milwaukee and New York to compare the experiences of black and white men seeking entry-level jobs. The study had two teams of black men and white men with identical resumes. The men applied for a wide variety of low-level jobs, including positions as couriers, telemarketers, and cashiers. In one team, the men told prospective employers that they had been incarcerated for a drug crime for eighteen months and listed their parole officers as a reference. In the other team, the men had no criminal records.

At this point the reader will probably not be surprised to learn that the men with criminal records had a difficult time. The reader probably will not even be surprised to learn that the black men with the drug conviction had a more difficult time than the white men with the drug conviction. But the Chokehold is even more insidious than one might realize. The studies found that the black men *without* criminal convictions got about the same number of callbacks as the white men *with* criminal convictions.[44]

CRUSHING THE CHOKEHOLD:
THE INTEREST-CONVERGENCE THESIS

One reason that it is important to understand who benefits from the Chokehold is that information helps inform a strategy to defeat the Chokehold. Derrick Bell was one of the founders of critical race theory, a school of jurisprudence that seeks to understand the relationship between law and racial justice. One of Bell's insights was that people of color make progress through the law only when what they seek aligns with some interest that white people have. Bell called this theory "interest convergence."

So, for example, the legal historian Mary Dudziak has demonstrated that the old Jim Crow segregation ended in part because it made the United States look so bad on the world stage during a time when the country was engaged in the Cold War. The United States looked hypocritical lecturing the Soviet Union about liberty and equality when southern states required blacks to drink out of separate water fountains. In *Brown v. Board of Education,* some lawyers explicitly argued to the Supreme Court that they should end "separate but equal" in public schools to help burnish the country's prestige. The Supreme Court credited that argument in its opinion.

How might interest convergence work to defeat the Chokehold? The story of Eric Lotke, a labor union organizer in Colorado, points us to a way. Lotke had a tough job. He worked for a progressive union—the Service Employees International Union—that had a platform critical of mass incarceration. The problem was that some of the workers SEIU represents are prison guards.

Correctional officers have been among the strongest advocates for tough-on-crime policies, not for public safety reasons but rather because incarceration guarantees their jobs. (The California Correctional Peace Officers Association, for example, might be the most influential lobbyist in the state and the main reason why California has one of the highest rates of incarceration in the world.)

In Colorado, there was an opportunity to close some prisons, but Lotke had to get the correctional officers he represented to buy in. They were dead set against it. Lotke started small. He got the men to agree that the prisons that were housed in decrepit buildings that were falling apart should be shut down and the workers transferred to other institutions. Next, because crime in the state had been falling, the men agreed to a moratorium on hiring—this was actually good for them because it reduced competition for promotions and the like.

Probably the most important thing Lotke did was talk to the men about their jobs. The men hated their work. Prisons are wretched places—loud, smelly, dirty, and violent—and to spend time in one, as an inmate or guard, drains the soul. When I was a prosecutor, whenever I had to go to a prison to interview a witness, the first thing I did when I left was go home and take a shower.

Prisons are often built in rural, white communities, and, in terms of the money and benefits, they provide good jobs. Correctional officers have even more of a warrior mentality than cops. The NYPD's slogan is "New York's finest"; the NY correctional officers' slogan is "New York's boldest." One effect is that there are generous pension plans to encourage early retirement, the idea being that a thirty-year-old makes a bolder warrior than a sixty-year-old.

Lotke discovered that pretty much all of the COs were just trying to hang on until they reached fifty or fifty-five and became eligible for retirement benefits. If the COs were able to reach this point, they didn't care what happened to the prison. Lotke got the state to offer the COs other employment that would still allow them to retire at the same age as if they had remained employed by the prison. Early retirement and not having to work at a prison? Hell, yeah, said the COs. It was a win-win, and Colorado ended up closing some prisons with the blessing of its prison guards.

There are things I don't like about that story—it seems weird that you have to be nice to jailers in order to reform criminal justice—but it worked. This story demonstrates both the strength of the Chokehold—it puts cash money in the pockets of many people—and also its vulnerabilities. The challenge now is to articulate a way to defeat the Chokehold, given the psychic and economic rewards that it brings many people. The last chapter of this book begins this crucial task. But first, in the next chapter, I break down the obsession that cops have with black male bodies. Then, in chapter 4, I go to a place where progressives have been reluctant to tread: the problem of black male violence. Chapter 5 explores the ways that some programs designed to help African American men actually fall prey to stereotypes about black men. Chapter 6 explains why traditional legal and policy reforms will not resolve the Chokehold. Chapter 7 offers practical advice to African American men who are trying to avoid getting locked up and suggests ways that brothers who have criminal cases can have better outcomes. Finally, Chapter 8 imagines a world without the Chokehold and presents some suggestions about how to get there.

3

Sex and Torture:
The Police and Black Male Bodies

The officer must feel with sensitive fingers every portion of the prisoner's body. A thorough search must be made of the prisoner's arms
and armpits, waistline and back, the groin and areas about the testicles, and entire surface of the legs down to the feet.[1]

—Police Manual, 1954

In an eight-block area of Brooklyn, New York, a neighborhood
called Brownsville, the police conducted almost 52,000 stop
and frisks over a period of about four years from 2006 to 2010.[2]
This was an average of one each year for every resident of this
community.

But the stops were not distributed randomly. Virtually all of the
people stopped were young African American and Latino males.
Men and boys fifteen to thirty-four years of age made up almost
70 percent of the stops. A young male citizen of Brownsville got
seized and searched about five times a year.

Less than 1 percent of these police detentions resulted in arrests. In other words, thousands of men and boys in this neighborhood were grabbed by armed agents of the state and then
subjected to "a careful exploration of the outer surfaces of a person's clothing all over his or her body,"[3] even though 99 percent
of the time, these people had committed no crime.

Here's what happens when you are stopped and frisked. You
are walking to work on a Monday morning. The cop car stops

suddenly, two men with guns jump out, and they order you to face
the building and put your hands up. They put their hands roughly
all over your body, one squeezes something in your pocket and
asks you "what's that?" You take out your asthma inhaler and show
it to him. They pat you down one more time and then they just
leave. They don't apologize. Your neighbors are walking by, some
looking at you sympathetically and others like they are wondering
what crime you committed. You feel humiliated.

Or you are going to visit your mom in the projects. The lock on
the door to the lobby is always busted, and the buzzer to her apartment is broken too. You just hope the elevator is working because
you don't feel like walking up eight flights of stairs. Again. You
open the door and enter the lobby. Four cops are waiting. You recognize a couple of them from your previous visits to the neighborhood. One officer asks where you are going. "To visit my mom,"
you say. "Put your hands against the wall," another cop says.
"Why? I'm just going to visit my mom." "Trespass" is the answer.
You tell them, "I'm not trespassing." They surround you. Now it's
a situation. You put your hands on the wall. They kick your feet
to spread your legs wider. They make you take off your cap, they
pat you up and down, they touch your private parts. Other people
entering the building look away partly to preserve your dignity
and partly because they hope that if they pretend not to notice the
cops, the cops will pretend not to notice them. Nobody coming
inside the building uses a key—it would be ridiculous because the
lock is broken. The cops write you up a citation for trespass. One
of the officers you have seen before pulls you aside and says when
you go to court just bring proof of your mother's address and the
judge will dismiss the case. Then they let you go. You hate them
with every fiber of your being.

The police got the power to stop and frisk from a 1968 Supreme Court decision called *Terry v. Ohio*. The Court said cops
can temporarily detain someone they suspect of a crime—that's
the stop, and they can "pat down" suspects they think might be

armed—that's the frisk. The "reasonable suspicion" standard that authorizes cops to stop and frisk is quite low. Even suspicion of a trivial offense like jaywalking, or spitting on the sidewalk, can give the police the authority to stop you. "*Terry* stops" are the most common negative interactions that citizens have with the police. Each year millions more people get stopped than arrested.

For African American men, stop and frisk is a form of government. It is the most visceral manifestation of the state in their lives. Most black men have never been convicted of a crime. About half of black men get arrested at some point during their lives. But virtually every African American man gets stopped and frisked. Of my black male friends and colleagues between the ages of twenty and seventy, I don't know one who hasn't been.

Stop and frisk is a central source of inequality, discrimination, and police abuse. It is a threat to democratic values. Yet stop and frisk has a strange prestige. It is the nation's leading crime control policy—despite scant evidence that it actually works to make communities safer. During his 2016 presidential campaign, Donald Trump, responding to a question in a town hall about "black on black crime" said, "Well, one of the things I'd do . . . is I would do stop and frisk. I think you have to. We did it in New York. It worked incredibly well."

As a police tactic, stop and frisk has been widely embraced. The number of stop and frisks in New York has been reduced, as a result of protests and litigation. But police in cities across the United States, including Philadelphia, Chicago, Baltimore, and Los Angeles, have taken the practice to heights far beyond what the NYPD did. Stop and frisk has been described by a leading legal scholar as "a practically perfect doctrine."[4] In this chapter, I'd like to diminish that prestige by demonstrating how stop and frisk is violent and destabilizing.

THREE WAYS OF FEELING A BLACK MAN

What does it mean when police go around touching people who are, in the eyes of the law, innocent? Stop and frisks are brutal assertions of police dominance of the streets, communicating to African American men through "three ways of feeling a black man"—sexual harassment, torture, and even terrorism—that they are objects of disdain by the state. The three frames are not mutually exclusive categories: Sexual harassment bleeds into torture. Torture bleeds into terrorism.

A NOTE ABOUT TERMS

Words have power. In 1997, the Federal Bureau of Investigation implemented an email-monitoring system called "Carnivore."[5] The system was widely criticized in the press, and by privacy advocates, even though it did not provide the FBI with any new legal authority (agents still had to get a court order to target particular users). A colleague jokes that if the FBI had called the system "Fluffy Bunny," rather than "Carnivore," it would not have inspired the same level of concern.[6] In fact, the FBI ultimately did change the name of the program, to "DCS1000."[7]

The police have not made the "Carnivore" mistake in embracing stop and frisk. The phrase connotes a slight intrusion, an inconvenience rather than a big deal. The Fourth Amendment to the U.S. Constitution regulates how the police can "seize and search," and in *Terry v. Ohio*, the prosecution argued that being stopped and frisked is so minor, it doesn't count as a search or seizure. But the Supreme Court "emphatically" rejected this notion:

> It must be recognized that, whenever a police officer accosts an individual and restrains his freedom to walk away, he has "seized" that person. And it is nothing less than sheer torture of the English language to suggest that a careful exploration of the outer surfaces of a person's clothing all over his or her

body in an attempt to find weapons is not a "search." More-over, it is simply fantastic to urge that such a procedure per-formed in public by a policeman while the citizen stands helpless, perhaps facing a wall with his hands raised, is a "petty indignity." It is a serious intrusion upon the sanctity of the person, which may inflict great indignity and arouse strong resentment, and it is not to be undertaken lightly.[8]

In this chapter, I will use the terms "stop and frisk" and "seize and search" interchangeably. The former is more familiar, but the lat-ter more accurately conveys the "serious intrusion on the sanctity of the person."

STREET LAW AND RACIAL
HUMILIATION: A BRIEF HISTORY

The Fourth Amendment is the part of the U.S. Constitution that governs arrests. It requires that the police have "probable cause" before they "book" a suspect. But often cops are suspicious of people they don't have grounds to arrest. Can those persons be detained—forced to stop and deal with the police—and searched, even if the police don't yet know that they have committed a crime? Prior to 1968, the Supreme Court had not decided this issue. Up until that time, unless the police had grounds to arrest you, they were not supposed to hold you.

But the law of the streets was quite different. The police had been conducting stop and frisks for decades before the Supreme Court got around to approving them in the *Terry* case. The prac-tice began in the 1930s. When cops saw African Americans doing things they thought were suspicious—it could be driving an ex-pensive car, socializing with white people, or just hanging out on the corner—police would routinely make them show identifica-tion and question them about where they worked and what they were doing.

Most stops did not lead to arrests, but that has never really been the purpose of stop and frisk. Rather, the benefit that police gained was a tool for "psychological warfare," according to Orlando W. Wilson, head of the Chicago police department from 1960 to 1967 and one of the pioneers of modern policing. Stop and frisk is an effective law enforcement strategy, Chief Wilson thought, because it creates the impression that the police are omnipresent.

"Field detentions" became a proactive police policy in the 1960s, not coincidentally during the time that the African American population of urban areas was increasing. The phrase "stop and frisk" was coined in New York in 1964, where the state passed a law allowing the police to temporarily detain people suspected of crime.

Every Supreme Court case is a creature of its times. In 1968, the year *Terry v. Ohio* was decided, the streets were wild. This was a new and troubling development, because for much of the early part of the century, at least since the Depression, crime had been relatively low. But between 1960 and 1970, the crime rate increased by 135 percent.[9]

For violent crimes like homicide and robbery, African American men were disproportionately the perpetrators and disproportionately the victims. There was a sense that the ghetto was out of control, and that the main culprits were black males. The police responded aggressively. James Baldwin, writing in 1962, observed:

> The only way to police a ghetto is to be oppressive. . . . The badge, the gun in the holster, and the swinging club make vivid what will happen should rebellion become overt. . . . He moves through Harlem, therefore, like an occupying soldier in a bitterly hostile country, which is precisely what, and where he is, and is the reason he walks in twos and threes.[10]

Many African Americans fought back—some literally. Alex Elkins, a graduate student at Temple University, has written about the forgotten practice of "cop fighting." During the 1960s African Americans would frequently intervene to prevent people from being arrested. The *Washington Post* reported, "In the Negro ghettos of cities across the Nation, there has been a rash of incidents in which slum dwellers have engaged police in 'tugs of war.' The charge of 'police brutality' is a rallying cry."[11] This happened all over the country. In Los Angeles one thousand people rescued a black man who had been arrested in a public park. Across the nation, the citizen reactions became so intense that, in 1961, FBI Director J. Edgar Hoover wrote an op-ed for the *Los Angeles Times* called "Stop Attacks on Police Men!" In New York, Elkins writes, "bystander interventions climbed to an average of five a day." A 1967 report stated that in Chicago, Boston, and Washington, D.C., in one-third of the cases in which the police arrested a black man, they had to deal with at least five bystanders.[12]

In Oakland, California, members of the Black Panther Party took a different approach to stop and frisk. When they saw a black driver being pulled over by the cops, they would approach and watch with their guns drawn.

From 2014 to 2016, protesters took to the streets to protest police violence against African Americans. In Ferguson some people threw rocks and bottles at cops. In Baltimore, a CVS drugstore was burned. In Charleston, people blocked highways and also threw objects at police officers, injuring sixteen officers. These protests were mild compared to the urban uprisings of the 1960s, many of which were also precipitated by police violence against African Americans. The summer before the Court decided *Terry*, the entire nation had been transfixed by the Twelfth Street Riot in Detroit. The city's police department was 93 percent white and notoriously racist. On July 23, 1967, cops raided a party for two African American soldiers coming home from the Vietnam War and arrested everyone present. Someone in the crowd watching the arrests threw a brick at the cops. Five bloody days later, forty-three people were dead, 7,200 people had been arrested, and two thousand buildings were destroyed. It took the Michigan National Guard and 82nd and 101st Airborne Divisions of the U.S. Army to restore order.

This was the atmosphere in which the Supreme Court had to decide how much power cops had to patrol the streets. Under the leadership of Chief Justice Earl Warren, the Court had been viewed as hostile to police. The year before, in *Miranda v. Arizona*, the Court had ruled that police have to advise arrestees that they don't have to talk to the police and that they have the right to a lawyer. Though *Miranda* was a 5–4 decision, and not expected by legal scholars to have much of an impact on actual police work, the case was reviled by many. Many people blamed the skyrocketing crime rate on the Supreme Court's "coddling criminals."

In the *Terry* case, a Cleveland police detective's attention was drawn to two African American men who were standing on a street corner. The detective couldn't say exactly why he had started watching them; he said he was "attracted" because "they didn't look right to me at the time." The detective observed the men walk up and down the street looking in the same store window several times. He claimed that he thought they were "casing" a store with the intention of robbing it. He also said that in more than thirty years on the force, he had never suspected anyone else of casing a store.

Next, the two men walked away from the store, and were joined by a white man. That's the point at which the officer approached. Why then? The Supreme Court's opinion doesn't mention this, but during this time in Cleveland (although not just Cleveland), police lore was that whenever black and white men were together, a crime was about to go down.[13] The detective asked the men to give their names, and when Mr. Terry "mumbled something" in response, the cop grabbed Mr. Terry and pushed him against a wall. The detective then patted down Mr. Terry and felt something that might have been a gun in his coat pocket. He ordered all three men inside a store, where he frisked them. Mr. Terry and one of the other men were carrying guns.

The Court held that even though the detective had no probable cause, he had acted legally. It said the beat cop needed the power to take "swift action predicated upon on-the-spot observations." The new standard the case created is that the police can briefly detain someone when they have "reasonable suspicion" that a crime may be occurring, or is about to occur.[14] Cops can "pat down" the person whom they have stopped if they have reasonable suspicion that the suspect is armed.[15]

To the extent *Terry* was a response by the Supreme Court to the charge that it was going too easy on criminals, it was a great success. The *New York Times*, in an editorial the day after the case was decided, said, "The Supreme Court's 8–1 decision will help persuade policemen that the Court does not lie awake nights dreaming up ways to increase the hazards of their jobs."[16]

Terry was not a close case for the Supreme Court. Even Thurgood Marshall, the newest member of the Court, and its first African American justice, went along with the majority, although years later he suggested that he regretted this vote.[17]

Justice Douglas was the lone dissenter. He called the decision "a long step down the totalitarian path" and warned that the country was entering "a new regime" where the police could seize and search at will.[18] William Douglas was known as the Court's "great dissenter" and he was right. The country had entered a new regime.

"THE WHITE HEAT RESENTMENT OF GHETTO NEGROES"

The National Association for the Advancement of Colored People believed that the *Terry* case had so much racial significance it asked the Supreme Court if it could participate in the oral argument. The Court denied this request, and the racial consequences of its decision weren't dwelt upon. The opinion never mentioned that Mr. Terry was African American.

The few sentences the opinion devotes to race are quite revealing; they directly acknowledge the potential for police to use their new power to stop and frisk as a mechanism for racial humiliation. The Court noted that "minority groups, particularly Negroes, frequently complain" about "wholesale harassment by certain elements of the police community."[19] The decision cited the President's Commission on Law Enforcement and Administration of Justice, which reported that frisking "cannot help but be a severely exacerbating factor in police-community tensions. This is particularly true in situations where the 'stop and frisk'" of youths or minority group members is "motivated by the officers' perceived need to maintain the power image of the beat officer, an aim sometimes accomplished by humiliating anyone who attempts to undermine police control of the streets."[20]

In a letter to Chief Justice Warren before the Court released the decision, Justice Brennan was even more forthright. He wrote:

> I've become acutely concerned that the mere fact of our affirmance in *Terry* will be taken by the police all over the country as our license to them to carry on, indeed widely expand, present "aggressive surveillance" techniques which the press tell us are being deliberately employed in Miami, Chicago, Detroit [and] other ghetto cities. This is happening, of course, in response to the "crime in the streets" alarums being sounded in this election year in the Congress, the White House [and] every Governor's office. . . . It will not take much of this to aggravate the already white heat resentment of ghetto Negroes against the police—[and] the Court will become the scape goat.[21]

And so it was. *Terry* became the gateway case for racial profiling, with the Supreme Court's blessing. Remember, the case allows the police to seize and search on the basis of "suspicious" factors.

The majority of federal and state courts have held that the police can consider your race when determining whether you are suspicious. Thus the fact that someone is African American can, coupled with other facts, legally be considered grounds for the police to detain you.

The Federal Court of Appeals for the Eighth Circuit, for example, allowed police to consider the fact that suspects were black when deciding who to investigate for suspicion of carrying drugs on flights from Los Angeles to Kansas City.[22] The court stated that "facts are not to be ignored simply because they may be unpleasant," and the unpleasant fact was that "young male members of black Los Angeles gangs were flooding the Kansas City areas with cocaine."[23]

Of course African Americans are not the only group that experiences group-based suspicion. Law enforcement agents have also relied on the *Terry* doctrine to profile Muslims and Arabs, particularly at airports.[24] Latinos are the subject of special attention by border patrol agents. As the next section details, however, stop and frisk by local police officers disproportionately burdens African American men. It's another example of the Chokehold at work.

Since *Terry* was decided, African American men appear to have been the primary targets of stop and frisks by local police officers. I say "appear" because there is no national database on who is subjected to stop and frisk. Some city police departments do maintain that data, however (see Table 5).

STOP AND FRISK AND PUBLIC SAFETY

Stop and frisk has become the principal technique in "proactive" or "order maintenance" policing. It is a practice that U.S. cops engage in millions of times a year. Cops have embraced their power to conduct brief detentions to see if "criminal activity is afoot." But the crimes they investigate are a far cry from the armed burglary Officer McFadden suspected in the *Terry* case. The crimes

TABLE 5: CITY-LEVEL STOP-AND-FRISK DATA

Boston		
Race	Percentage of population (2010 census)	Percentage of stops (2007–2010)
White	53.9 percent	21.8 percent
Black	24.4 percent	63.3 percent
Hispanic	17.5 percent	12.4 percent
Other races/ unknown data	13.2 percent	2.5 percent

Chicago		
Race	Percentage of population	Percentage of stops
White	32 percent	9 percent
Black	32 percent	72 percent
Hispanic	29 percent	17 percent
Asian or Pacific Islander	5 percent	1 percent

Newark		
Race	Percentage of population (2010 census)	Percentage of stops (2011–2015)
Black	52.4 percent	54 percent
White	26.3 percent	21.5 percent
Hispanic (Latino)	33.8 percent	7 percent (2014 only)

Philadelphia		
Race	Percentage of population	Percentage of stops
White	43 percent	19.77 percent
Black	43 percent	71.58 percent
Hispanic	9 percent	8.65 percent
Asian or Pacific Islander	5 percent	N/A

African American men are the primary targets of stop-and-frisk policing in Chicago, Boston, Newark, and Philadelphia.

Sources: Stop and Frisk in Chicago, ACLU of Illinois (Mar. 2015), www.aclu-il.org/wp-con tent/uploads/2015/03/ACLU_StopandFrisk_6.pdf; Stop and Frisk Report Summary, ACLU of Massachusetts (October 2014), aclum.org/app/uploads/2015/06/reports-black-brown-and -targeted-summary.pdf; Newark Stop-and-Frisk, ACLU of New Jersey (February 25, 2014), www.aclu-nj.org/theissues/policepractices/newark-stop-and-frisk-data; Census Newark, New Jersey, Census Bureau (2010), www.census.gov/quickfacts/table/PST045215/3451000#flag -js-X; Plaintiffs' Fifth Report to Court and Monitor on Stop and Frisk Practices, *Bailey v. City of Philadelphia*, C.A. No. 10-5962, 6–7 (2015), www.aclupa.org/download_file/view _inline/2230/198.

most frequently used by cops as an excuse to stop and frisk are minor misdemeanors like drinking in public or trespassing on private property. The detentions are a pretext to allow the police to frisk.

In the proactive policing context, stop and frisk has two purposes: first to provide a means to search people who the police have no cause to arrest to see if those people have guns or drugs; and second, to deter people from carrying contraband—if people know there is a significant chance that they may be searched, the theory goes, that should make them less likely to carry.

This theory, though widely embraced, has never been proven. In jurisdictions like New York City that have employed aggressive stop and frisks, crime went down. But crime also went down in jurisdictions that did not use stop-and-frisk tactics in the way that New York has.

Let's keep it real. In neighborhoods like Brownsville, where young men of color got stopped and frisked all the time, they probably were deterred from carrying contraband. Normally if all a police officer has is a hunch or a feeling that a person might have a weapon, he is not allowed to search. *Terry*'s gift to cops is that it allows a search, as long as the police have reasonable suspicions that any crime, such as jaywalking or loitering, has been committed, and reasonable suspicion that the suspect might be armed. A brother would have to be crazy to walk down the street packing, knowing the odds that he could be frisked. But all this means is that he would give the gun to his girlfriend to carry, or stow it away until it was needed. In fact, the homicide rate went up in Brownsville during the years when the police were doing the most stop and frisks.

Whether stop and frisks reduce crime is an important question. Since defenders of stop and frisk frequently extol its crime reduction virtues, let's see whether the data support those claims.

A study by the *New York Times* of an eight-block area of Brownsville, a predominately black and Latino neighborhood, revealed that the arrest rate from *Terry* stops is less than 1 percent. Police made 13,200 stops in 2010, for example, and arrested 109 people, a "hit rate" of .05 percent; in the city as a whole for the same period, the hit rate was .15 percent, three times as high as the Brownsville rate. Aggressive stop and frisk is actually less effective at finding actual criminal activity.[25]

In the more than fifty thousand stops between 2006 and 2010, the police recovered twenty-five guns. Yet, while hundreds of police officers were stopping hundreds of innocent people every week in Brownsville, and almost never finding guns, shootings in the community increased by 39 percent in 2011. Stop and frisk has been completely ineffective in preventing Brownsville from having one of the highest rates of violent crime in New York.

Figure 10, provided by an expert witness in the New York stop-and-frisk case, shows that crime in New York City began decreasing years before the NYPD started its aggressive stop-and-frisk campaign. The biggest drop in crime actually happened between 1998 and 2003, before the NYPD dramatically ramped up its use of stop and frisk. Crime continued to go down after the NYPD's aggressive policing increased, but not at the same rate as before. In 2012, because of community activism against the policy, the police began to make fewer stops. Between 2012 and 2015, as the number of stop-and-frisk incidents decreased from more than 500,000 to fewer than 25,000, the murder rate in NYC dropped by 32 percent.[26] In 2016, the NYPD was on track to make the lowest number of stops since reporting began, and major felony crimes, including homicide, also reached record lows.[27] The data is clear: stop-and-frisk does not make communities safer. Instead it causes many men of color to hate the police, and makes them less willing to engage with the government in any way, because the primary manifestation of the government in their lives—the police—treats them with such contempt.[28]

FIGURE 10: STOPS AND CRIMES, 1998–2009

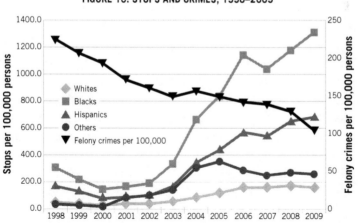

Stop-and-frisk policing does not appear to meaningfully deter crime.

Source: Expert Report of Jeffrey Fagan, David Floyd v. City of New York, ccrjustice.org/sites /default/files/assets/files/Expert_Report_JeffreyFagan.pdf.

In 2013, a federal judge found that the NYPD had gone too far with stop and frisk. The police were using it in a way that violated the Constitution, because the stops were not based on reasonable suspicion. The court ruled that the police were discriminating against African Americans and Latinos. The judge did not say that the NYPD had to end stop and frisk, just that it must be used in a way that is constitutional. But as we have seen, the police still have extraordinary power to stop and frisk within the bounds of the law.

THE EFFECT OF STOP AND FRISK

It is not hard to imagine authoritarian law enforcement practices that would enhance public safety; indeed a hallmark of many police states is low crime rates. If the police could randomly enter any home they wanted at any time, they would absolutely find more guns and drugs. But stop and frisk is ineffective even on its own terms. The evidence from New York demonstrates that *Terry* stop and frisks have an almost negligible public safety benefit. If stop and frisk is not actually protecting citizens from crime, is it fair to ask what purpose is being accomplished by the harsh tactic? The next sections suggest some answers.

A predictable retort to the claim that stop and frisks are like torture, sexual harassment, and terrorism is that the perpetrators—the police—do not intend them that way. One response is that it does not matter. Numerous legal scholars have catalogued the problems of constructing injustice based on "intent."[29] One concern is that intent may not be conscious, and thus it is difficult, if not impossible, to prove, because the person herself may not be aware of her intent. A more pressing objection to an "intent" standard is that, from the standpoint of the victim of an injury, the wrongdoer's intent is not the most salient feature; the victim's immediate concern is redressing her injury rather than blaming a particular bad actor.

Some scholars have observed that Fourth Amendment analysis has been distorted by a failure to weigh effects properly. Under the Constitution, searches and seizures must be reasonable; to determine whether they are, the Supreme Court has engaged in a cost-benefit analysis, balancing the government interest versus the individual interest. In the context of race-based assessments of suspicion, many scholars have argued that courts discount the effect on victims (and overstate the value to the government of using race as a cause for suspicion). Professor Jody Armour vividly describes the feeling of being the target of race-based suspicion as having "waves of strangers successively spit in my face."[30]

Likewise, people who have been stopped and frisked use words like "violated," "invaded," and "chumped" to describe how it made them feel.[31] It also may affect their actions: African American and Latino men, in particular, tell stories about the measures they take to avoid being stopped and frisked; these steps may range from decisions about clothing and hair style to the kinds of cars they drive or the neighborhoods in which they choose to live.

While not overtly brutal, stop and frisks have more consequence than what race theorists have defined as "microaggressions."[32] Racial microaggressions are "brief and commonplace daily verbal, behavioral, or environmental indignities whether intentional or unintentional that communicate hostile, derogatory, or negative racial slights and insults toward people of color. Perpetrators of microaggressions are also often unaware that they engage in such communications when they engage with racial/ethnic minorities."[33]

Stop and frisks cause injury more like police brutality than racial microaggression. The *Terry* opinion characterized stop and frisk as a "serious intrusion on the sanctity of the person, which may inflict great indignity and arouse strong resentment." I would go further and say that the invasive aspect of the frisk—the "feel with sensitive fingers every portion of the prisoner's body [including] the groin and areas about the testicles," in the words of the police manual referenced in *Terry*—makes the injury analogous to sexual assault. Frisks are frequently experienced as offensive sexual touchings.

STOP-AND-FRISK SEX

Abuse of African American men has often had a sexual component.[34] Black male victims of lynching were frequently castrated,
and then their penises were stuffed in their mouths. A New York
police officer inserted a broom handle into the anus of Abner
Louima. In 1970, Philadelphia cops raided three offices of the
Black Panther Party, ordered the men to line up against a wall
and strip, and then took photos of them. Police sometimes obtain
confessions by warning male suspects if they don't cooperate with
the cops, they will be raped in prison.[35]

Stop and frisk is also gendered, and sexual. Frisks are frisky. The
police "cop" a feel. To "assume the position" is to make oneself
submissive—one turns and offers his backside to another person.
Often other cops participate, either as voyeurs, or by doing another guy at the same time. In African American neighborhoods,
it is not uncommon to see a row of young men facing a wall,
each waiting his turn to be patted down by one officer, or a group
pat down, involving several officers and several young men. The
journalist Richard Goldstein, writing about the assault of Abner
Louima, observed:

> Several false assumptions shape our obliviousness to the
> erotic element in police brutality: that men are rarely the
> victims of sexual assault, that straight men have no homo-
> sexual feelings, and that sexuality is limited to what we do in
> bed. The first perception allows police to force young black
> men to drop their pants—a common practice during street
> frisks—without risking charges of sexual harassment (imag-
> ine what would happen if black women were subject to this
> treatment); the second notion prevents us from imagining
> that cops who specialize in such tactics might find them
> exciting; and the third blinds us to the connection between
> sadism and racism.[36]

Many hip-hop artists have, in their lyrics, depicted frisks as a form of sexual harassment.[37] I should note that hip-hop is notorious for the homophobia of some of its artists, as well as for the distaste with which many members of the hip-hop nation regard the police. These two factors may combine to make the police prime candidates for what is, from the homophobe's perspective, the ultimate insult—an "accusation" of homosexuality. I use hip-hop lyrics as on-the-ground reporting of lived experiences; they are victim testimony. Indeed, since part of the gratification that some police officers derive from stop and frisks is sadistic, the fact that a victim might be homophobic enhances the pleasure.

The seminal hip-hop group NWA states, "I don't know if [the police] are fags or what / search a nigga down and grabbin' his nuts."[38] The most interesting aspect of this analysis isn't the homophobia, which, sadly, is a trope in hip-hop culture. Rather, it is the words "or what," which suggest that the male-on-male sexual harassment is not just for gays. Indeed these lyrics support all three of Goldstein's claims about the eras of police brutality: the NWA character is a male victim of sexual assault—by officers who may or may not be gay but regardless are gratified by "grabbin' [a "nigga"'s] nuts."

In fact hip-hop's endemic homophobia makes the absence of antigay epitaphs to describe the sexual component of frisks especially revealing. Lupe Fiasco complains about "crooked police that's stationed at the knees and they do drive-bys like up and down the thighs."[39] Likewise, Webbie raps, "The police pull me over and they raid my cash / Man they be wishin' they could take my ass."[40] Commercial hip-hop, unfortunately, does not subscribe to a civility that prohibits the use of words like "fag"; indeed, rap music seems almost to encourage pejorative terms. Thus their absence, when the artists describe male-on-male sexual harassment, seems a recognition—from victims of frisks—that it's possible for "straight" men to get off by doing sexual things to other men.

African American men other than hip-hop artists have also

observed the erotic nature of frisks. In an article for the *Village Voice* titled "The Gropes of Wrath: The NYPD Loves Touching Black Men," the journalist Nicholas Powers wrote that "for black men, being stopped and frisked by the police is a rite of passage. But I've never been touched by a cop. I'm a virgin." Recounting statistics about the number of African American and Latino men who have been stopped and frisked by the New York Police Department, Powers observed, "The NYPD is fondling our bodies."[41]

The Urban Dictionary, an online wiki that defines street slang and provides an example of usage, contains this entry for "frisk": "When cops search you for drugs and guns by feeling you all over from behind. The big, tall, muscular security guard leaned right down behind me and felt me all over because his orders were to frisk me."[42]

I do not want to be too grandiose about hip-hop's analysis. There certainly are artists who view frisks as standard homosexual sexual gratification, and who don't have a problem using antigay terms to castigate the harassers. Dead Prez, for example, claims, "Every police is a punk ass bitch / this is for my niggas in the streets getting frisked gun to your head."[43] I simply make two points: first that several hip-hop artists have described frisks as sexual harassment and, second, that some of the artists have constructed the meaning of the touching as outside of the usual sexual norms.[44]

The legal scholar Bernard Harcourt has also observed a sexual element in stop and frisk.[45] He describes an encounter, recorded in the appendix of a study of police searches by scholars Jon Gould and Stephen Mastrofski, between a white police officer and an African American male, both in their late twenties.[46] The black man, who had been riding a bike, was stopped and frisked by the police, who found no contraband. The cop then said to the black man, "I bet you are hiding [drugs] under your balls. If you have drugs under your balls, I am going to fuck your balls up." As Harcourt relates, quoting from the study by Gould and Mastrofski, "The police officer then tells the young black suspect to 'get behind the police car, and pull his pants down to his ankles.' The white police officer puts on some rubber gloves. He then begins 'feeling around' the black suspect's testicles."

The officer still found no contraband. He told the black man, "I bet you are holding them in the crack of your ass. You better not have them up your ass." Harcourt writes, "The black man, at this point very compliant, 'bent over, and spread his cheeks.' The white cop, still with his rubber gloves, then 'put his hand up [the black man's] rectum.'"

The police still found no evidence of a crime. They told the black man he could leave, he said "thank you" and rode off on his bike. Harcourt poses a series of questions, including, "What must have been going through the officer's mind when he started putting on those rubber gloves? . . . Did he feel embarrassed about being white and putting his hands up a black man's rectum? Or did that excite him? Do you think he experienced some pleasure at the idea of penetrating a black man?"

It is difficult for some to understand sexuality between men when one or both men are perceived to be heterosexual. If I were describing a practice of police officers choosing, at will, which women they want to touch (and especially men of color choosing white women), the sexual element would seem obvious.[47] Heteronormativity obscures what is going on between the police and black men.

MAN-ON-MAN SEXUAL HARASSMENT

Civil rights law has recognized that man-on-man sexual harassment is possible even when the harasser is heterosexual. Title VII of the Civil Rights Act of 1964 prohibits sex discrimination but does not specifically outlaw harassment between people of the same gender. The U.S. Supreme Court then extended the protection in 1998, holding in *Oncale v. Sundowner Offshore Services, Inc.*, that sexually harassing conduct "need not be motivated by sexual desire." Justice Scalia, writing for the majority of the Supreme Court, stated, "male-on-male sexual harassment in the workplace was assuredly not the principal evil Congress was concerned with when it enacted Title VII. But statutory prohibitions often go beyond the principal evil to cover reasonably comparable evils."

Some men who have been touched by the police have brought lawsuits, but usually courts have responded skeptically. In *Njaka v. Wright County*, police officers responded to a call that a black male was behaving suspiciously near a water treatment facility.[48] One officer frisked the suspect and, in so doing, "deliberately pinched his testicle while patting him down."[49] The subject of the frisk sued, alleging that the pat down was a "homosexual harassing; a 'come-on,' and a 'homosexual fantasy.'" The court ruled that the plaintiff's theory was "highly implausible particularly in light of the fact that the search was conducted in front of another officer."[50]

A few judges have been more receptive. In *Myers v. James*,[51] a man accompanied a female friend to her vehicle, which was parked in an area notorious for burglaries.[52] A police officer approached the man, frisked him, and "grabbed the plaintiff's testicles and asked him if he liked the way that felt."[53] This court found "grabbing a citizen's testicles under these circumstances is plainly unconstitutional."[54]

Likewise, in *Marrie v. Nickels*, military prisoners sued prison guards for sexual assault.[55] The plaintiffs alleged that, during frisks, one guard would regularly "[place] his hands into [an inmate's] pants, [caress] his buttocks, and [stroke] his genitalia."[56] The plaintiffs also challenged another policy whereby frisks were used as a punishment in which the guards "formed up to create a shakedown gauntlet wherein inmates are frisk searched dozens of times in a mere 150 feet," causing the plaintiffs to suffer "uncountable assaults." The prison guards tried to get the case dismissed, but the judge refused.[57]

"DON'T TOUCH MY JUNK"

In recent years, a large cross section of the public has come to know what it feels like to be felt up by law enforcement officials. Transportation Security Administration (TSA) pat downs, introduced at airports in 2010, met with swift public outcry. Stories of angry and humiliated passengers have steadily flowed forth through the media and the Internet. A poll showed that half of the public are bothered or angered by the pat downs.[58] Many people perceive a sexual component in this touching.[59] Some sexual assault survivors reported feeling traumatized by pat downs.[60] One man's "don't touch my junk" video protest recording went viral on the Internet.[61]

Since many people who have been subject to TSA frisks have not been frisked by police officers, the TSA experience may help some people empathize with the sexual nature of these searches. Still, there are important differences. By going on an airplane, one implicitly consents to a TSA frisk, while people who are subject to *Terry* frisks have no say in the matter. African American men, especially, are repeat players for police frisks. Most white people, however, don't get pulled aside frequently for TSA "secondary screening," although many Arabs, South Asians, and people who are perceived to be Muslim do. Finally, stop and frisks are communicative of degraded citizenship and the TSA frisks generally are not (except, again, for Arabs, South Asians, and people who are perceived to be Muslim).

My claim is not that seize and search is the same as sexual harassment. My point is that stop and frisk shares certain features with this form of subordination, and the fact that it does should enter into our assessment of the practice.

STOP-AND-FRISK TORTURE

Sometimes the police have literally tortured African American men. I grew up in an all-black neighborhood in Chicago. One day when I was about thirteen years old I rode my bike to the public library, which was in the white neighborhood a few miles away. When I got close to the library, a cop car pulled up next to me and an officer rolled down his window and asked if the bike I was riding belonged to me. "Yes," I replied. "Does that car belong to you?" And I sped off.

When I got home I told my mother what I had done. She spanked me good. Didn't I know what happened to black boys who talked to the police like that? I was lucky to be alive. It was one of those whoopings when the parent cries as much as the child.

It turns out that my mother was right about the police. During this time, Chicago police commander Jon Burge was overseeing the torture of 118 black men. He and his "midnight crew" of cops coerced confessions from suspects by methods that included sticking electrical devices up their rectums, pouring soda in their noses, and burning them with curling irons. Burge's method of choice was the "black box." This was an electrical device that would be attached to people who were shackled to tables or chairs. One wire from the box would be placed on their hands, and another on their ankles. An officer would then place a plastic bag over the suspect's head and crank up the electricity.

Anthony Holmes, one of Burge's victims, told prosecutors, "When he hit me with the voltage, that's when I started gritting, crying, hollering. . . . It [felt] like a thousand needles going through my body. And then after that, it just [felt] like, you know—it [felt] like something just burning me from the inside, and, um, I shook, I gritted, I hollered, then I passed out."[62]

Chicago has now spent more than $100 million investigating Burge's midnight crew and compensating its victims. Some of the people tortured into confessing have been freed, while others are still in prison. In 2011, Burge himself was convicted of obstruction of justice and perjury and did four years in federal prison. He still receives his pension from the Chicago Police Department.

In 1883, some African Americans brought a case to the Supreme

Court arguing that Jim Crow segregation violated the Thirteenth Amendment's prohibition against "the badges and incidents" of slavery. The Supreme Court rejected the argument, saying that the black litigants were "running the slavery argument into the ground."[63] Today, however, many more people understand the relationship between slavery and segregation. By comparing stop and frisk to torture, I might be accused of "running the torture argument into the ground." But one of the lessons of history is that it is hard to see the picture when you are inside the frame.

Stop and frisk can be seen as a "badge and incident" of lynching, the gendered and racialized violence directed against African American men (among others) around the turn of the twentieth century.[64] Lynching was expressive. It was not only about destroying individual bodies; it was designed to terrorize all blacks, especially African American men. It worked. Indeed it was so effective that the nation's first civil rights organization, the National Association for the Advancement of Colored People, was formed in response to it.

Stop and frisk is not as violent as some forms of police brutality, like the atrocities the NYPD perpetrated against Abner Louima in 1997, which included raping him with a broom handle.[65] Nobody has ever died from a stop and frisk per se, although police are allowed to use deadly force when the suspect is noncompliant and the officer believes there is a risk to life. Police routinely draw their guns during *Terry* stops in high-crime neighborhoods.[66] For example, the expert witness's report in the recent New York City stop-and-frisk case found that "force was 14 percent more likely to be used in stops of Blacks compared to White suspects, and 9.3 percent more likely for Hispanics."[67] In any event the fact that stop and frisk does not typically draw blood does not mean it is benign.

TORTURE-LITE

When we think of torture, lurid images of the Iron Maiden or victims shrouded in black hoods come forth. But while all torture is "the deliberate infliction of suffering and pain," a continuum exists.[68] As philosopher David Luban has noted, "There is a vast difference . . . between the ancient world of torture, with its appalling mutilations, its roastings and flayings, and the tortures that liberals might accept: sleep deprivation, prolonged standing in stress positions, extremes of heat and cold, bright light and loud music—what some refer to as 'torture lite.'"[69]

In human rights law, torture-lite refers to interrogation techniques that don't leave physical marks on the body. Beth Van Schaack, writing on a blog for human rights lawyers, described these techniques as "psychological humiliations (forced nudity), disguised rape (e.g., body cavity searches), prevention of personal hygiene, forced grooming, denial of privacy, infested surroundings, threats against self or family, witnessing or hearing the abuse of others, attacks on cultural values or religious beliefs, and mock executions."[70] The purpose of torture-lite is "to induce hopelessness and despair. . . . Small gestures of contempt—facial slaps and frequent insults—drive home the message of futility. Even the rough stuff, such as 'walling' and waterboarding, is meant to dispirit, not to coerce."[71]

Stop and frisks are like the torture-lite that some military police officers have conducted to obtain intelligence from suspected terrorists. They are, as Susan Sontag described, the "bestial practices" at Abu Ghraib "general or nonspecific information-gathering. . . . Softening them up, stressing them out."[72] They are designed to humiliate and control. I do not mean that police who use stop and frisk would be formally guilty in a U.S. court or under international law of a crime or a human rights violation. Just as the Thirteenth Amendment to the U.S. Constitution, which abolishes slavery, contains an exception for prison, the torture law has an exception for "lawful sanctions." My claim is that the police practice of stop and frisk in minority communities causes injuries similar to torture-lite and has the same kinds of benefits.

In *Discipline and Punish*, the French philosopher Michel Foucault described the evolution of punishment in the Western world away from torture to the modern prison.[73] Foucault noted that torture blurred the line between investigation and punishment.

One might make the same observation about a stop and frisk. The purpose of the detention is for the police to investigate: the problem, however, is that the Supreme Court didn't say what the police are supposed to do, beyond not allowing the suspect to leave. The cops can ask questions, or see if witnesses to a crime can identify the detainees as the culprits, but even if the suspects pass this part of the ordeal by providing nonsuspicious answers to questions, the police remain wary. As Foucault put it, "Guilt did not begin when all the evidence was gathered together; piece by piece it was constituted by each of the elements that made it possible to recognize a guilty person. Thus a semi-proof did not leave the suspect innocent until such time as it was completed; it made him semi-guilty; slight evidence of a serious crime marked someone as slightly criminal."[74]

Stop and frisk is not supposed to be punishment, but it feels that way to its victims. After the police have detained you, felt all over your body, and then let you go, you are supposed to go about your business as if nothing of consequence has happened.

Most citizens don't take it personally when they are detained by a traffic light. Proponents of stop and frisk seem to feel that the *Terry* rule requiring you to submit, often spread-eagle, and almost always in public, while the police physically investigate you to see if they can arrest you for a crime, is somehow regulatory in the same sense as a traffic light. Except that the red light does not prefer to stop black men; the red light does not stop people as part of a performance that demonstrates its dominance and control; the red light engages in no kinky sexual violation while you're waiting for it to turn green; and the red light derives no pleasure from the public spectacle of submission to its order. And the police do.

Stop and frisks signal that the police control the streets, and they signal this in a way that is, as Foucault described torture, "public," "spectacular," "corporal," and "punitive." When one sees a row of black men spread against a wall, one is witnessing what Foucault called "the very ceremonial of justice being expressed in all its force."[75]

A 2000 Supreme Court case called *Illinois v. Wardlow* offers a compelling example of Foucault's concept of torture as a "continual gradation" between investigation and punishment.[76] Chicago police were patrolling a high-crime area and noticed Mr. Wardlow standing next to a building. What Mr. Wardlow did to justify being stopped and frisked was stated succinctly by Chief Justice Rehnquist: Mr. Wardlow "looked in the direction of the officers and fled." This was enough of an affront to the power of the officers that they gave chase and "eventually cornered him on the street."[77] They frisked him and discovered he was carrying a gun.

The issue before the Supreme Court was whether the police can stop you when they have no reason to suspect you of a crime, other than that you have tried to evade them. The Court ruled that the police did have this power—but only in high-crime areas. In other words, if you see the police and run in a middle-class community, the police have to leave you alone. But if you see the police and run in a "high-crime" area, the police can stop and frisk you.

The detention that *Wardlow* authorizes is ceremonial because often it will be useless as a matter of investigation. The Court conceded that suspects who are detained maintain the right to "stay put and remain silent in the face of police questioning."[78] The police purpose then is served not so much by the investigation but by the stop itself, which is, in Foucault's words, a "reassertion and public declaration of power by the sovereign."[79] The goal is to make citizens aware of the presence and authority of the cops. It is "the ceremony of the public torture . . . displayed for all to see the power relation that gave . . . force to the law."[80]

When the cops detain someone from running away from them

it seems punitive because they don't have a specific crime to investigate. After *Wardlow*, this is now not a barrier to detention; just as with torture, "penal demonstration did not obey a dualistic system, true or false, but a principle of continual gradation."[81] It isn't your suspiciousness that makes the police interested in you but, rather, because the police are interested in you, you must be suspicious. In Foucault's description of the torture subject, "The suspect as such always deserved punishment; one could not be the object of suspicion and be completely innocent."[82]

In an African American neighborhood, the real offense *Wardlow* addresses is not displaying sufficient deference to the police; this then becomes grounds for being detained, and, only afterward, "[if] the officer does not learn facts rising to the level of probable cause, the individual must be allowed to go on his way."[83] Mr. Wardlow was suspicious because he communicated that he wanted to avoid the police. As redress for this affront to the state, the Supreme Court allowed his detention and search, and, sure enough, the police discovered an actual crime for which Mr. Wardlow could formally be punished.

Wardlow is an emblematic Chokehold case. It stands for the proposition that when African American males see the police, they must communicate submission—otherwise they can be detained and touched. The effect of the *Wardlow* doctrine in African American and Latino neighborhoods is hard to overstate. The arbitrary nature of being stopped—it is now a de facto offense to demonstrate that you do not want to be near the police—contributes to an atmosphere of fear of the police. The result is that citizens are more compliant—or they risk the consequences.

The Supreme Court opinion, by limiting its holding to "high-crime" neighborhoods, ensures that affluent white people need not submit to the cops. Imagine a white man in Chicago's tony Gold Coast neighborhood who takes off running as soon as he spies a police officer. After *Wardlow*, the police have no grounds to stop him. It's suspicious only when it happens in a "high-crime" area, which almost always means minority communities. Yet the

Chokehold makes even the act of imagining the white man running when he sees the police a difficult thought experiment. The white man would not run because he, going about his daily business, is likely to be ignored by the police. The black man, however, reasonably expects that he might be stopped and frisked and that is why he bolts. And then *Wardlow* authorizes the black man's detention, precisely on the ground that he sought to avoid being detained. It is a perfectly vicious cycle.

In Baltimore, Freddie Gray was stopped by the police not because they suspected him of a specific crime, but because, according to one of the officers, he fled "unprovoked upon noticing police presence." Two cops on bikes chased him down and stopped and frisked him. They found a small knife, which they wrongly thought was illegal, arrested him, and put him in the back of a police wagon. As the whole world now knows, by the time Mr. Gray got to the police station, his spine was crushed, and one week later he died of the injuries he sustained in the police van.

STOP-AND-FRISK TERROR

Recently in the District of Columbia, the police, while driving squad cars, were under orders to flash their cruise lights (the bar of lights on top of the car) at all times. The practice was commanded by the chief of police after he visited Israel, where police also do this. It was, for D.C. motorists, very confusing: you were never quite sure, when a squad car with flashing lights was behind you, whether the police were ordering you to pull over. In a city that has more police per capita than any other city in the country, a more symbolic concern was also expressed: What is the effect on a community when the government makes its surveillance so omnipresent? For many, it was disquieting. It created a heightened and pervasive sense of alarm.

The practice of stop and frisk has this same effect on African American men, but it is much more pronounced. The sight of any police officer is a signal to any black man that you are subject to being detained and searched. The instinct is to avoid the intrusion, but the standard is so low, and so arbitrary, that sometimes it is not clear what you can do. Your best option is to avoid being detected by the police and, if you are noticed, to show submission.

Stop and frisk punishes black men, its most consistent repeat targets. It punishes them for being black and male. In "99 Problems," Jay-Z is asked by the officer who has stopped him, "Son, do you know what I'm stopping you for?"[84] Jay-Z replies, "Because I'm young and I'm black and my hat's real low."[85] The legal scholar Bennett Capers writes, "Stops are a dressing down, a public shaming, the very stigmatic harm that the Court has often, but not often enough, found troubling."[86]

Black's Law Dictionary defines "terrorism" as "the use or threat of violence to intimidate or cause panic."[87] This is also how the police use their Terry power to seize and search. During the 2013 Floyd trial in New York City, in which the NYPD's stop-and-frisk policy was being challenged, a former police captain testified that Ray Kelly, then the city's police commissioner, stated that stop and frisk focused on African American and Latino men because Kelly "wanted to instill fear in them, every time they leave their home they could be stopped by the police."[88]

In 2012, the New York Times published an article about Tyquan Brehon, an African American male who claimed that he had been "unjustifiably stopped by the police more than sixty times" before he turned eighteen years old.[89] Brehon explained that he "did whatever he could to avoid the police, often feeling as if he were a prisoner in his home."[90] The consistent behavior of the NYPD had created an automatic behavioral response. The mere presence of the police might cause Brehon, at least, to avoid the police while walking in his neighborhood, and at worst, to confine himself to his own home in order to completely avoid the risk of being stopped and frisked.

Now, consider that many other black and Latino men share Brehon's response. They have shifted their otherwise innocent behavior, in fear of being stopped and frisked. For example, one witness testified in the New York stop-and-frisk trial that the first time the police stopped and then frisked him on his block in the Bronx, he remembered wanting only "to get home" and "be in my own space." The second time it happened, the witness testified, he was left with the impression that "I needed to stay in my place, and my place was in my home."[91]

The witness's sense that, in order to avoid violent encounters with the police, he needed to stay at home is the type of result terrorists hope for. An innocent individual restricts his freedom out of fear that he will be terrorized once again. Effecting this kind of community-wide behavioral change is the essence of terrorism.

Many law-abiding African American men have stories about how fear of the police modifies their behavior. Law professor James Forman is one of the founders of a high school for at-risk students, mainly African American, in the District of Columbia. He observes that when these students see the police approach, they immediately "assume the position," without even being asked.[92] Harvard professor Henry Louis Gates, long before the famous incident in which he was arrested in his home, wrote that, whenever he moved to a new city, he would go and introduce himself to the police, so he would not be stopped.[93] Randall Kennedy, a Harvard law professor, does Professor Gates one better: he offers to volunteer at police stations so that they will know him. A football coach in Brownsville told the New York Times that his players wear their bright orange helmets going home on the streets at night so the police will leave them alone. Otherwise, he said, "My players were always calling me saying 'Coach, the police have me.'"[94] Capers, an African American law professor, has spoken of preferring to walk through his own neighborhood in Brooklyn with his white husband, because being accompanied by a white person communicates that he is safe.[95]

In another context, we might describe these behavior modifications by saying "the terrorists won." Terrorism is successful when it creates the kind of fear that controls the activities of the terrorized. That the Supreme Court, in *Terry*, gave the police this kind of power over minority communities is no accident. It's how the Chokehold works.

An African American mother, writing on a blog about parenting, said this about her son's experience growing up in New York City:

> The saddest part of all of this is he'd begun to become "immune" to being stopped. He, like too many other men of color in this city, had become desensitized to being treated criminally. They take it as par for the course; they shrug it off and most will laughingly share their war stories. But listen closely and you can hear anger comingled with humiliation and a weary, reluctant acceptance.[96]

The Supreme Court got it right in *Terry* when it noted, in the majority opinion, that frisks might be "motivated by the officers' perceived need to maintain the power image of the beat officer, an aim sometimes accomplished by humiliating anyone who attempts to undermine police control of the streets."[97] The "weary, reluctant acceptance" of humiliation is how torture-lite succeeds. It induces in its victims a learned helplessness. One African American resident of Brooklyn told the *New York Times*, residents "fear the police because you can get stopped at any time."[98] Professor Luban describes the torturer's work as inflicting "pain one-on-one, deliberately, up close and personal, in order to break the spirit of the victim—in other words, to tyrannize and dominate the victim."[99]

The stories of many black men who are subject to seize and search are the stories of men who have had their spirits broken. They are afraid of the police. Stop and frisk demonstrates who is in charge, and the consequences of dissent. It does not leave a physical mark, but as one study of torture-lite noted, "Psychological manipulations conducive to anxiety, fear, and helplessness in the detainee do not seem to be substantially different from physical torture in terms of the extent of mental suffering they cause, the underlying mechanisms of traumatic stress, and their long-term traumatic effects."[100]

In *Terry*, to decide whether stop and frisk meets the Fourth Amendment requirement of reasonableness, the Court balanced the government interest in the search and seizure versus the nature of the intrusion to the individual. Some forty years after *Terry*, we have a better sense of the calculus. The data from New York suggests that the government interest—crime detection—is not served well by stop and frisk. And the experience of hundreds of thousands of victims of the practice helps us to understand the harm to the individual in a much more visceral way.

Still, *Terry* is likely to remain good constitutional law for a long time. What this truth helps us understand is that the Constitution may be an insufficient instrument for regulating the police.[101] But just because the police can legally maintain a practice does not mean that they should.

The good news is that we the people have the power to make them stop. We did it in New York City. As pictured in Table 6, in 2013, the number of stop and frisks dramatically declined.[102]

Significantly, the stops began falling well before August 2013, when a federal judge issued an opinion requiring the police to stop unconstitutional proactive stop and frisks.[103] It is also important

TABLE 6: NEW YORK'S STOP-AND-FRISK RATES HAVE FALLEN

Year	Stops
2011	685,724
2012	532,911
2013	191,558
2014	45,787
2015	22,939

Since 2011, the number of stops in New York has been decreasing.

Source: New York Civil Liberties Union, "Stop-and-Frisk Data," 2016, http://www.nyclu.org/content/stop-and-frisk-data.

to note that from 2012, when the NYPD began curtailing stop and frisk, to 2015, the murder rate dropped by 32 percent, and in 2016, all major crimes in New York, including homicide, reached record lows.[104]

It is likely that some combination of activism, political protests, and litigation made the police reduce the number of stop and frisks. The effect of the court case alone gets less credit when one recalls that there had been an earlier case, *Daniels v. City of New York*, which required the police to reform the way they carried out stop and frisk in minority neighborhoods.[105] Yet this case failed to make the police stop in the way that the social movement to end stop and frisk did. Activists need to capture and transport the factors that led to success in New York to the broader national campaign of criminal justice transformation. In the final chapter, I suggest ways to make this happen.

Recall Justice Douglas's dissent in *Terry*.[106] He warned that giving the police the power to stop and frisk citizens based on innocent conduct was a step toward totalitarianism.[107] If Justice Douglas's view of the law had prevailed in *Terry*, the police would still have plenty of power to enforce the criminal law. The detective in *Terry*, for example, could have observed the three men until they seemed about to commit a crime, and then he would have had probable cause to arrest them. It has made law-abiding American citizens outsiders to democracy. It is a primary means of racial subordination of African American and Latino men. In allowing the police to forcibly detain and search based on innocent conduct, the Supreme Court opened the door to giving the police the kind of power they should not have in a free country.

4

Black Male Violence:
The Chokehold Within

Many African American men asked me not to publish this chapter. They said that it would confirm the worst of the stereotypes about us. They said that no matter what I said in the rest of the book, this is the chapter that would get the most attention, for the wrong reasons. They said that writing about violent crime committed by African American men would undermine the cause of criminal justice reform, and make the grip of the Chokehold even tighter. But I had to write about the problem of violence by African American men because the problem has not received sustained analysis in the new discourse about criminal justice reform.

Murder is the leading cause of death of young African American men. In the past fifteen years, more black men have been killed in the city of Chicago alone than the total number of U.S. soldiers who died in the wars in Iraq and Afghanistan.[1] And contrary to popular belief, violent crimes—not drug crimes—have created mass incarceration. In 2013, only 16 percent of state prisoners were serving time for drug offenses.[2] If no one was locked up for any drug offense whatsoever, the United States would remain the world's largest jailer, and a large percentage of the people in prison would be African American. Until we stop using prison to treat black male violence, the United States will continue to have the highest incarceration rate in the world.

One reason African American men asked me not to write about this issue goes to the familiar fear, in any vulnerable community, of airing dirty laundry. The concern is that "inside" problems should not be exposed to the hostile outside world. But thinking of black male violence as an inside issue for the African American community to solve is actually part of the problem. This chapter makes the case that black male violence is as much a symptom of the Chokehold as brutal policing and mass incarceration. It is a plague that the United States has caused, and it will take the resources of the United States to cure it. Believing that African American men alone can resolve the problem is like thinking that they can, by themselves, end climate change.

In any case, African American men are already talking about this issue, in public, a lot. Our dirty drawers have been flapping in the wind for a long time.

Jesse Jackson (civil rights leader)[3]:

> There is nothing more painful to me at this stage in my life than to walk down the street and hear footsteps . . . then turn around and see somebody white and feel relieved.

Richard Sherman (professional athlete, National Football League)[4]:

> We need to solidify ourselves as people and deal with our issues, because I think as long as we have black-on-black crime and, you know, one black man killing another . . . if black lives matter, then it should matter all the time. You should never let somebody get killed—that's somebody's son, that's somebody's brother, that's somebody's friend. So you should always keep that in mind.

A$AP Rocky (rapper)[5]:

> Black on black crime. So, one cop shoots a black person, let's march, let's protest. But I feel like; if you're not going to talk about the main topic, don't talk about it at all. We have

to do something first. That's within us, internally. We can't blame the police officers; that kind of shit is inevitable.

Stephen A. Smith (journalist, ESPN)[6]:

Where is all the noise about #BlackLivesMatter when black folks are killing black folks?

Jay-Z (rapper)[7]:

And we're still killing each other. We need to understand that we are kings and queens. We are kings and queens and we're under attack. A young man trying to make a way out of the hood. We can't have it both ways. We say, "People, they leave the hood and never wanna come back." When people go to the hood, they get killed. We can't have it both ways. We gotta protect our own.

Kendrick Lamar (rapper)[8]:

But when we don't have respect for ourselves, how do we expect them to respect us? It starts from within. Don't start with just a rally, don't start from looting—it starts from within.

James Pate is an African American artist. He has a controversial series of drawings called kin-killin'-kin that compare black-on-black violence to violence by the Ku Klux Klan. His artwork depicts young black men wearing KKK hoods and pointing guns at each other. When an exhibit of the work was shown at the National Civil Rights Museum in Memphis, the local chapter of Black Lives Matter protested. The group issued a press release that stated: "To equate the KKK to a group of people who have been enslaved, segregated, and degraded into second class citizenship is callous and outright offensive. Moreover, this exhibition fails to address the root causes of crime in predominately Black neighborhoods, which is that crime is a reaction to a lack of resources."[9]

Pate responded, "We're just hearing repeatedly people in my community say that we as black people have put the Ku Klux Klan out of business, so as an artist I decided I wanted to respond to that."[10]

Clearly the cat is out of the bag. It's impossible, in the age of Twitter, Facebook, Snapchat, and Instagram, to keep something within the community, if that were ever possible in a group as large and diverse as the African American community. I want to have an open, no-holds-barred conversation about why brothers are disproportionately at risk for violence, as victims and as harm doers, and how we as a society can make things better. In inviting this conversation my role is not so much truth teller as illuminator. It is crucial to put the issue in a broader context than the typical, simplistic "pull your damn pants up" critiques of black masculinity.

THE UGLY FACTS: PART 1

Black men are about 6.5 percent of the population but they are responsible for approximately half of all murders in the United States.[11] Black men commit more murders, in absolute numbers, than Latino men, who slightly outnumber them, and white men, who greatly outnumber them.[12]

Because violent crime is mainly intra-racial, black men are also about 50 percent of murder victims.[13] While overall violent crime is decreasing in the United States, in some cases to historic lows, the percentage of victims of homicides who are black males is increasing.[14]

Homicide Victimization Rate[15]
White: 3 per 100,000
Black men between 15 and 34: 80 per 100,000

Black men are also vastly overrepresented among violent felons other than murderers. According to U.S. Department of Justice statistics, African Americans committed 54 percent of robberies and 39 percent of assaults.[16] Overall, blacks are responsible for 41 percent of all violent felonies.[17] An urban myth is that the ten cities with the highest crime rates are the cities with the largest percentages of blacks. This is not true, but what is true is that since the Great Migration, urban areas in which the black population has increased have also experienced increases in crime.[18]

Sometimes we think of black-on-black crime as a new thing, a consequence of the woes of de-industrialization, or even integration. Most African Americans have listened to an elder wax romantic about a gentler time in black history where people treated each other with more kindness out of a shared sense of kinship. But the reality is that there never has been a golden age for black people in the Unites States. There are bad times, and then there are worse times. In 1950 black men were about twelve times more likely to be a victim of homicide than white men.[19] In 2013 black men were about ten times more likely to be a victim of homicide than white men.[20] The good old days were actually more dangerous for black men than now. And now is still quite bad.

The bottom line is that African American men commit a disproportionate share of certain serious crimes, including homicide, assault, and robbery, and are disproportionately victims of those same crimes. I'll explain why I think these statistics are reliable and then break down why black male violence should not distract from also focusing on state violence by the police.

SHOULD WE TRUST THE DATA ABOUT BLACK MEN AND VIOLENT CRIME?

Some people just don't believe the statistics. Certainly black people have good reason to be dubious that government data about crime is somehow neutral or color-blind. Today most people know that "the war on drugs" has been selectively waged against African Americans. No one thinks that the arrests and incarceration rates for drug crimes reflect the actual rates of offending. Blacks are still the majority of people who are incarcerated for drug offenses, even though the evidence suggests that they do not commit these offenses more than other racial or ethnic groups. For drug crimes, African Americans are about 13 percent of people who do the crime, but about 60 percent of people who do the time.

So, considering the racialized enforcement of drug laws, it's fair to ask how trustworthy the data is about violent crime. Is that data also the result of selective enforcement?

The best answer is "probably not." Every year the United States Census Bureau performs the National Crime Victimization Survey (NCVS). It asks a representative sample of residents of the United States (which included 82,000 households in 2010) about victimizations in the past six months and whether they reported them to the police.[21] As Figure 11 demonstrates, a huge number of crimes are not reported to the police.

Obviously it's impossible to know anything about the racial demographics of crime that is not reported to the police. But what we do know is that, generally speaking, the more serious the crime, the more likely it is to be reported (with the exception of rape, as I explain below). Indeed because African Americans are less likely to report crimes than white people, and most victims of black offenders are also black, the official statistics might actually underestimate the risk of violent crimes for African Americans.

For serious violent crime, the race of the *victim* makes the biggest difference in how the criminal justice system responds. Cases with white victims tend to be taken more seriously by police and prosecutors. The Supreme Court blessed this practice in a case called *McCleskey v. Kemp*.[22] The Court was presented with compelling statistical evidence that people convicted of killing whites were more likely to get the death penalty, and that people convicted of killing African Americans were less likely to get the death penalty. A black convicted of killing a white was twenty-two

FIGURE 11: VICTIMIZATIONS NOT REPORTED TO THE POLICE, BY TYPE OF CRIME, 1994–2010

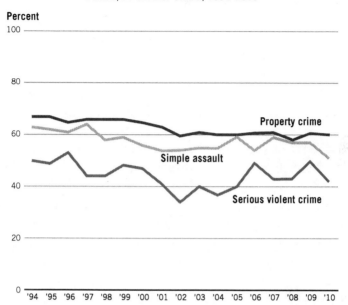

With the exception of rape, serious crimes are more likely to be reported.

Source: Lynn Langton, Marcus Berzofsky, Christopher Krebs, and Hope Smiley-McDonald, "Victimizations Not Reported to the Police, 2006–2010," U.S. Department of Justice, Bureau of Justice Statistics, August 2012, www.bjs.gov/content/pub/pdf/vnrp0610.pdf.

times more likely to get the death penalty than a white convicted of killing a black. Still the Court said that the data did not demonstrate a "constitutionally unacceptable" risk. Some legal scholars have said that *McCleskey* is actually a worse case than the infamous *Plessy v. Ferguson*, the case in which the Supreme Court allowed "separate but equal" Jim Crow segregation. In *McCleskey*, the Court actually permits an unequal "good enough for black people" kind of justice.

So, to be clear, it's not that violent crime statistics are somehow immune from the Chokehold's construction of the black man as thug. Rather, because white lives matter more in the eyes of the law and most crime is intra-racial, the police might actually be more invested in arresting those offenders who hurt white people—and those offenders are more likely to be white than African American.

THE RAPE EXCEPTION

African American men are less likely to be arrested for rape than for other violent crimes. In 2012, black men were about 31 percent of rape arrestees, as compared to about 56 percent of those arrested for robbery.[23] According to the U.S. Department of Justice, at least half of survivors of sexual assault do not report the crime to the police. Susan Estrich was one of my criminal law professors at Harvard. She wrote *Real Rape*, a classic text about sexual violence against women that starts with an account of her own rape.[24] The only reason the police took her claim seriously, Estritch writes, is because she is white and her rapist is African American. At the same time, African American women might actually underreport rape.[25] We know that sexual victimization of black women, by men of all colors, remains a horrific problem. In the end, the data about rape is insufficient to make any reliable inferences.

FALSE EQUIVALENCE: POLICE VIOLENCE VERSUS BLACK MALE VIOLENCE

Some people say that racial justice activists should focus their attention on crime by African American men, rather than violence perpetrated against black men by the police. For example, Rudy Giuliani, former mayor of New York City, said:

> Ninety-three percent of blacks are killed by other blacks. . . . I would like to see the attention paid to that that you are paying to [Ferguson]. . . . What about the poor black child that was killed by another black child? . . . Why aren't you protesting that? . . . Why don't you cut it down so that so many white police officers don't have to be in black areas? . . .

White police officers wouldn't be there if [African Americans] weren't killing each other.[26]

The historian Khalil Gibran Muhammad calls this move "playing the violence card." I'll admit, if you just look at the numbers, the violence card has a certain rhetorical appeal.

Number of African Americans shot by other African Americans in 2015: 4,900 (approximately)
Number of African Americans shot by the police in 2015: 305 (approximately)

The problem with the violence card is that it misunderstands both African American history and the problem that black folks have with the police. African Americans have always been concerned about violent crime, even if, at times, we have tried to shield this debate from white people. You can't sit through a sermon at a black church without hearing exhortations from the pulpit about the need for the brothers to stop smoking each other.

But there are crucial differences between the violence that the police do to black people versus the violence that African Americans do to each other. Cops are agents of the state. And when police shoot unarmed black people, they almost always get away with it.

Between 2005 and 2014, only forty-seven cops were charged with homicides. It gets worse. Of those forty-seven, only eleven were convicted.[27] However, when African Americans commit homicide, they are usually prosecuted, convicted, and sentenced to long years in prison. This is one of the main reasons U.S. prisons are filled with black men. There was a period in U.S. history when crimes that victimized African Americans were largely not prosecuted. There is evidence that even now, police do not take those crimes as seriously as they do crimes with white victims.[28] But even so, African American men do not get the same kind of pass that police officers get when they kill—even when the cops kill unarmed people. That is the concern of activists. There is a categorical moral difference between antisocial conduct that is harshly punished, on the one hand, and authorized violence by the state committed with impunity, on the other hand.

Still, as I will discuss below, everyone concerned about black lives should do more to address holistically black people's vulnerability to violence, as victims and as harm doers. This approach is entirely consistent with the activist critique of white supremacy; the focus is "both/and" not "either/or." One of the ways that the United States has failed its African American citizens is by not providing them the equal protection of the law.

BLACK MEN AND THE CONSTRUCTION OF "CRIME"

Right or wrong, I don't make the law.

—Erykah Badu

The idea that black violence speaks to the character of the people and is endemic while white violence is deviant and rare is disgusting.

—Touré[29]

Are African American men really more dangerous than other men? Or, on the other hand, is the way that we define concepts like "danger," "crime," and "violence" influenced by race?

There are certainly greater threats to the well-being of Americans than the harm caused by some black men. For centuries, many white men, sanctioned by the law of the land, enslaved, tortured, raped, and lynched black people, but we've conveniently started our narrative about who's dangerous with the spike in violent crime in the 1960s, a move that puts the focus on African American men. Today, we ought to be more concerned, some people say, about threats like pesticides in our food and lead in our water, radiation from nuclear power plants, or corporate greed that pays CEOs millions and not enough for an average worker to feed her family than about the threat posed by black men. Cars kill more people than black men do, but the local news leads with black suspects, not automobile accidents.[30]

We should take this claim very seriously. It reveals how the law really works and who it protects. It does not mean that we should ignore the conduct of African Americans who victimize others, but it should make us think deeply about the kind of antisocial conduct that we choose to punish, and the kind of antisocial conduct that is legal. Unsurprisingly this has something to do with race and class. The ways that rich white people victimize others are often quite legal.

The people who make the law get to decide what crime is. Conduct that results in the loss of life or the taking of property might not necessarily be criminal—it's all up to lawmakers. And, as we have seen, the law is not blind to race and class. Thus it is not surprising that the law frequently insulates rich people from being called criminals—even when their conduct is very destructive.

In the years leading up to the housing crisis in 2008, greedy mortgage bankers provided loans to poor people that were virtually guaranteed to fail. Investors who bet against the loans being repaid got very rich, but millions of Americans lost their homes, or had their retirement savings decimated, or became unemployed due to the tanked economy. One of President Obama's first major acts, upon his election, was to provide a $700 billion rescue plan *to the banks*. But no one has gone to jail for behavior that devastated the lives of millions of Americans. Yet when Eric Garner sold a single tobacco cigarette on the streets of Staten Island, he was arrested and put into a chokehold.

We know that some crimes were created specifically to target people of color. In 1971, Daniel Patrick Moynihan, then an aide to President Nixon, wrote a memo to the president identifying African American men as public enemy number one:

The incidence of anti-social behavior among young black males continues to be extraordinarily high. Apart from white racial attitudes, this is the biggest problem black Americans face, and in part it helps shape white racial attitudes. Black Americans injure one another. Because blacks live in *de facto* segregated neighborhoods, and go to *de facto* segregated schools, the socially stable elements of the black population cannot escape the socially pathological ones. Routinely their children get caught up in the anti-social patterns of the others.[31]

The president agreed. "[Nixon] emphasized that you have to face the fact that the whole problem is really the blacks," Haldeman, his chief of staff, wrote. "The key is to devise a system that recognizes this while not appearing to."[32] Soon thereafter, the Nixon administration implemented the "war on drugs." Years later, in 1995, John Ehrlichman, White House counsel to President Nixon, explained the rationale:

Look, we understood we couldn't make it illegal to be young or poor or black in the United States, but we could criminalize their common pleasure. We understood that drugs were not the health problem we were making them out to be, but it was such a perfect issue . . . that we couldn't resist it.[33]

Thus, one need not be paranoid to think that subordination of black men is deeply embedded in American crime and punishment. Too often the concept of danger as embodied in the criminal law is being used not for public safety purposes but to do some other kind of work—controlling black men.

The Chokehold means that many people see African American men through the lens of crime. As we have seen, people tend to overestimate their chances of being a victim of crime.[34]

One study showed that the number of blacks in a neighborhood affected whether residents perceived it as disorderly.[35]

Even the way that we think of a concept like "gun violence" is raced.

It is well known that there is a huge problem of gun violence among African American males. But less well known is the fact there is also a huge problem of gun violence among white males. Figure 12 illustrates the issue.

When a black man takes a life, it is most often the life of another black man. When a white man takes a life, it is most often his own. Today, the black male homicide rate is close to the white male suicide rate. Black men kill each other. White men kill themselves. Blacks are less likely to kill themselves. White men are less likely to kill someone else. Because there are many more white men than black men, many more white men die of suicide than black men die of homicide.

So both black men and white men are at similar risks when it comes to guns.

A black man is as dangerous to another black man as a white man is to himself. I am not suggesting that we should use the criminal justice system to treat the problem of suicide (although

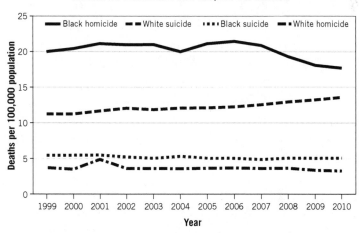

FIGURE 12: DEATH RATE PER 100,000 POPULATION

When white people use a gun to take a life, it is most likely to be their own.

Source: "Morbidity and Mortality Weekly Report, Quickstats: Annual Age-Adjusted Death Rates for Suicide and Homicide, by Black or White Race—United States, 1999–2010," April 5, 2013, www.cdc.gov/mmwr/preview/mmwrhtml/mm6213a7.htm.

people who survived suicide attempts used to be prosecuted in some jurisdictions). We correctly recognize the problem as one requiring a public health intervention. I think the same thing is true of many people who use guns against other people rather than themselves. The problem might be better solved with a public health approach rather than a criminal one. One reason that that concept is hard for many people to grasp is because the Chokehold makes punitive approaches to black male issues seem natural or intuitive.

IS "BLACK-ON-BLACK" CRIME A THING?

Some people say that "black-on-black" crime is a racist concept, because most crime is intra-racial, but there is no corresponding analogue called white-on-white crime. As Figure 13 demonstrates, most homicide, not just African American homicide, is intra-racial. The phrase "black-on-black crime" is a trope, designed to deflect a holistic conversation about the root causes and structural racism, and to emphasize the Chokehold construction of black men as thugs.

At the same time, it is legitimate, and indeed crucial, for activists and policymakers to devote time and attention to the problem of black male violence. The African American community's risk for violence is of a different magnitude than, say, the white community's or the Asian American community's. A black man is ten times more likely to be a homicide victim than a white man.[36]

Here are three reasons why people concerned about racial justice should lead the discussion of black male violent crime:

1) There is an overlap between the root causes of black-on-black violence and police violence against black people. They are different points on an axis of African American vulnerability. In a neighborhood in Baltimore, Maryland, neighbors were alarmed to see children fighting outside of a school. They were also alarmed to see police gathering

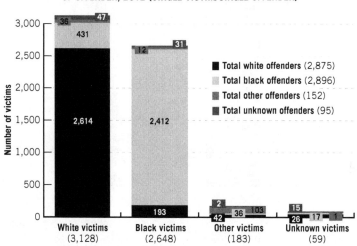

FIGURE 13: MURDER: RACE AND SEX OF VICTIM BY RACE OF OFFENDER, 2012 (SINGLE VICTIM/SINGLE OFFENDER)

For whites and African Americans alike, homicide is typically intra-racial.

Note: This table is based on incidents where some information about the offender is known by law enforcement; therefore, when the offender age, sex, and race are all reported as unknown, these data are excluded from the table.

Source: "Murder: Race and Sex of Victim by Race and Sex of Offender, 2012 [single victim/single offender]," Crime in the United States, 2012, U.S. Department of Justice, Federal Bureau of Investigation, Criminal Justice Information Services Division, 2012, ucr .fbi.gov/crime-in-the-u.s/2012/crime-in-the-u.s.-2012/offenses-known-to-law-enforcement /expanded-homicide/expanded_homicide_data_table_6_murder_race_and_sex_of_vicitm _by_race_and_sex_of_offender_2012.xls.

outside of the school to respond to the fight. In both instances they were concerned that people might be needlessly hurt. The neighbors ended up calling a local church to send somebody to break up both the fighting children and the gathering police officers.[37]

2) The debate about how to respond to black vulnerability to violence should not be ceded to conservative "law and order" types. The movement for black lives has brought a new energy and creativity to the struggle for racial justice. We need those bright minds fashioning solutions to the violence crisis that don't involve locking everybody up and throwing away the key.

FIGURE 14: STATE AND FEDERAL PRISONERS BY OFFENSE, 2010

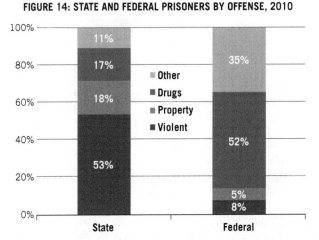

The fact that most federal prisoners are serving time for drug crimes is misleading. Because most prisoners in America are incarcerated at the state level and most state prisoners are serving sentences for violent crimes, violent crime rather than drug crime is actually fueling mass incarceration.

Source: E. Ann Carson, "Prisoners in 2011," U.S. Department of Justice, Office of Justice Programs, Bureau of Justice Statistics, December 2012, tables 10 and 11, https://www.bjs.gov/content/pub/pdf/p11.pdf.

FIGURE 15: STATE PRISONERS BY RACE AND OFFENSE, 2010

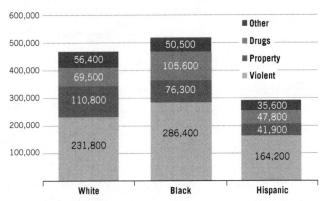

Violent crime, not drug crime, is fueling mass incarceration.

Source: E. Ann Carson, "Prisoners in 2011," U.S. Department of Justice, Office of Justice Programs, Bureau of Justice Statistics, December 2012, table 9, https://www.bjs.gov/content/pub/pdf/p11.pdf.

3) As shown in Figures 14 and 15, violent crime, much more than drug crimes, is fueling mass incarceration.[38] Right now African Americans make up about 37 percent of state and federal prison inmates.[39] If no one were incarcerated for drug crimes, blacks would constitute about 36 percent of America's prisoners.

OK, SO WHY DO BLACK MEN DISPROPORTIONATELY COMMIT VIOLENT CRIME?

First, let's define a term. Is it black men who commit crimes, or black male criminals? Most African American men do not commit violent crimes. Indeed most African American men will never be incarcerated for any crime. It's true that far too many black men do have criminal cases: among black men in their twenties, one in three is either in prison, on probation or parole, or awaiting trial.[40] Among some other segments of the black male population, for example high school dropouts in their forties, most of the group is incarcerated.[41] But as a group, the majority of black men are law-abiding.[42]

The more precise question that this section explores is what it means that, among all violent offenders, black men are greatly overrepresented. To say that men kill more than women (91 percent of murderers are male) does not mean that all, or most, men kill; it just means that men as a group kill more than women as a group. The same is true of African American men compared to men of other races in the United States.

The question explored here is whether there is something about black males—something that happens to them, that is done to them, and/or something they do or believe (in that sense, their culture)—that contributes to their disproportionate involvement in violent crime.

Before I describe different ideas about why African American men disproportionately commit violent crime, an important disclaimer is necessary. The most accurate answer to the question of why anyone commits a crime is "we do not know."

At best, we have a series of correlations. Even analysis of the correlations is unsatisfactory because we do not know why most people with a certain set of attributes do not commit crime, but some do. For violent offenders, the most consistent correlation is gender. Men are much more violent (in the corporal ways that concern the law) than women. The gender effect outweighs the race effect: a larger percentage of white men, for example, are incarcerated for violent crimes than African American women.

Another correlation is age: violent offenses tend to be the work of the young. Males between fifteen and thirty years old are most at risk of becoming perpetrators or victims.

BLACK MALE CULTURE AND
BLACK MALE VIOLENCE

A community of victims, unaware of its history and unable to control its destiny, tends to victimize itself viciously.

—Frantz Fanon[43]

We've all seen them or heard about them. The black boys wilding out on the subway. The teen on the front page of the newspaper for robbing the elderly woman. The brawl at the high school football game in the hood. The drive-by shooting at the hip-hop club.

What is going on?

Some commentators have emphasized the influence of black male culture. They attribute violence and lawbreaking to moral failures of African American men. There are conservative and progressive versions of this critique. The right-wing pundit Bill O'Reilly said, "The reason there is so much violence and chaos in the black precincts is the disintegration of the African American family. . . . Raised without much structure, young Black men often reject education and gravitate towards the street culture, drugs, hustling, gangs. Nobody forces them to do that. Again, it is a personal decision."[44]

Don Lemon, a black anchor on CNN, responded that O'Reilly "didn't go far enough." He admonished African American men to "Please, pay attention to and think about what has been presented in recent history as acceptable behavior. . . . Pay close attention to the hip hop and rap culture that many of you embrace, a culture that glorifies . . . thug and reprehensible behavior."[45]

President Obama expressed the same sentiment: "There's no contradiction to say that there are issues of personal responsibility that have to be addressed, while still acknowledging that some of the specific pathologies in the African American community are a direct result of our history."[46] On the fiftieth anniversary of the March on Washington, Obama stated:

> And then, if we're honest with ourselves, we'll admit that during the course of 50 years, there were times when some of us claiming to push for change lost our way. The anguish of assassinations set off self-defeating riots. Legitimate grievances against police brutality tipped into excuse-making for criminal behavior.[47]

Do brothers really make excuses for criminal behavior? How much should we blame black male culture for perpetrating the violence? How fair is it to demand that they improve their outcomes, and how much can we expect them to do on their own?

These are important questions, because the structural causes described below are unlikely to be resolved anytime soon. If another route to reducing violence and incarceration is following Don Lemon's five-point plan (black men should "hike up" their pants, finish school, not call each other "nigger," take care of their communities, and not have children outside of marriage[48]), that would seem to be in everyone's best interest. I understand the strong lure of black self-help, but in the end that is not going to solve the problem. Still, because the behavioral critique of

African American men has so much resonance, with everyone from Barack Obama on down, it is important to interrogate it.

Some old-school discussions about causes of crime create a false distinction between "culture" and "environment." Now sociologists understand that it's impossible to discuss those as separate and distinct entities. Culture is determined by environment in significant ways.[49] This is a key insight in order to avoid the Chokehold's dynamic of blaming African American men. I am making the commonsense observation that when a group of people are treated with disdain and fear every time they enter a public space, this impacts what they believe and how they interact with the world.

Scholars don't agree on one single definition of culture but many say that it includes values, frames (ways of understanding how the world works), and coping systems. The question of whether black male culture exists and, if so, how it informs things like propensity for violence and lawbreaking, is in part empirical. There is not much research on whether black men hold common values and beliefs and, if so, what those values and beliefs are.

I want to make some tentative assertions about black male culture as it might relate to violent conduct. These are evidence-based, but this does not mean they are irrefutable. They are also experiential. I was raised a black man. By that I mean, as I was growing up the people around me taught me what it meant to be African American and to be a man, and at the intersection of those things, what it meant to be an African American man. My "acculturation" is in accord with the stories of many other black men, and that gives me some confidence that the idea of African American male culture is a coherent concept.

One construction of masculinity is that it is a violent performance. This isn't limited to African Americans—in the famous phrase of the black revolutionary H. Rap Brown, "violence is as American as apple pie"—but African American men might be particularly susceptible to it. After all, for most of American history, blacks have been the target of brutal violence: first during slavery, then during the convict leasing that replaced slavery in the South, followed by lynching and the terrorism of the Ku Klux Klan. The sociologist Michael Eric Dyson notes, "[T]he notion of violent masculinity is at the heart of American identity. The preoccupation with Jesse James and the outlaw, the rebel, much of that is associated in the American mindset, the collective imagination of the nation, with the expansion of the frontier. In the history of American social imagination, the violent man using the gun to defend his family, his kip and kin, becomes a suitable metaphor for the notion of manhood."[50] Just as elements of American culture glorify some outlaws, elements of African American culture glorify some African American outlaws, including those who use violence for self-defense or to attain wealth.[51] The genre of hip-hop music known as gangsta rap frequently presents approving narratives of men who get rich through illegal means.

BLACK MACHO: THREE THEMES

BE HARD: Acting hard (tough) is a coping skill employed by many black men. The rapper Fat Joe said, in Byron Hurt's documentary *Hip Hop: Beyond Beats & Rhymes*, "Everybody wants to be hard. This is one of the flaws . . . of being from the hood. . . . I'm wondering why can't we just walk around and smile at each other."[52] In high-poverty areas it may be seen as a survival skill. Men who do not act hard may be perceived as more vulnerable. The historian Jelani Cobb notes, "There's a whole lineage of black men wanting to deny their own frailty and so in some ways, you have to do that, like a psychic armor to walk out into the world every day."[53]

PROTECT YOURSELF: A black man has to take care of himself and his family. Being willing to fight is part of being hard. The hip-hop artist Mos Def notes that as a kid he was a "nerd" and a "bookworm" but "when shit got critical, you know you can't be no punk. I know how a lot of young black men is growing up, how I grew up. You got to be a limit. You got to let niggas know, like yo, I'm no pussy. And you will get tested."[54] In some communities, having access to a gun is a way to communicate that one is hard. It is part of a performance of masculinity. This does not mean that everyone approves of guns, only that having one makes one more masculine.

DEMAND RESPECT: Being respected is a big deal. Being disrespected is an even bigger deal.

These are frames that many black men tell themselves about how the world works. I don't want to be overly judgmental about these attitudes. That's not easy for me as a former prosecutor. When I was going after someone for a violent crime, I loved working myself up in a frothy-mouthed closing statement about what an evil dude he was. In retrospect I think that I, like most prosecutors, was assigned a task—holding African American men accountable for crimes—that I simply did not have the skill set to do. I relied on a sense of morality that was itself hypocritical: I prosecuted black men for marijuana possession, a crime that I had stopped committing myself only because as a law enforcement officer I was subject to drug tests. Ultimately, though, understanding the appropriate response to antisocial conduct by black men requires a depth of knowledge about economics, psychology, sociology, U.S. history, and brain development that virtually no prosecutor has.

The unemployment rate for young black men in the hood can be as high as 50 percent.[55] Teens from all backgrounds tend to be conspicuous consumers, but many African American teens do not have legitimate ways to buy stuff. Their parents can't afford it, and they can't get a job to buy it themselves, so some of them use illegal means to get what they want.

Science has also given us new insight into the factors that contribute to violence in high-poverty communities. Lead paint poisoning, for example, reduces people's ability to control their impulses—one of the primary risk factors for violence. One of the tragedies of the lead crisis in Flint, Michigan, is that years from now, it may cause elevated levels of crimes such as assault and homicide. And, when that happens, many people will bemoan "black-on-black" crime and not acknowledge the direct role of the government in creating the madness.

I don't experience personally the stresses of people who live in the high-poverty areas where African Americans are most at risk for violence. But if I lived in the hood, I probably would not have much respect for the law. I might carry a gun if it made me feel safer.

As a teenager, I did my share of stupid things. Scientists have discovered something almost any parent of a young person could have told them: human brains are not fully developed until we are around twenty-five years old. The dumb things I did as a teen would have much more severe consequences today, both because the system has become more punitive and because I would be watched in a way that was not true thirty years ago.

Mix all these factors together—the survival skills for staying safe in the hood, the vast deprivations of high-poverty neighborhoods, the disproportionate and intense surveillance of black men—and add easy access to guns, and you get a toxic stew.

Traditional methods of crime control are also less effective in communities where too many people are locked up. Offenders are not deterred by the threat of incarceration because incarceration seems inevitable. Their norms of ethical behavior are influenced by standards outside the law, because the law seems so hostile to them.[56] This creates a vicious cycle because incarceration itself is criminogenic after a certain tipping point, meaning that interactions with the criminal justice system—including brief, pretrial stays in jail—have been shown to increase the likelihood that a person will subsequently be convicted of a criminal act. Furthermore, few people in prison receive the services they need to equip them to successfully come home. This is one reason why more than half of prisoners who are released from prison will return within eighteen months.

WHY DON'T MORE BLACK MEN COMMIT CRIME?

Sometimes African Americans discuss among ourselves what would happen to white people if they had to experience what black people experience on a daily basis. Blacks often tell ourselves that white people would react in more antisocial ways than we do. In the context of violent crime, there is intriguing data from social science. It turns out that when white men are exposed to the same level of structural impediments as black men, white men are more likely to commit homicide than black men.[57] The "racial invariance" theory asks whether certain factors better predict outcomes for one race than another. For example, does unemployment affect African Americans differently than Latinos? Several sociologists have done sophisticated regression analysis to try to answer those questions. Graham Ousey, a sociologist at the University of Kentucky, was interested in racial invariance for predictors for homicide. He found that conditions like poverty, unemployment, and family structure are stronger predictors for white men than black men.[58] Another study found that being unemployed was a stronger predictor of violent crime for white men than black men.[59] These studies suggest that black masculinity is not a cause of disproportionate violence by black men but rather, in some instances, a protector against it. So for all of the criticism that African American masculinity receives, it turns out that there is something redemptive about it. It prevents black men from responding violently when similarly situated white men would.

In the end, the problem with focusing too much on black male behavior is that it does not lead to a productive solution that stops the violence. It puts too much blame on black men. It makes it sound like they should just stop killing each other and everything will be fine. And most importantly it absolves the dominant culture—white society, and especially elite white people—of any responsibility. The late Supreme Court justice Antonin Scalia

famously said, "There are no debtor or creditor races." But Justice
Scalia was wrong.

WHITE CULTURE AND BLACK MALE VIOLENCE

What white Americans have never fully understood—but what the
Negro can never forget—is that white society is deeply implicated in
the ghetto. White institutions created it, white institutions maintain it,
and white society condones it.

—National Advisory Commission on Civil Disorders, 1965

In the United States there is no poor like black "po." In the old
joke, it's so po it can't even afford the extra letters to make "poor."
    There are many poor white people in the United States. As
a group, they have a significantly lower risk of being incarcerated for a violent crime than African Americans. The same is true
of Latinos. Sometimes people use those facts to suggest that you
can't blame poverty for why blacks disproportionately commit
some crimes. But low-income African Americans have categori-
cally different life experiences than low-income Americans of
other races, with the exception of American Indians.

THE UGLY FACTS: PART 2

Median household wealth:
    White: $111,145
    Hispanic: $8,348
    African American: $7,113[60]

Those numbers actually don't tell the whole story. More than
60 percent of African American kids are raised by a single black
woman. The average net worth of a single black woman is one
hundred dollars. Twenty-five percent of black families have less
than five dollars in savings.[61]

Percent of children who live in high-poverty neighborhoods:
   Asian American: 8 percent
   Latino: 24 percent
   American Indian: 31 percent
   African American: 32 percent
   White: 5 percent[62]

Nobody should think that poor white people have it good. But their experiences are more comparable to middle-income African Americans than to poor black people. Indeed in some ways poor white people have better outcomes than wealthier African Americans. A family headed by a white high school dropout has more wealth than a family headed by a black college graduate.[63] Middle-class black children are more likely to go to prison than poor white children.[64] Blacks who make more than $100,000 per year live in more disadvantaged neighborhoods than whites who make $30,000 per year.[65]

Why does poverty make things so much worse for black people than whites? Why, in some ways, does race seem to limit middle-class blacks more than class limits poor white people? One reason is that low-income African Americans tend to live in much more economically segregated spaces than low-income whites. They don't have the same proximity to middle-class people, and the goods and services that attach to them, including better schools. This entrenched poverty greatly constrains educational attainment, upward mobility, and even health. Professors Robert Sampson and William Julius Wilson wrote, "Racial differences in poverty and family disruption are so strong that the 'worst' urban contexts in which whites reside are considerably better than the *average* context of black communities."[66]

The law has played an instrumental role in creating the concentrated poverty that allows violence to flourish. In his important article "The Case for Reparations," Ta-Nehisi Coates described how racist housing policies steered African Americans to certain communities and locked them out of opportunities to build wealth.[67] The Federal Housing Administration declined to insure mortgages in neighborhoods where black people lived. Practices like redlining "spread to the entire mortgage industry, which was already rife with racism, excluding black people from most legitimate means of obtaining a mortgage."[68] As a result, black families were "herded into the sights of unscrupulous lenders who took them for money and for sport," leading to further exploitation and ultimately to declining property values in black communities.[69] This "concentration of disadvantage," Coates points out, was a consequence of federal government policy rather than just the actions of private individuals.[70]

We have seen that the structural conditions of high-poverty neighborhoods are strongly correlated with people being at risk for violence. In the United States, seven out of eight people who reside in those communities are people of color. To state the obvious, people don't live in the most deprived neighborhoods because they choose to. They live there because white supremacy severely constrains their choices. One study found that racial inequality raises the rate of black-on-white homicide. Black-on-black homicide, at the same time, increases the more deprived and segregated a neighborhood is.[71]

White supremacy is "the belief that white people are superior to those of all other races, especially the black race, and should therefore dominate society."[72] Although the phrase calls to mind the night riders of the Ku Klux Klan, it is more helpful to think of white supremacy as law scholar Frances Lee Ansley defines it: "A political, economic and cultural system in which whites overwhelmingly control power and material resources, conscious and unconscious ideas of white superiority and entitlement are widespread, and relations of white dominance and non-white subordination are daily reenacted across a broad array of institutions and social settings."[73]

White supremacy means that white people are complicit in, and derive benefits from, the conditions that hold African Americans back. In a system of racial inequality, as black people lose, white people win. This is not the same as saying that all white people are racist. Individual white people may or may not be; the fact that every white person benefits from white supremacy is simply another description of the role that race plays in their lives. Where white people live, who they marry, how they worship, how much money they make, and which politicians they vote for are based on choices they get to make, and opportunities they get to have, because they are white. Thinking of these as cultural practices helps us understand the role of white culture in creating the black criminal.

Indeed the recognition that race-based structural deprivation was the most important explanation of black criminality used to be commonplace. Thinking about crime in black communities, President Truman in 1947 and President Johnson in 1965 both blamed racism. But as the United States has become, since the 1970s, the most punitive nation in the world, the way we think about causes of crime fails to take racism into account. Our harsh sentencing laws are premised on personal responsibility and free choice. But a young black man in South Central Los Angeles does not have the same kinds of choices as a young white man in either Beverly Hills or Appalachia.

The bad news, and the good news, is that none of these vast differences in opportunity is an accident. All are the result of government policies. It's bad news because the fact that the government created the hood demonstrates its antipathy to its black citizens. It's good news because government policies can also do substantial work in making things better now.

We know this because African Americans are not the only group in U.S. history that have had some of their members turn to crime because they were shut out of other ways to achieve the American dream. Immigrant communities in the late nineteenth and early twentieth centuries were often involved in criminal activity. According to historian Daniel Bell in his classic 1953 essay "Crime as an American Way of Life," Irish Americans, Jewish Americans, and Italian Americans represented "a distinct ethnic sequence in ways of obtaining illicit wealth." Yet as they were afforded a wider array of economic choices, each of these groups assimilated and crime went down. As legal scholar David Wade writes, "As each group acquired the wealth and social position accompanying the profits of illicit activity, they invested in legitimate businesses and assumed a greater political role in the dominant, legitimate society."[74]

Ira Katznelson points out in his book *When Affirmative Action Was White* that white ethnic groups were also aided in their economic rise by "Social Security, key labor legislation, the GI Bill, and other landmark laws that helped create a modern white middle class."[75]

By contrast, African Americans were locked out of these social programs. For example, farmworkers and maids—who made up "more than 60 percent of the black labor force in the 1930s"— were "excluded from the legislation that created modern unions, from laws that set minimum wages and regulated the hours of work, and from Social Security until the 1950s."[76]

Compounding this lack of a social safety net for many African Americans, the government subsequently implemented harsh criminal justice policies that led to mass incarceration, turned a blind eye to housing discrimination, and failed to invest seriously in education and effective job training in low-income communities. Given the lack of economic opportunity, it is not surprising that many young men in these communities turned to criminal activity and participated in illegal markets with higher rates of violence.

There are two things we need to do to dramatically reduce black male violence, though it is not clear that we have the political will to do either. First we need to get rid of the hood— segregated, high-poverty communities that are breeding grounds for homicide. This requires financial assistance to help families move places where they would have better outcomes, and a shift in white culture such that middle-class white Americans are comfortable with having poor black families as neighbors. Policies to promote this kind of economic and racial integration include the national "Moving to Opportunity" project, in which poor people were given housing vouchers they could use only to move to middle-class communities.[77] Children who moved at a young age had significantly better outcomes than kids who remained in the high-poverty neighborhoods.[78]

One study found that if black men graduated from college and received the same incomes as white men, the homicide disparity would be reduced by more than 50 percent.[79] People in high-poverty neighborhoods could be offered free college educations and subsidized jobs to make this happen. Taxpayers seem okay with handing out the $25,000 per year to house and feed these men in prisons and jails across the country. And most citizens seem quite content with the significantly larger sums the government hands out to middle-class and wealthy Americans, including $400 billion every year in subsidies to citizens to promote home ownership, retirement savings, and economic investment. In fact, half of government handouts go to the wealthiest 5 percent of taxpaying households. The bottom 60 percent receive only 4 percent of those benefits.[80] But a transfer of wealth that would reduce black male violence by offering black men education and jobs would be seen as an unacceptable government "handout."

Near the end of his administration, President Obama endorsed the concept of some form of race-based government investment in the African American community. In an interview with the journalist Ta-Nehisi Coates, Obama said, "Theoretically, you can make obviously a powerful argument that centuries of slavery, Jim Crow, discrimination are the primary cause for all those gaps. That those were wrongs to the black community as a whole, and black families specifically, and that in order to close that gap, a society has a moral obligation to make a large, aggressive investment, even if it's not in the form of individual reparations checks but in the form of a Marshall Plan." A large-scale intervention to eliminate high-poverty segregated neighborhoods would save the lives and enhance the safety of countless African American men.

Second, we need to greatly limit access to guns. In an article entitled "How the Gun Control Debate Ignores Black Lives," Pro-Publica reporter Lois Beckett describes how the debate about gun control frequently leaves out black men. Beckett writes, "Gun control advocates and politicians frequently cite the statistic that more than 30 Americans are murdered with guns every day. What's rarely mentioned is that roughly 15 of the 30 are black men."[81] Conservative politicians like Donald Trump who harp on "black-on-black" crime are often the most protective of gun rights. Limiting access to guns on a national basis, in the way that most other Western nations do, would also save the lives of thousands of black men each year.

But again, there seems to be no political will for this crucial intervention to reduce black male victimization. After the tragic incident at Sandy Hook Elementary School, when a gunman killed twenty-six people, including twenty children, some activists sensed an opening. They were concerned, however, that the reforms that were being discussed, like banning the kind of assault rifle the Sandy Hook shooter used, would not have much of an impact on gun violence in the hood, where people are killed with guns that are easier to obtain than the Bushmaster XM15-E2S that the Sandy Hook shooter used. According to ProPublica, a group of activists met with Vice President Joe Biden's task force on gun violence to lobby for interventions that would have more of an impact on the urban communities that were most at risk for gun violence. The activists were turned down. As ProPublica reports:

> "What was said to us by the White House was, there's re- ally no support nationally to address the issue of urban violence," said the Rev. Charles Harrison, a pastor from Indianapolis. "The support was to address the issue of gun violence that affected suburban areas—schools where white kids were killed."

The Rev. Jeff Brown, from Boston, was angered by the

administration's calculated approach. "When you say some-thing like that and you represent the President of the United States, and the first African-American President of the United States, you know, that's hugely disappointing," he said.

Former administration officials said they thought it was tragic that the everyday killings of black children did not get more political attention. "I totally agree with their frustra-tions," a former official said. "At the same time, when the nation listens, you've got to speak, and you don't get to pick when the nation listens." [82]

There is one remedy intended for African American men that has been endorsed by many politicians, policymakers, and ordi-nary citizens, regardless of their political affiliations. Given what we have learned about the Chokehold, that should make us suspi-cious. The next chapter explains why the suspicion about "black male achievement" programs is warranted, and explores both the pitfalls and potential of this kind of intervention.

5

Do the Brothers Need Keepers?
How Some Black Male Programs
Perpetrate the Chokehold

Being a black man is demanding.

— Black Star, "K.O.S."

The launch of President Obama's signature racial justice project, the My Brother's Keeper initiative, was the most bipartisan moment of his presidency. February 27, 2014, was a mild winter day in Washington, D.C., with no sign of the near-record cold the next day would bring. Gathered in the East Room of the White House were what had to be a record number of African American men. They included Colin Powell, the former secretary of state, Magic Johnson, the entrepreneur and NBA Hall of Famer, and Kenneth Chenault, the CEO of American Express. The leaders of the major civil rights organizations showed up as well, along with politicians including Mayors Mike Bloomberg of New York and Rahm Emanuel of Chicago.

In his remarks, the president joked about seeing the civil rights activist Rev. Al Sharpton and conservative Fox News host Bill O'Reilly at the event. He said, "If I can persuade Sharpton and O'Reilly to be in the same meeting, then it means that there are people of good faith who want to get some stuff done, even if we don't agree on everything. And that's our focus."[1]

Seated in the front row were the parents of Trayvon Martin,

the unarmed seventeen-year-old who had been gunned down by George Zimmerman, a self-appointed "neighborhood watch man," in Sanford, Florida. Trayvon, wearing a hoodie, had been walking home to his father's residence from a 7-Eleven store when Zimmerman called 911 and told the dispatcher, "This guy looks like he is up to no good or like he is on drugs or something." The dispatcher told Zimmerman not to follow Trayvon, but Zimmerman disregarded the dispatcher. An altercation ensued, and Zimmerman fired a bullet into Trayvon's chest. Zimmerman was prosecuted for murder but was acquitted.[2]

Obama said that the concept for My Brother's Keeper came to him after Trayvon's death. The president did not explain what he saw as the relationship between Trayvon's homicide and a program designed to foster achievement among African American and Latino males. Obama's other remarks, however, were more revealing about the problems that he saw afflicting African American men and that his new program would address. He observed that growing up, "I didn't have a dad in the house. And I was angry about it. . . . I made bad choices. I got high without always thinking about the harm that it could do. I didn't always take school as seriously as I should have. I made excuses. Sometimes I sold myself short."[3]

My Brother's Keeper was rolled out in the middle of Obama's second term, a time when there was widespread disenchantment among black progressives with the president's record on racial justice. There was a sense that Obama had not been as proactive on issues of importance to the African American community as he had on issues affecting other constituencies, for example the LGBT community. Some African Americans felt that the usual civil rights advocates weren't pushing Obama hard enough. A couple of years earlier, the chairman of the Congressional Black Caucus had admitted that if Bill Clinton had showed the same inattentiveness to race that Obama did, the Black Caucus would "probably be marching on the White House," but the caucus was giving Obama a pass because its members didn't want to empower the president's detractors.[4]

The death of Trayvon Martin represented a turning point. The homicide and subsequent trial and "not guilty" verdict attracted international attention. Commentators noted the irony of a racially motivated killing of a young black man during the administration of the first African American president. They urged the president to comment, and when he did, finally, his statement—Trayvon "could have been my son"—was classic race speak from Obama.[5] It was ambiguous enough that people could project on it whatever they wanted it to be.[6] But the journalist Tavis Smiley, a prominent critic of the president, called the remarks "as weak as pre-sweetened kool-aid."

The times seemed to demand that Obama use the power of his presidency to do something specifically for black people. And so he did. There was an almost celebratory atmosphere in the East Room on that February day. But some people, outside the room, had questions. Why would the most feminist president in U.S. history create a racial justice initiative that left out women and girls? Obama is, after all, married to a woman with a law degree from Harvard, father to two daughters, and given to boasting that his first official act as chief executive was signing a bill promoting pay equity for women. What were people like Bill O'Reilly and Michael Bloomberg, reviled in the black community because of their critiques of young black men, doing at the launch? And what did it mean that My Brother's Keeper raised little outcry from the president's usual conservative critics, who one might have thought would be the first to complain about a race-based program from the White House?

There is nothing like the topic of black male achievement to create strange bedfellows. As every word in this book has demonstrated, African American men need help. But "keepers" is an interesting way to describe the kind of help they need. Some black male programs do more harm than good. They fall squarely within the Chokehold dynamic of blaming the victim. They are designed to fix African American men—to get them to pull their pants up—with the suggestion that once black men act right, everything will be fine.

These programs also make the plight of African American women invisible. In writing a book about African American men, I want to avoid the mistake that many others have made before me—a mistake that is replicated in the rationale for many black male achievement programs. While some of the problems that African American men face are particular to them, I never want to suggest that their situation is worse than that of some other groups, especially African American women. Policymakers and activists often make this error. They claim that by almost every measure of inequality, black males are on the bottom—exceptionally burdened and marginalized. For example, in a recent Supreme Court affirmative action case, a coalition of black male achievement organizations "acknowledged that many young Americans other than black male youth face serious life course obstacles in need of attention, but . . . the depth and breadth of the negative life outcomes experienced by black males are sufficiently grave to warrant independent investigation and policy prescription."[7]

"Black male exceptionalism" is the term I use to describe the claim that African American men are worse off than anybody else, including African American women. The concept has been endorsed by organizations ranging from the federal government to big foundations to Afrocentric and black nationalist groups. Black male exceptionalism is a billion-dollar industry. But the premise—that black women are doing better than black men—is not only factually wrong, it reinforces the Chokehold.

Can we imagine interventions for African American men that recognize the unique race and gender discrimination they face but that do not position them as the only blacks worth caring about? Some black male achievement programs that now exist, however well intentioned, are anti-women. And other programs are not well intentioned—they are premised on stereotypes of violent, hyper-masculine black men. They are designed to tame the savage beast.

I come sympathetic to the cause of black male achievement. I want, however, to reconfigure the programs, to transform the black male exceptionalist project into a progressive one. How should we respond to white supremacy's insults to black masculinity? Is it possible to specifically support men in a way that is not anti-feminist?

In this chapter I discuss the myth that created black male exceptionalism—the claim that black men are an "endangered species." This problematic metaphor has had a major impact on public policy and the way many people think about black men. I then explain why it's a myth that African American women are doing better than African American men, and the damage the myth does to both sisters and brothers. Finally I imagine black male–specific interventions that are not based on stereotypes and that don't hold black women down.

BLACK MEN AS "ENDANGERED SPECIES": A BRIEF HISTORY OF A TROUBLING METAPHOR [8]

Most importantly, the statistics . . . are reflections of a society which is, in some respects, an organized conspiracy against black masculinity.

— "The Crisis of the Black Male," *Ebony*, August 1983

The Mack, a film released in 1973, is about the different paths taken by two African American brothers, and their ultimate reconciliation. Olinga is a black nationalist and Goldie is a pimp. The brothers come together to kill two white racist cops who are responsible for the death of their mother. The only women with significant roles in the movie are "Mother" and "Lulu," who is Goldie's head prostitute.

The Mack is viewed as a classic "blaxploitation" film, although its producers saw it more as social commentary. Its soundtrack is as well known as the film, especially Willie Hutch's "Brothers Gonna Work It Out," which has been sampled by a "who's who" of hip-hop legends including Public Enemy, 2Pac, Dr. Dre, Wale, A$AP Rocky, and Chance the Rapper.

> *All brothers sing*
> *Stop the pimps, the hustler and*
> *The pusher man as fast you can*
> *Open your ears and eyes to the fact*
> *Of what's truly holding you back!*
> *OoOoOoOoOoOoOoh*
>
> *Brother needs your help*
> *Now, can't you see?*
> *Aw he's got to have it*
> *Oh right on*
> *Ohhhh yeah*
>
> *Brother's gonna work it out (brother's gonna work it out)*
> *Brother's gonna work it out (brother's gonna work it out)*

Think of "Brothers Gonna Work It Out" as the soundtrack of black male exceptionalism. It says the behavior of African American men—the pimping, hustling, and (dope) pushing—is "what's truly holding them back." Black men "got to have . . . help," but ultimately they will work it out.

"Brothers Gonna Work It Out" contains only one reference to women.

> *Instead of brother turning on sister*
> *Sister turning on brother*
> *Now how you gonna get it together*
> *Being against one another?*

The idea that black women bear some responsibility for the plight of African American men is a subtext of many interventions designed for black men. Willie Hutch, the artist who wrote and performed "Brothers Gonna Work It Out," does not provide evidence of "brothers turning on sisters" or "sisters turning on brothers." The former is easier to come by than the latter. Homicide is the second leading cause of death of young black women, and the vast majority of the perpetrators are black men. Ways that African American women might injure African American men are more difficult to imagine. Still the song's critique of black women is consistently reproduced in discourse about black male achievement.

A few years before *The Mack* was released, the United States government issued a report that also suggested that African American men are threatened by African American women. "The Negro Family: The Case for National Action," written in 1965 by Assistant Secretary of Labor Daniel Patrick Moynihan, the same person who went on to write the memo to President Nixon in 1971 about the threat presented by African American men, was to have a profound impact on public policy.

Moynihan wrote:

The Negro community has been forced into a matriarchal structure which, because it is so out of line with the rest of the American society, seriously retards the progress of the group as a whole, and imposes a crushing burden on the Negro male and, in consequence, on a great many Negro women as well. . . . There is, presumably, no special reason why a society in which males are dominant in family relationships is to be preferred to a matriarchal arrangement. However, it is clearly a disadvantage for a minority group to be operating on one principle, while the great majority of the population, and the one with the most advantages to begin with, is operating on another.

The Moynihan Report contains what we can think of as the five rules of "brothers gonna work it out." These rules are helpful in understanding contemporary racial justice policy, especially the emphasis on programming for African American men.

Rule 1: Fixing black male problems is a way to establish racial justice.

Rule 2: African American women bear some responsibility for the subordination of African American men.

Rule 3: Black male problems are more deserving of remedies than black female problems.

Rule 4: Racism, discrimination, and white supremacy have impacted black men more adversely than black women.

Rule 5: A specific kind of African American masculinity should be championed as a matter of public policy.

The "brothers gonna work it out" rules are evident in a famous *Ebony* magazine issue in 1983 devoted to "The Crisis of the Black Male." In his "Publisher's Statement," John H. Johnson reported that black men have "borne the brunt" of the struggle for racial justice, and that the "special issue breaks new ground by presenting the first definitive analysis of an urgent national problem: The Crisis of the Black Male." Johnson claimed to have received "hundreds of letters" from men and women who "cited alarming statistics on the mortality, unemployment and homicide of black males." The letters said "almost without exception that something strange and ominous is happening to black males in this country and someone should sound the alarm before it is too late."

Ebony editor Lerone Bennett Jr. wrote in the introduction that the "institutions of American society have been systematically and mercilessly manipulated to keep the black man down." Bennett noted that African American men are "losing ground to white men, white women, and black women in offices and colleges. The black male-female ratio at some colleges is three, four, five to one!" He stated that there is an "organized conspiracy against black masculinity" but "history tells us it is a losing proposition to bet against black men." His introduction ends with a quote from a poem by Sterling A. Brown:

One thing they cannot prohibit
The strong men . . . coming on
The strong men gittin' stronger.
Strong men . . .
Stronger . . .

The articles in the special edition included "Are Black Women Taking Black Men's Jobs?," "The Challenge to Black Supremacy in Sports," "What Black Men Should Know About Black Women," and "Black Men–White Women: An Update." Significantly, the *Ebony* issue contains the first reference I could find to an enduring metaphor in black male exceptionalism: the black male as an "endangered species."

In "Is the African American Male an Endangered Species?" the author, Walter Leavy, answers the question in the negative because "the black man has been incredibly creative in finding ways to adapt to society's demands." Still the article reads like a pop-psychology version of the Moynihan Report's embrace of patriarchy. Explaining the black homicide rate, the author writes, "America has always defined the male role as that of protector and provider but the black male is, in many cases, incapable of playing that role for a number of reasons. While he may understand that racism is frequently the cause of his failure, the black male's structured inability to play his role can take a psychological toll and lead to violence, drugs, alcohol, and other elements that can be responsible for his removal from society."

The *Ebony* special issue deploys statistics in two ways that are commonplace in black male exceptionalism. First, data about African Americans that includes both men and women is used to support the case for special interventions for African American men. For example, one article states, "Since the unemployment rate is traditionally higher in the black community, many black men accept jobs that call for them to work under very hazardous conditions." Likewise, "the black male is more likely than his white counterpart to die at a younger age due to the lack of, or inability to pay for, proper health care."

Second, statistics about African American males are used to support the necessity of special interventions, with no description of what the corresponding data is for black women. For example, one article claims that because of "a lack of prenatal and postnatal care, the infant mortality rate of black males is more than double that of white males." This fact would seem to support the case for a race-based intervention, but without the corresponding data for black females there is no way of knowing whether the intervention should be focused exclusively on black males. For the record, I am not aware of any data that suggests that black male babies have higher mortality rates than black female babies.

The article's point about infant mortality also exposes another common move in black male exceptionalism: advocacy of interventions for African American women when, or because, the interventions will benefit African American men. So the problem with the lack of prenatal care for African American women is that it risks the mortality of African American male infants. The implicit "ask" is for better health care for black women so that more black male infants will survive.

The focus on black men at the expense of black women is not a relic of the 1960s. A June 2013 cover story in *Newsweek* magazine by Joshua Dubois entitled "The Fight for Black Men" employed many of the "brothers gonna work it out" rules. It states, "When one single group of people is conspicuously left behind, it never bodes well for society as a whole. In many ways, black men in America are a walking gut check; we learn from them a lot about ourselves, how far we've really come as a country, and how much further we have to go." This is an example of Rule #1: fixing the problems of African American males is a way of establishing racial justice overall.

Dubois writes:

> We focused our social investments in this period—our brief War on Poverty—on women and children, because men were supposed to figure it out. But in the 1970s and 1980s, many of these black men didn't. Just like their great-grandfathers never fully figured out how to teach their sons about manhood while being lashed in a field. Just like their grandfathers never completely figured out how to pass on lessons about building wealth when theirs was stolen through peonage and sharecropping.

But black women are as injured by white supremacy as black men. Intersectionality certainly helps us understand that African American men can, and do, experience different injuries, and that therefore different kinds of remedies might be necessary. My concern is not about claims that black men have been specifically disadvantaged by discrimination but rather with the implicit ranking of black male harms as more severe than black female harms.

Sometimes the endangerment narrative is meant literally. In an article titled "Screw the Whales, Save Me! The Endangered Species Act, Animal Protection, and Civil Rights," Joseph Lubinski recommended the founding of a coalition of animal rights groups and civil rights activists. The idea reached its logical conclusion in a satirical documentary broadcast on the cable station Comedy Central in 2012 in which comedian D.L. Hughley lobbied the Environmental Protection Agency to have black males placed on the endangered species list.[9]

Here are the problems with thinking of African American men as an "endangered species." First, African American men are not dying off; as with other people of color, their numbers are actually increasing. In 2014, for example, the life expectancy of African American men increased to 72.2, while that of white people decreased, to 78.8. Even if the term "endangered species" is meant more symbolically, it objectifies black men in a way that does not advance their cause. There is something at once aggrandizing and victimizing about describing African American men as an "endangered species." "Species" connotes an otherness, as though black men are not human beings. It is dehumanizing, implying an analogy to animal conservancy rather than a response to social injustice as it impacts human beings. It draws on a long history of analogizing African Americans to nonhuman animals.

"Endangered" is more suggestive. Among other things, it stakes a claim in the debate about the cause of the problems that African American men face. Some people have attributed blame to African American men. The 1995 Million Man March—the largest political formation of African American men in history—was framed as a day of "atonement." Exactly what black men were supposed to atone for was left unstated.

In the same vein, in a Father's Day speech, President Obama criticized "too many" black fathers for "abandoning their responsibilities, acting like boys instead of men." In a bit about interracial homicide in the Comedy Central program *DL Hughley: The Endangered List*, Hughley states that black men are "the only species in history complicit in our demise. The passenger pigeon didn't have shit to do with making himself extinct." Hughley is right that we typically do not blame endangered animals for their own potential extinction. "Endangered" communicates that the danger comes from without, not within; it seems more of a structural critique than a behavioral one. Unfortunately that idea has not traveled to black male programs, most of which focus on changing how black men respond to society rather than how society responds to black men.

Still, apart from being too naturalistic, the endangerment narrative gets the problem wrong. Survival is an act of resistance. African American men are still here; they, along with African American women, have survived in a country that for most of its history has been extremely inhospitable to them. As a group, African Americans have survived slavery, de jure segregation, and terrorism by white supremacists. "Endangered species" is inexact enough that it is careless. It is bad history and bad science. It is patriarchy masquerading as racial justice.

ARE BLACK MEN REALLY THE WORST OFF?

Policymakers often use the rhetoric of black male exceptionalism to justify racial justice programs and initiatives. For example, Washington, D.C., Attorney General Karl A. Racine defended the city's establishment of a $20 million boys-only public school, with no equivalent school for girls, by arguing that, as the lowest performing demographic, African American males require particularized academic support.[10] Similarly, in an amicus brief in *Fisher v. Texas*, a coalition of "black male achievement" organizations "acknowledged that many young Americans other than Black male youth face serious life course obstacles in need of attention, but . . . the depth and breadth of the negative life outcomes experienced by Black males [are] sufficiently grave to warrant independent investigation and policy prescription."[11] Former White House senior adviser Valerie Jarrett, responding to critics of the My Brother's Keeper initiative, stated that President Obama's "approach is to create a society where nobody gets left behind, and right now our young boys of color are falling farther and farther behind than everybody."[12]

The claim that black men are in a state of crisis is, upon a review of the evidence, entirely sound. Black men are 6.7 times more likely to be incarcerated than white men, and 14.3 times more likely than black women. And black men are 4.3 times more likely to drop out of high school than white men, and 2.5 times more likely to drop out compared to black females.[13]

But African American women, who after all live in the same communities as African American men, are in a state of crisis as well. Black men actually do better than black women by several important measures. For example, black women have lower incomes than black men, and are more likely to live below the poverty line than black men.[14] African American women drop out of high school at higher rates than both white men and women.[15] And black girls are also suspended from schools more than six times as often as their white counterparts.[16] In what is frequently seen as an indicator of social status, African American women are the least likely of any women of color to marry outside their race. In 2013, one out of four black men married a person of a different race, compared with only 12 percent of black women.[17]

The point I am making here is not that it's a "race to the bottom" between black women and black men. In fact, I am anxious to avoid this type of comparison. The point is that we need to be thoughtful about the way that interventions supposedly designed for racial justice are framed. The focus on black men only distorts the pervasiveness of white privilege, which harms black women as much as it harms black men. Policies that ignore this fact not only make the plight of African American women invisible, they often lead to the wrong kinds of solutions for black men.

HOW SOME BLACK MALE PROGRAMS HURT BLACK MEN

Shortly before his presidency ended, Barack Obama met with young black men in North Carolina who had participated in My Brother's Keeper. The writer Ta-Nehisi Coates was also present. The men told the president how, through mentoring or job training programs, they had the opportunity to go to college or get a job. The president replied, "It doesn't take that much. It just takes someone laying hands on you and saying 'Hey, man, you count.'"[18]

But the issues faced by all African Americans, including young black men, require much more than a laying on of hands. The deprivations faced by black men are not due to a lack of self-esteem. In fact when Obama asked the young men in North Carolina what message they would give to policymakers, one replied that they still had to live in the same neighborhoods where they had gotten in trouble. "It's your environment," he said. "You can do what you want, but you still gotta go back to the hood."

Not long after Trayvon Martin was killed, a series of high-profile police shootings and other acts of violence against African Americans took place in cities across the country. When President Obama was asked how the White House was responding, he frequently invoked his My Brother's Keeper initiative, which focuses on mentoring, job training, and college prep for young men of color. But Trayvon Martin did not need a male role model. He was on his way to his father's house when he was killed. Michael Brown, the unarmed black man killed by a white police officer in Ferguson, Missouri, was supposed to start college the week after he died. It is far from clear what a program premised on black male achievement has to do with the problem of state and private violence against black men. Unless, of course, one thinks that African American men bear some responsibility for that violence.

In a speech about race and policing at Georgetown University, FBI Director James Comey asked, "Why are so many black men in jail? Is it because cops, prosecutors, judges, and juries are racist? Because they are turning a blind eye to white robbers and drug dealers?" [19] Comey answered his own question by saying, "I don't think so" and that "what really needs fixing" was being addressed by My Brother's Keeper, which is "about doing the hard work to grow drug-resistant and violence-resistant kids, especially in communities of color, so they never become part of that officer's life experience." Comey attributed the involvement of young black men in the criminal system to their "lacking role models, adequate education, and decent employment." The problem is, as the FBI director sees it, that black men "inherit a legacy of crime and prison. And with that inheritance, they become part of a police officer's life, and shape the way that officer—whether white or black—sees the world. Changing that legacy is a challenge so enormous and so complicated that it is, unfortunately, easier to talk only about the cops. And that's not fair." Comey's use of the word "inherit" implies a kind of genetic determinism, consistent with stereotypes about black men as natural-born thugs. But his idea that, to resolve the crisis in policing, the focus should be on repairing African American men rather than the police is consistent with the ethos of many black male achievement programs.

The rhetoric of black male exceptionalism seldom involves critiques of patriarchy or white privilege. In some ways it resonates more with the ideology of conservatives than with a progressive vision of social justice. Indeed many of these programs became popular at the same time that the right wing was complaining about a breakdown in traditional gender roles and "a war against boys."[20]

It follows, then, that some black male achievement programs appear to be premised on the Chokehold construction of black men as violent, hyper-masculine criminals. Other interventions supported by some of the programs can be seen as implicit behavioral critiques of black men as dysfunctional or pathologic.

The legal scholar Verna Williams has shown how the drive for single-sex public schools in the inner city, while presented as in the best interest of black boys and girls, "posits black males as dangerous and threatening," "irresponsible and undependable," and "oversexed."[21] Created to help "at-risk boys," these schools often emphasize black gender stereotypes in their curricula and student discipline systems, and reinforce "a vision of masculinity that focuses on disruptive behavior, athleticism, and being 'bad.'"[22] Many single-sex schools for African American boys rely on regimented discipline systems that have resulted in hyper-masculinized environments in which "Men [are] either positioned as the protector and provider, or as the predator." Thus in these environments intended to help black boys and girls, there is in fact little flexibility about what it means to be a black "male."[23]

Many other programs for black men contain elements of behavior modification interventions for African American men. The mentoring program of 100 Black Men of America, Inc., includes workshops that focus on social and emotional skills, moral character, and work ethic. The United Negro College Fund Black Male Initiative states that strong African American male initiatives should incorporate activities that help young men "better handle frustration and anger." New York's Young Men's Initiative (YMI) references training men for careers as commercial truck drivers, but not doctors, artists, or professors.[24] Indeed $52 million out of the $127 million allocated to the YMI program is spent on males placed under the authority of the correctional system.[25] Certainly some money should be spent on helping people who have been incarcerated successfully reenter society, but the program's allocation of 40 percent of its funds to criminal justice–based interventions seems excessive, unless, perhaps, one sees a close relationship between law enforcement supervision of African American men and public safety.

In this regard it is worth noting that New York City's Young Men's Initiative was created during a time in which the New York City Police Department was defending its aggressive stop-and-frisk tactics, which, as chapter 3 describes, disproportionately burdened young African American and Latino men. Mayor Bloomberg's private foundation contributed millions of dollars to the city's black and Latino male youth initiative, at the same time that the mayor vigorously defended the stop-and-frisk program. The *Huffington Post* reported, "In a speech brimming with vitriol, Mayor Michael Bloomberg took aim at all who have criticized the NYPD's controversial stop-and-frisk policy, accusing them of encouraging a lawless mayhem state. Mayor Michael Bloomberg unleashed a 45-minute tirade in defense of the police tactic." The *New York Times* reported Mayor Bloomberg responded to critics of the city's stop-and-frisk policy by stating that "They just keep saying, 'Oh, it's a disproportionate percentage of a particular ethnic group.' That may be, but it's not a disproportionate percentage of those who witnesses and victims describe as committing the murder. In that case, incidentally, I think we disproportionately stop whites too much and minorities too little."[26]

It is revealing that black male achievement programs have not engendered the same kinds of conservative backlash that other race-conscious remedies have. For example, they have not generally been challenged by the conservative groups that have attacked affirmative action programs. I would argue that this is because the patriarchal rhetoric of these programs resonates with conservative values. Jonah Goldberg, writing in the *National Review*, stated that conservatives should support black male achievement programs, despite the usual right-wing antipathy to race-based interventions. Goldberg noted, "A strong male role model can tell boys to 'act like a man' in ways women can't. Sure, a woman can say the words, but she can't be a man. For some boys, particularly ones without fathers at home (the majority of at-risk youths), that's still a huge distinction."[27]

TOWARD BLACK MALE INTERSECTIONALITY

Gender is a social system that divides power. . . . Women, by contrast with comparable men, have systematically been subjected to physical insecurity, targeted for sexual denigration and violation; depersonalized and denigrated; deprived of respect, credibility, and resources; and silenced—and denied public presence, voice, and representation of their interests. Men as men have generally not had these things done to them; that is, men have had to be black or gay (for instance) to have these things done to them as men.

—Catharine MacKinnon[28]

There is nothing inherently wrong with interventions that are designed for African American men; indeed, if done right, these programs have the potential to be transformative. As this book has pointed out, some of the issues that black men experience are based on race and gender, and attention must be paid to both those aspects of their identity (as well as others like sexual orientation, disability, age, etc.) in order for them to succeed. But these programs should not pit men against women in the fight for racial justice. An equivalent amount of resources should be devoted to black women. Any government office, business, or foundation that sponsors an intervention for African American men should also sponsor one for African American women. The programs should receive equal funding. This equality goal will strike some as impractical and will raise feelings of a sense of sacrifice in some advocates for black men. It is a key component, however, of an intersectional strategy for black male interventions.

Civil rights law contains a model of this kind of approach: the regulations implementing Title IX of the Education Amendments of 1972 establish general standards for public schools receiving federal funding, allowing gender-segregated programs as long as "substantially equal" provisions exist for the other gender. It's a gender version of "separate but equal."

Why defend black male programs at all, if there are so many potential problems and if, as a practical matter, there are not likely to be the same number of programs for black women? Let's keep it real. Black men are still black. Many black women accrue some benefit when black men are better educated, are less likely to be incarcerated, live longer, and so on.

I realize that there is no guarantee that, if funding exclusively black male programs were not an option, funders would reallocate resources to black women. It would be revealing if funders did not, because it would demonstrate that they were more interested in black men than in racial justice, or at least less interested in racial justice if that includes black women. But that revelation would be at the expense of black male programs. I understand that some will view strict equality as too idealistic a standard in a community—the African American community—where the need is so great and the resources so limited. Any charity that thoroughly interrogates the motives of its donors is bound to be disappointed by some of them. But in the end, I am simply not persuaded by a "money is green" argument against any standards or ethical expectation of donors to racial justice projects.

My defense of black male programs is not simply "all about

the Benjamins"; intersectionality not only allows different interventions for different identity groups but also provides a basis for understanding why they are necessary. If they can be properly implemented, programs and initiatives targeting black males are appropriate as part of a comprehensive racial justice strategy. Just because one is not exceptional does not mean that one does not merit special attention. The premise of an intersectional intervention is not "best at being the worst."

Black males also have an intersectional identity. They are black. And they are male. Their experience is unique because of the interplay between these two (and many other) categories. Scholarly analysis of the plight of the black man frequently has been limited to racial discrimination. In reality, their experience has much to do with their status as males. Only recently has analysis pointed to the ways that race and gender combine to affect African American men.

The rhetoric about black men as an endangered species must be dismissed. Black male intersectionality is a more accurate way of conceptualizing the issues. It acknowledges that black men have specific issues, but they are not "worse" than black women's and do not require a hierarchy that displaces black women and girls.

Black male programs should be closely examined to eradicate any hint of anti-female ideology or practice. Some African American men have always supported feminist causes. After the Fifteenth Amendment extended the right to vote to black men, the abolitionist Frederick Douglass became a prominent advocate of suffrage for women. When President Obama's My Brother's Keeper initiative was announced, hundreds of African American men signed a letter requesting a program for African American women.[29] The legendary singer and activist Harry Belafonte, speaking to a black fraternity in 2014, told them to "man up" and let their new mission be preventing abuse against women. "It is men who created violence against women," Belafonte said. "It is men who should end the violence against women." The *Washington Post* reported that the audience of black men "rose up in applause."[30]

Understanding male privilege means acknowledging that black men's issues have historically been prioritized over black women's issues. Black male interventions should create space for African American women to be racial standard-bearers, a conversation that would position poverty and reproductive freedom as racial justice issues, in the way that advocates for black men have already done with criminal justice. Attention to women's issues is justified in part because African American men have been complicit in their subordination. Black men are still men. The scholar Michael Eric Dyson notes, "If we have a glorified sense of our own victimization as black and brown men, what we must not miss and what we often do, is to understand that black and brown women themselves are so victimized, not only by white patriarchy but by black male supremacy and by the violence of masculinity that is directed toward them."

In addition to fighting for African American women, an intersectional black male intervention would focus on attacking the structures, like white supremacy and patriarchy, that keep African American down, rather than just focusing on fixing black men. Imagine young men of color being schooled in the tradition of African American protest, studying how activists in New York City made the police end the stop-and-frisk program, and studying the history of the Black Panther Party (where they would learn, among other things, that most of the Panthers were women[31]).

Finally an intersectional black male intervention would affirm the diversity of African American men. One of the functions of white supremacy is to defeat black masculinity. I am a proud black man. I want to fight back against all the ways that white supremacy denigrates my manhood. At the same time, I worry that maleness—even black maleness—remains a problematic site for empowerment. Many African American men are thinking about new ways to define what it means to be a black man. Some brothers have always subverted the stereotypes. Little Richard, the flamboyant soul singer, wore mascara long before Prince ever picked up a makeup brush. The actor Jaden Smith and the best-selling hip-hop artist Young Thug appear on magazine covers in frilly frocks. Young Thug declared, in a Calvin Klein advertisement campaign, "In my world, you can be a gangsta with a dress or a gangsta with baggy pants. I feel like there is no such thing as gender." The professional football player Odell Beckham Jr. breaks into an expressive dance every time he scores a touchdown. Some of the most prominent leaders of the movement for black lives, including activists DeRay Mckesson and Darnell Moore, are proud gay men, in the tradition of James Baldwin and Bayard Rustin, who was selected by Martin Luther King to organize the March on Washington. All of these brothers, simply by living their truth and not being bound by rigid stereotypes, are creating a transformative vision of what it means to be an African American man.

Some programs are beginning to reflect this new wave of black masculinity. The Open Society Foundation's "Black Male Re-Imagined" campaign is an effort to move media portrayals of African American men beyond the stereotypes.[32] Question Bridge, a video art installation that has toured the United States, is intended to "deconstruct stereotypes about arguably the most opaque and feared demographic in America." It seeks to "represent and redefine Black male identity in America."[33] #BlackBoy Joy has used Twitter to deconstruct stereotypes of black men as thugs and gangsters by portraying joyful moments and expressions of African American men and boys.

The route from black men as "endangered species" to black male intersectionality creates equal space for African American women, and celebrates all brothers in our glorious diversity. That is the only way that racial justice will be achieved.

6

Nothing Works: Why the Chokehold Can't Be "Reformed"

Well, if one really wishes to know how justice is administered in a country, one does not question the policemen, the lawyers, the judges, or the protected members of the middle class. One goes to the unprotected—those, precisely, who need the law's protection the most!—and listens to their testimony. Ask any Mexican, any Puerto Rican, any black man, any poor person—ask the wretched how they fare in the halls of justice, and then you will know, not whether or not the country is just, but whether or not it has any love for justice, or any concept of it.

—James Baldwin[1]

Much of the conventional wisdom about racial justice is wrong. The civil rights movement did not do nearly as much good for African Americans as many people think. Having more black police officers does not mean that cops treat African Americans better. When the federal government takes over a police department, it does not necessarily improve the situation it seeks to address. About half the time, police violence actually increases after an intervention by the U.S. Department of Justice.

Why don't most Americans—and especially most white Americans—understand, despite having had a black president, how little progress this country has made on race? It's because, as Malcolm X told an audience in Harlem, "You been hoodwinked! Bamboozled! Led astray! Run amok!" The prominence of celebrities like Oprah Winfrey, Beyoncé, and Shonda Rhimes obscures the reality that black women on average are among the poorest people in the United States. What some scholars have described as our "celebratory tradition" of describing racial advancement is ahistorical and not evidence-based.

I want to disrupt the celebration. I don't relish the role of Debby Downer, the party pooper from the *Saturday Night Live* skit. My goal, however, is to help free my brothers from the tight grip of the Chokehold. Many people of all races share that goal, and the United States is now focused on race in a way that it has not been since the 1960s. Criminal justice has been the main source of concern. But, as I will demonstrate, the idea that the system can be reformed is shortsighted. If black lives are to matter, we must dream bigger.

WHAT, EXACTLY, IS THE PROBLEM?

Many people regret some racial effects of police practices, including that unarmed African Americans are disproportionately killed by the police, and that there are vast racial disparities in arrest and incarceration rates, although people differ about what causes these circumstances. As we think about whether the problems can be fixed, we need to be clear on what it is that needs fixing. Among the many who agree that something is broken, there is no consensus.

Some people say it is African American men, and others say it is police departments. Still others view the project of reforming a police department as enabling a system of white supremacist law enforcement to operate more effectively. These very different sets of critics are too often lumped together into one category of reformers. This is not helpful to any of their causes.

Let's examine the four leading articulations of the crisis.

CRISIS 1: BLACK MALE BEHAVIOR

If more African American men obeyed the law, they would not have to worry about being shot by police or being stopped and frisked. The problem is the antisocial way that many black men perform masculinity. Throughout this book we have seen several versions of this critique. Bill O'Reilly stated that "Young black men often reject education and gravitate towards the street culture, drugs, hustling, gangs. Nobody forces them to do that. . . . It is a personal decision."[2] After George Zimmerman was acquitted for killing Trayvon Martin, an unarmed African American teenager, CNN anchor Don Lemon said black male teenagers could "fix the problem" by pulling up their pants.[3]

During his first presidential campaign, Barack Obama joked about the work ethic of "gangbangers," mocking them as saying, "Why I gotta do it? Why you didn't ask Pookie to do it?"[4] Similarly, in a speech at an African American church, President Obama said, "Too many fathers . . . have abandoned their responsibilities, acting like boys instead of men. . . . You and I know how true this is in the African American community."[5]

If the problem is African American male behavior, one obvious response is to attempt to modify black male behavior. This is, as chapter 5 suggests, one of the goals of black male "achievement" programs, like the White House's My Brother's Keeper initiative.

CRISIS 2: UNDER-ENFORCEMENT OF LAW

In *Race, Crime, and the Law*, law professor Randall Kennedy writes that "the principal injury suffered by African Americans in relation to criminal matters is not overenforcement but underenforcement of the laws."[6] As an example of "racially selective underprotection,"[7] Kennedy points to the South's practice—during both the slavery and Jim Crow eras—of not seriously prosecuting black-on-black violence.[8] More recently, he notes, blacks do not demand more law and order because they "fear racially prejudiced misconduct by law enforcement officials. History re-inforced by persistent contemporary abuses gives credence and force to this fear."[9] This is the race problem that President Donald Trump has identified. He believes that "crime and violence are an attack on the poor."[10]

In this way of thinking, law enforcement is a public good. For a group to complain about having too much of it would be like complaining about having too many public parks or libraries. In the words of President Trump, "The problem in our poorest com-munities is not that there are too many police, the problem is that there are not enough police."[11]

Some scholars have asserted that many African Americans endorse this point of view. Exploring the support in Harlem for tough law enforcement in response to a heroin epidemic in the 1970s, Michael Javen Fortner found that "mass incarceration had less to do with white resistance to racial equality and more to do with the black silent majority's confrontation with the 'reign of criminal terror' in their neighborhoods."[12] James Forman has documented a similar dynamic in crime policy in majority-black Washington, D.C.[13]

If under-enforcement is the problem, then more enforcement is one solution. This brings us Chokehold police tactics like stop and frisk. According to former New York City mayor Michael Bloomberg, eliminating aggressive policing strategies such as stop and frisk would result in "far more crimes committed against black and Latino New Yorkers. When it comes to policing, politi-cal correctness is deadly."[14]

Sometimes proponents of this viewpoint recognize that in-creased enforcement may create tension in relations between blacks and the police, but they view this as a cost of increased public safety. Bloomberg, for example, asserted that police depart-ments must balance competing considerations: the "right to walk down the street without being targeted by the police because of his or her race or ethnicity" and the "right to walk down the street without getting mugged or killed."[15] "Both are civil liberties—and we in New York are fully committed to protecting both equally, even when others are not."[16]

CRISIS 3: POLICE–COMMUNITY RELATIONS

Perhaps the most common articulation is that the crisis concerns the relationship between the police and the African American community.

Cleveland police chief Calvin Williams said, "If we don't ensure that our officers and our community have a better relationship, then a lot of what we're trying to implement . . . is going to be hard to do."[17] Likewise, a federal investigation of the Cincinnati Police Department determined that officers had "superficial relationships" with the community.[18]

The Obama administration most often talked about criminal justice reform through this frame. It created the National Initiative for Building Community Trust and Justice, which is designed "to improve relationships and increase trust between communities and the criminal justice system."[19] The initiative's website highlights three areas "that hold great promise for concrete, rapid progress."[20] They are reconciliation, procedural justice, and implicit bias.[21]

This frame focuses on fairness rather than race per se. Former U.S. attorney general Eric Holder said that reform should ensure "that *everyone* who comes into contact with the police is treated fairly,"[22] that reforming drug sentencing laws "presents a historic opportunity to improve the fairness of our criminal justice system,"[23] and that preventing felons from voting is "unfair."[24]

In this construct, the race problem arises when law enforcement officers treat people of color differently.[25] The fix is the traditional civil rights–based approach of attempting to eradicate the discrimination. One of the main tools civil rights activists seek to use to repair police–community relations is the intervention of the U.S. Department of Justice. I discuss this remedy at length below. Here I want to note that this is the response that tends to

be championed by mainstream civil rights organizations like the
NAACP and the NAACP Legal Defense Fund.

CRISIS 4: ANTI-BLACK RACISM/
WHITE SUPREMACY

At the same time that police violence against African Americans
commands substantial attention in the media, a group of blacks
and sympathetic allies who hold radical racial ideologies have ascended to prominence. These activists, scholars, and journalists
represent the most radical movement among African Americans
since the Black Panther Party of the 1960s. Their critique of criminal justice generally, and police practices specifically, creates the
fourth explanation of the crisis. It views police brutality against
blacks as a symptom of structural racism and white supremacy.
To describe this point of view, I will focus on the movement for
black lives and the work of the scholar Michelle Alexander and
the journalist Ta-Nehisi Coates.

The movement for black lives is a collective of individuals
and community organizations who have come together "in response to the sustained and increasingly visible violence against
Black communities in the United States and globally."[26] Black
Lives Matter is the best-known organization in the collective. According to its website, "#BlackLivesMatter is a call to action and
a response to the virulent anti-Black racism that permeates our
society. Black Lives Matter is a unique contribution that goes
beyond extrajudicial killings of Black people by police and vigi-
lantes."[27] Its activists intend to "broaden the conversation around
state violence to include all of the ways in which Black people
are intentionally left powerless at the hands of the state" including "Black poverty and genocide," mass incarceration, and discrimination against the LGBT community and undocumented
immigrants.[28]

In *The New Jim Crow*, one of the most influential books
about race in many years, Michelle Alexander argues that mass

incarceration is a form of social control of blacks.[29] Alexander proposes a multiracial coalition to address the causes of mass incarceration.[30] She argues that unless the root causes are addressed, even if mass incarceration is defeated, another mechanism for controlling African Americans will rise in its place.[31]

Ta-Nehisi Coates is a leading public intellectual on race relations in the United States. In his best-selling *Between the World and Me*, he writes, in an open letter to his son, "all you need to understand is that the [police] officer carries with him the power of the American state and the weight of an American legacy, and they necessitate that of the bodies destroyed every year, some wild and disproportionate number of them will be black."[32]

Coates situates his critique of the police in a historical context. He notes, "White supremacy does not contradict American democracy—it birthed it, nurtured it, and financed it. That is our heritage. It was reinforced during 250 years of bondage. It was further reinforced during another century of Jim Crow. It was reinforced again when progressives erected an entire welfare state on the basis of black exclusion."[33]

This frame advocates broad economic and political transformation, extending well beyond police reform. For example, the Movement for Black Lives website states:

> The violence inflicted on Black communities goes far beyond police brutality. It can be seen in the continued suppression of our history, the exploitation of our culture, and the reality that many of our people live in communities that have been systematically denied resources and jobs. The violence includes inadequate health care, dirty water, failing schools, and a lack of resources. Every day we contend with the indecencies of racism and poverty, which wear on our spirit and make our communities more vulnerable to state violence and fuel community conflict. These varying forms of violence are perpetrated by government and corporate institutions and actors, at both the local and national level.[34]

The radical critique has received a surprisingly favorable reception. Both Alexander's *The New Jim Crow* and Coates's *Between the World and Me* have been widely acclaimed. They were national bestsellers, both won NAACP Image awards, and Coates's book also won the National Book Award. The movement for black lives has become an important force in progressive politics. Its members met with Democratic presidential candidates Hillary Clinton and Bernie Sanders.[35]

The pop music star Beyoncé Knowles released a video for the song "Formation" that alluded to iconography of the movement, including the "hands up, don't shoot" gesture that activists often make at protests.[36] In protest of police violence against African Americans, the professional football player Colin Kaepernick refused to stand when the U.S. national anthem was played during games.[37] Some other athletes joined him in these protests.[38] These developments represent a new acceptance, if not mainstreaming, of racial ideology that is left of traditional civil rights discourse.

CIVIL RIGHTS VERSUS BLACK LIVES MATTER

These categories are not mutually exclusive. Barack Obama, for example, employed Crisis 1 when he gave the commencement address at Morehouse College, the prestigious African American men's college. He said, "We know that too many young men in our community continue to make bad choices. And I have to say, growing up, I made quite a few myself. Sometimes I wrote off my own failings as just another example of the world trying to keep a black man down."[39]

Speaking after the decision by the grand jury not to bring charges against Darren Wilson in the shooting of Michael Brown, Obama invoked Crisis 3, saying, "We need to recognize that the situation in Ferguson speaks to broader challenges that we still face as a nation. The fact is, in too many parts of this country, a deep distrust exists between law enforcement and communities of color."[40]

But there are tensions between these explanations. In particular, I want to point out a tension between Crisis 3, the liberal/civil rights construct that focuses on police–community relations, and Crisis 4, the radical construct identified by the movement for black lives and the influential public intellectual Ta-Nehisi Coates, among others, that focuses on white supremacy.

While Crisis 4 centers white supremacy, each of the other three articulations acknowledges some role of race-based subordination in creating the crisis. Probably people who subscribe to any of the frames would say that a significant contributing factor to the crisis is the concentration of poverty in African American communities.

So, in the Crisis 1 black male culture frame, liberals, at least, blame the environment for over-determining the behavior of the African American men they critique. People who think law is under-enforced in black communities frequently point to the historic denial of "equal protection" of law and the current failure of the white majority to take black-on-black crime seriously.[41] The "relationship between police and the community" frame, Crisis 3, frequently highlights implicit bias as an explanation for why police patrol African American neighborhoods differently.[42]

Acknowledging that the problems are both complex and interrelated should cause advocates to understand that piecemeal solutions to the race and criminal justice crisis are unlikely to succeed. This understanding, in turn, could lead to two different responses.

On the one hand, we could embrace incremental reform in all four areas—black male conduct; under-enforcement in African American communities; police–community relations; and white supremacy/anti-black racism—in the hope that incremental reforms are likely to have some effect on the problem, even if none will solve it.

On the other hand, we could identify and focus on the root of the problem. If the root is concentrated economic disadvantage, the solution might be to advocate for more equitable distribution of wealth, rather than focus on policing. If the root is race discrimination, we could try to implement the most effective laws and practices to combat the discrimination. If the root is white supremacy, we could attack that problem at its core, as opposed to, say, promoting greater investments in inner-city communities.

While the articulations may share some common understandings, there are also important tensions between them. In particular, I want to identify Crisis 3, the police–community relations critique, as liberal, and Crisis 4, the white supremacy critique, as radical.

The civil rights interventions sought by liberals are intended to make the criminal justice system fairer. They address racial inequality in a narrow sense, to ensure that similarly situated people are treated the same, regardless of their race or ethnicity. They are especially focused on improving the perceptions of people of color about the police. For example, the Final Report of the President's Task Force on 21st Century Policing begins with this quote from President Obama: "When any part of the American family does not feel like it is being treated fairly, that's a problem for all of us."[43]

Elsewhere Obama made it clear that he does not think the problem is particularly widespread. After the grand jury failed to indict Ferguson police officer Darren Wilson for the death of Michael Brown, the president said: "There are still problems and communities of color aren't just making these problems up. Separating that from this particular decision, there are issues in which the law too often feels as if it is being applied in a discriminatory fashion. I don't think that's the norm. I don't think that's true for the majority of communities or the vast majority of law enforcement officials."[44]

But if you believe, as many people in the movement for black lives do, that the police are the enforcers of a white supremacist regime, then having a good relationship with them is not a desirable goal. The radicals argue for broader forms of relief. Coates, for example, is a prominent advocate for reparations for African Americans.[45] The Movement for Black Lives website states, "We believe that we can achieve, and will seek nothing less than, a complete transformation of the current systems, which make it impossible for many of us to breathe."[46] While liberals think reform is sufficient, radicals believe that until there is fundamental change in the structure of U.S. society, the problems will persist.

Both proponents of the police–community relations and the white supremacy frames have looked to the law, among other things, to help achieve their agenda. In Ferguson, for example, people allied with the movement for black lives were among the strongest voices for prosecution of Officer Wilson, and for the intervention of the U.S. Department of Justice in the police department. The question I turn to now is whether reform can actually help, for the change that either liberals or radicals seek.

RACIAL REALISM

Our nation/empire was and is established and constituted through the plunder, extermination, and exploitation of human beings, rationalized and justified by racialization.

—Charles Lawrence, University of Hawaii law professor[47]

How much [does] a dollar cost?

—Kendrick Lamar

Problems in the criminal justice system are just one set of problems that African Americans face. Despite the civil rights movement of the twentieth century, African Americans still experience extreme inequality in almost every aspect of life. Because African American history is often presented in a "celebratory" narrative of forward progress, it is important, especially in light of the strong claims that follow, to focus on the depth of the inequality.[48] Black people in the United States are not doing well. Their median net worth has gone down, not up.[49] In 2013, the median white household had thirteen times the wealth of the median black household:

the median net worth of a white household was $141,900 and the median net worth of a black household was $11,000.[50] Between 1954 and 2013, the unemployment rate for black people has consistently been double the unemployment rate for white people.[51] The disparity is similar for those with a college degree. In 2013, the unemployment rate for black college graduates between the ages of twenty-two and twenty-seven was 12.4 percent, compared to the overall unemployment rate of 5.6 percent for all graduates in the same age range.[52] Racial discrimination is against the law in the United States, but that law seems to have little impact on the lived experiences of black people.

AN IPOD HELD BY A BLACK HAND

Indeed, there is widespread evidence that African Americans face discrimination virtually every time they enter the marketplace. A 2012 study by the U.S. Department of Housing and Urban Development found that while the most blatant forms of housing discrimination, such as refusing to meet with a minority home seeker, have declined, other forms of discrimination still exist.[53] African Americans who want to rent an apartment are informed about 11.4 percent fewer units and shown 4.2 percent fewer units than white renters.[54] Blacks who try to purchase homes are told about 17 percent fewer homes and shown 17.7 percent fewer homes.[55]

African Americans also encounter discrimination on the travel website Airbnb. The Twitter hashtag #AirbnbWhileBlack chronicles incidents where black travelers were initially denied a rental based on their profile picture or having an "African American–sounding name" but were subsequently granted a rental after changing their picture or name.[56] A study conducted by Harvard Business School provided statistical backing to this phenomenon.[57] Inquiries by guests with white-sounding names were approved by the renter roughly 50 percent of the time.[58] However, inquiries by guests with black-sounding names were approved by the renter roughly 42 percent of the time. There was a 16 percent negative disparity in the acceptance rate for guests with black-sounding names.[59]

Black applicants for employment are less likely to get callbacks than white applicants. A 2003 study found that applicants with white-sounding names needed to submit ten resumes to receive one callback, and applicants with black-sounding names needed to submit fifteen resumes to receive one callback.[60] A study released in 2014 using additional metrics to separate data by the prestige of the applicant's degree found similar results.[61] White applicants from elite universities received responses 17.5 percent of the time and similarly situated black applicants received responses 12.9 percent of the time.[62] White applicants from less selective universities received responses 11.4 percent of the time and similarly situated black applicants received responses 6.5 percent of the time. The disparity continued for salaries, with black applicants receiving offers approximately $3,000 less than white applicants.[63]

A study of loans by the University of Chicago Booth School of Business found that requests from a profile with a black person in the profile picture were 25 to 35 percent less likely to receive a loan than profiles with a white person in the profile picture, even with similar credit ratings.[64]

African Americans even encounter bias in a transaction as mundane as selling a used iPod. A 2013 study using classified ads featuring an iPod being held by either a black or a white hand found that black sellers received fewer and lower offers for iPods.[65] Specifically, black sellers, compared to white sellers, received 13 percent fewer responses, 18 percent fewer offers, and offers that were $5.72 (11 percent) lower.[66]

Small wonder there is a robust debate about exactly what good the civil rights movement did African Americans![67] Why has the law not worked better to remedy these problems? How much racial justice should African Americans ever expect?

An important school of race theorists has attempted to answer these questions. Critical race theorists ("crits") have made strong claims about race and the law. These claims resonate with the analysis of crisis 4, including the movement for black lives and the work of Ta-Nehisi Coates. I want to set out some of those claims and see how they might inform the project of police reform.

THE LAW CREATES RACIAL HIERARCHY AND WHITE SUPREMACY

Critical race theorists assert that the law "constructs race" by separating people into groups, assigning social meaning to these groups, and instituting hierarchical arrangements.[68] Racial inequalities persist because race informs all areas of the law—"not only obvious ones like civil rights, immigration law, and federal Indian law, but also property law, contracts law, criminal law, and even [corporate law]."[69] Legal institutions such as "legislatures and courts have served not only to fix the boundaries of race in the forms we recognize today, but also to define the content of racial identities and to specify their relative privilege or disadvantage in U.S. society."[70] For example, legal scholar Ian Haney López in his book *Dog Whistle Racism* cites a series of Supreme Court decisions from the late 1800s and early 1900s in which the Court defined various groups as white or nonwhite, a determination that carried important consequences for naturalization and citizenship.[71] Racial beliefs "were quickly translated into exclusionary immigration laws."[72]

Critics built on the arguments of black nationalists like the Black Panthers and others who felt that allegedly neutral goals such as integration were actually imprinted with white cultural practices.[73] As a result, so-called objective tests that rely on the determination of what a "reasonable person" would do could prove problematic. These insights loom large in the criminal justice context because, as we have seen, the Supreme Court's adoption of "reasonableness" standards for stop and frisk and the use of deadly force have enabled police violence against African Americans.

RACISM IS NEVER GOING AWAY

While racial categories are dynamic, critical race theorists assert that racism[74] is a deeply ingrained feature of American society. Devon Carbado and Daria Roithmayr write, "Racial inequality is hardwired into the fabric of our social and economic landscape."[75] Derrick Bell and others have argued that racism, rather than an unfortunate accident, represents an "integral, permanent, and indestructible component" of American democracy.[76] Roithmayr has analogized white supremacy to a monopoly, in which "whites anticompetitively excluded people of color to monopolize competition, and then used that monopoly power to lock in standards of competition that favored whites."[77] Given the central role race has played in shaping allocation of societal resources, addressing racial injustice is not merely a matter of clearing up misconceptions through dialogue or adopting modest reforms.[78]

The crits' assertion of the durability of racism is a marked contrast to rhetoric, after the election of Barack Obama, about a "post-racial" or "color-blind" society. In acknowledging the extent to which racism is deeply ingrained in American society, critical race theorists posit a more systemic critique of legal institutions and policies than liberal advocates of improved police–community relations.

RACIAL PROGRESS COMES AND GOES

The dominant narrative of American race relations is one of forward progress. In this story, the United States has moved "from segregation to integration and from race consciousness to race neutrality."[79] Critical race theorists believe that the more accurate model is a cycle of reform and retrenchment. Charles Lawrence writes, "When people's movements successfully challenge and disrupt racist structures and institutions, and contest the narratives of racial subordination, the plunderers will respond with new law."[80] One example is the passage of civil rights legislation. The civil rights movement of the 1950s and 1960s led to important developments like the Supreme Court's decision in *Brown v. Board of Education*,[81] the Civil Rights Act of 1964,[82] and the Voting Rights Act.[83] As Kimberlé Crenshaw points out, civil rights laws "nurtured the impression that the United States had moved decisively to end the oppression of Blacks."[84] However, the rhetoric of color blindness and equal opportunity was then deployed to block further remedial measures and "undermined the fragile consensus against white supremacy."[85] Now the Supreme Court has gutted the Voting Rights Act, often considered the most successful civil rights law, and weakened affirmative action.

RACIAL PROGRESS OCCURS WHEN IT IS GOOD FOR WHITE PEOPLE

Derrick Bell developed the theory of interest convergence, the notion that the United States has adopted racial justice measures only when "the interest of blacks in achieving racial equality . . . converges with the interests of whites."[86] For example, Bell cites global public opinion during the Cold War, the participation of black soldiers in World War II, and segregation as a barrier to industrialization in the South as reasons for the Supreme Court's decision in *Brown v. Board of Education*.[87]

After the backlash to integration began taking root in the 1950s and 1960s, the Court turned away from robust enforcement and emphasized local autonomy, even though it would likely "result in the maintenance of a status quo that will preserve superior educational opportunities and facilities for whites at the expense of blacks."[88] These "second thoughts" about school desegregation reflected the "substantial and growing divergence in the interests of whites and blacks."[89]

FERGUSON AND THE CRITS

The ideas from critical race theory help us understand why the crisis in criminal justice stems more from legal police conduct than illegal police misconduct. As discussed in chapter 2, many of the concerns about the police are about conduct that is legal. The problem is not as much "bad apple" cops as police work itself—what the law actually allows. That's why even when police officers are charged with brutality, they are often found "not guilty."

The Justice Department's Ferguson Report depicts a police department that is brutal and discriminatory. It found that bias against blacks affected "nearly every aspect of Ferguson police and court operations." [90] Ninety percent of the time that FPD officers used force, it was used against African Americans. [91] Every single time they deployed a police dog to bite a suspect, the suspect was African American. [92]

But the Ferguson Report was not the only report issued on March 4, 2015. The Department of Justice also issued a specific report about the shooting of Michael Brown, an unarmed African American teenager, by a Ferguson police officer, the "Department of Justice Report Regarding the Criminal Investigation into the Shooting Death of Michael Brown by Ferguson Missouri Police Officer Darren Wilson," referred to as the "Wilson Report." [93] There are some notable tensions between the themes of these two reports.

The Wilson Report found that Officer Wilson's shooting of Brown did not meet the Justice Department standard for criminal prosecution because Wilson had reasonably perceived a threat from Brown. [94] The Wilson Report stated, "While Brown did not use a gun on Wilson at the SUV, his aggressive actions would have given Wilson reason to at least question whether he might be armed, as would his subsequent forward advance and reach toward his waistband. This is especially so in light of the rapidly-evolving nature of the incident. Wilson did not have time to determine whether Brown had a gun and was not required to risk being shot himself in order to make a more definitive assessment." [95]

The Wilson Report carefully cites case law that allows an armed police officer to kill an unarmed suspect in self-defense.[96] It discounts the credibility of witnesses who said that Michael Brown was shot despite having his hands up in surrender.[97]

But the Wilson Report also suggests that even if Officer Wilson had shot Michael Brown while Brown's hands were in the air, Officer Wilson's shooting Brown could still be reasonable.[98] The report states, "The Eighth Circuit Court of Appeals' decision in *Loch v. City of Litchfield* is dispositive on this point. There, an officer shot a suspect eight times as he advanced toward the officer. Although the suspect's 'arms were raised above his head or extended at his sides,' the Court of Appeals held that a reasonable officer could have perceived the suspect's forward advance in the face of the officer's commands to stop as resistance and a threat."[99]

The Wilson Report also discounts the claim that Wilson should have used non-deadly force against Brown:

> Under the law, Wilson has a strong argument that he was justified in firing his weapon at Brown as he continued to advance toward him and refuse commands to stop, and the law does not require Wilson to wait until Brown was close enough to physically assault Wilson. Even if, with hindsight, Wilson could have done something other than shoot Brown, the Fourth Amendment does not second-guess a law enforcement officer's decision on how to respond to an advancing threat. The law gives great deference to officers for their necessarily split-second judgments, especially in incidents such as this one that unfold over a span of less than two minutes.[100]

In sum, the Ferguson Report described the Ferguson police department as a racist organization that consistently used excessive violence against African Americans. The Wilson Report, by

contrast, found that a white officer of the Ferguson Police Department acted legally when he shot an unarmed African American man.[101]

There is no direct contradiction between these two reports. It
is possible that even in a prejudiced and brutal police department
a shooting of an unarmed African American man could be justified. What is revealing, however, is the different focus of the
two reports. The Ferguson Report uses data and stories to present
a troubling case of a police department that has targeted black
people.[102] The Wilson Report relies on law to suggest that Officer
Wilson's act of killing an unarmed black man was not illegal.[103]
These two reports, read together, demonstrate a problematic reality. It is possible for police to selectively invoke their powers
against African American residents and, at the same time, act consistently with the law. This resonates with the critical race theory
ideas about race. Those ideas gain even more credibility based on
the settlement reached between Ferguson and the Department of
Justice. In March 2016 the United States Department of Justice
and the City of Ferguson entered into a consent decree regarding the allegations in the Ferguson Report. After the Ferguson
consent degree was approved, Vanita Gupta, the head of the U.S.
Justice Department's Civil Rights division, said that the city had
taken "an important step towards guaranteeing all of its citizens
the protections of our Constitution."[104]

In reality, however, the consent decree provides Ferguson residents far more protection than does the Constitution. It reads as
an implicit critique of the cases in which the Supreme Court has
blessed the cops with super powers. The following examples are
illustrative.

In *Whren v. United States*, the super power to racially profile
case discussed in chapter 2, the Supreme Court held that the
Fourth Amendment does not prohibit the police from making
pretextual stops. The Ferguson consent decree bars pretextual
stops other than in limited circumstances.[105]

In *Atwater v. Lago Vista*, the super power to arrest case discussed in chapter 2, the Supreme Court stated that the police can arrest for minor offenses, even if the offenses themselves do not carry jail time. The Ferguson consent decree limits the offenses for which people can be arrested.[106]

In *Pennsylvania v. Mimms*, the Supreme Court granted the police the power, during a traffic stop, to automatically order the driver out of the car.[107] The Ferguson consent decree, on the other hand, requires an "articulable basis" in order for police to command the driver to leave the car.[108]

The Supreme Court has never required any showing of suspicion for the police to seek consent to a search.[109] The Ferguson decree prohibits officers from seeking consent for a search unless they have reasonable suspicion.[110]

In *Schneckloth v. Bustamonte*[111] and *United States v. Drayton*[112] the Supreme Court ruled that suspects do not have to be informed that they have the right to refuse consent. The Ferguson decree requires that officers inform suspects of this right.[113]

In sum, the consent decree prohibits the Ferguson police from exercising the scope of the super powers that the Supreme Court has granted them. In order to try to prevent the Ferguson police from treating African American residents unfairly, the police department's constitutional powers have to be curtailed. Not only is the Constitution, as interpreted by the Supreme Court, insufficient to protect black people from police abuse, it actually aids and abets the police abusers.

Even if the changes provided for in the consent decree are implemented, the question remains, will they be enough? Or will the Ferguson police find ways to backslide? The Department of Justice, during the Obama administration, increased its oversight of police, but it has never done an evidence-based analysis to see whether they make a difference. Next I take a look at the data.

FEDERAL TAKEOVER OF LOCAL POLICE
DEPARTMENTS: DOES IT WORK?

As we have seen, critical race theory also suggests the possibility of interventions that improve racial justice. Could federal oversight of local police departments be one of those interventions?

I focus on Department of Justice investigations because they are probably the most sought-after legal remedy for complaints about the police. High-profile cases of allegations of police misconduct almost always elicit calls for the federal government to intervene. When the federal government acts, these investigations are the action it undertakes. I also focus on these cases because they provide a limited set of data that lends itself to analysis more than some other kinds of remedies. There have been a total of sixty-seven Department of Justice investigations since the first one in 1995 and just sixteen cases in which the department imposed its strongest oversight.[114]

As part of the Violent Crime Control and Law Enforcement Act of 1994, Congress included a provision that made it illegal for police departments to engage in "a pattern or practice" of unconstitutional conduct.[115] This statute allows the Department of Justice to "seek injunctive or equitable relief to force police agencies to accept reforms aimed at curbing misconduct."[116] The Department of Justice selects its cases by monitoring existing civil litigation, media reports, and research studies that indicate widespread misconduct within a police department.[117] The department then engages in a preliminary inquiry, followed by a formal investigation.[118] Figure 16 shows cases from 2000 to 2013.

This investigation has the potential to lead to a negotiated settlement in the form of a consent decree; there is also the possibility of an appointed monitor to supervise the department's implementation of required reforms.[119] Incredibly, the Department of Justice has never done a quantitative analysis of whether its interventions in local police departments are successful.[120] The *Washington Post* looked at available data about use of force after

FIGURE 16: VIOLENT CRIME CONTROL AND LAW
ENFORCEMENT ACT CASES, 2000–2013

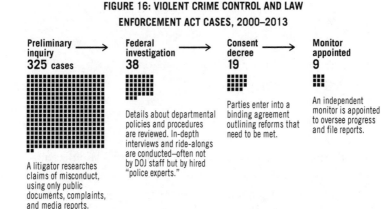

Preliminary inquiry	Federal investigation	Consent decree	Monitor appointed
325 cases	**38**	**19**	**9**

A litigator researches claims of misconduct, using only public documents, complaints, and media reports.

Details about departmental policies and procedures are reviewed. In-depth interviews and ride-alongs are conducted—often not by DOJ staff but by hired "police experts."

Parties enter into a binding agreement outlining reforms that need to be met.

An independent monitor is appointed to oversee progress and file reports.

Although DOJ conducted hundreds of preliminary inquiries between 2000 and 2013, only nineteen consent decrees were entered into, and only nine monitors were appointed to supervise local agencies' required reforms.

Source: Stephen Rushin, "Federal Enforcement of Police Reform," *Fordham Law Review* Fol 82, page 3190, 2014, fordhamlawreview.org/wp-content/uploads/assets/pdfs/Vol_82/No _6/Rushin_May.pdf.

Department of Justice interventions. It found that use of force decreased in half of the departments, and stayed the same or increased in the other half.[121]

The investigation of Los Angeles is often presented as a success story. In the aftermath of high-profile incidents of police brutality, Los Angeles entered into a consent decree with the Department of Justice. A study conducted from 2002 to 2008 (the consent decree was lifted in 2009) revealed lower crime and fewer use-of-force incidents.[122] Both property crimes (down 53 percent) and violent crimes (down 48 percent) decreased in Los Angeles more than in several adjacent communities.[123]

During this time the level of law enforcement increased. Stops increased by 49 percent from 2002 to 2008.[124] Pedestrian stops nearly doubled, and motor vehicle stops increased almost 40 percent.[125] Still, there was a dramatic increase in the proportion of stops resulting in arrests, suggesting that police officers "stopped people for good reasons and were willing to have the District Attorney scrutinize those reasons."[126]

An extensive survey of Los Angeles residents conducted after the decree found: "Public satisfaction is up, with 83 percent of residents saying the LAPD is doing a good or excellent job."[127] The number of satisfied residents includes more than two-thirds of Hispanic and African American residents.[128]

Over the course of the consent decree period, "the incidence of categorical force used against Blacks and Hispanics decreased more than such force used against Whites."[129] At the same time, black residents remained a disproportionate percentage of individuals arrested and injured in the course of a use-of-force incident.[130]

Pittsburgh also reformed its police department in compliance with a federal consent decree. As in Los Angeles, crime decreased (although crime decreased across many cities during the 1990s). In Pittsburgh, between 1994 and 2000, arrests decreased by more than 40 percent.[131] Moreover, the proportion of African Americans among those arrested for serious crimes declined.[132] A survey of Pittsburgh residents "showed that public opinion of the police has improved in a number of respects, although improvements are generally larger among whites than among blacks."[133]

Cincinnati too is often cited as one of the success stories of the pattern and practice approach. A recent report on the Cincinnati reform effort indicates: "Between 1999 and 2014, Cincinnati saw a 69 percent reduction in police use-of-force incidents, a 42 percent reduction in citizen complaints, and a 56 percent reduction in citizen injuries during encounters with police. . . . Violent crimes dropped from a high of 4,137 in the year after the riots, to 2,352 last year. Misdemeanor arrests dropped from 41,708 in 2000 to 17,913 [in 2014]."[134] Because of the consent decree, "CPD officers . . . chose to use less harmful methods of force to make arrests."[135] There is also evidence that police–community relations improved over the course of the implementation of the consent decree.[136] At the same time, these results were not easy to achieve. It took years "to get police to actually buy into the reforms," and "the federal government had to apply constant pressure, reminding all parties about the need to stay vigilant about reform."[137] Moreover, "Cincinnati is not completely free of police shootings or citizen complaints. In 2014, police officers shot and killed three people—all black males."[138] Community activists assert that there is still substantial distrust between police and the black community in Cincinnati.[139]

The investigations are very expensive. The Los Angeles investigation is estimated at $300 million.[140] The difficulty of achieving meaningful reform raises doubts about whether this success is sustainable and can be reproduced in other cities. For example, because the Department of Justice investigates only a few departments per year, it may be difficult for pattern and practice investigations to produce large-scale change.[141] Even in cities where there have been reduced disparities in arrests and use-of-force incidents, institutionalizing reform has been a challenge.[142] As seen in Figure 17, the level of interest in the Justice Department in bringing these cases varies depending on whether there is a Democrat or Republican in the White House.

While focusing on use-of-force policies and community engagement strategies is important, federal investigations do not directly address issues like overcriminalization, prosecutorial discretion, and sentencing disparities.

To summarize, federal investigations work, some of the time, to reduce police violence and to improve community perceptions about the police. They are expensive, and the benefits may be only short term. But, in the jurisdictions where the federal intervention is successful, fewer people are killed or beat up by the police, and that is a good thing.

Reform does not, however, do the work of transformation. It does not bring about the kind of change that the radical critics are seeking.

The point I am making about reform is unremarkable to

FIGURE 17: NUMBER OF OPEN CONSENT DECREES, BY ADMINISTRATION

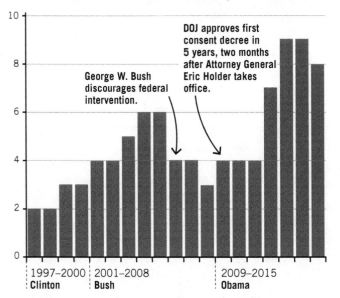

The Department of Justice's willingness to bring these cases varies depending on whether there is a Democrat or Republican in the White House.

Source: "A 'Pattern or Practice' of Violence in America," *Bloomberg,* https://www.bloomberg.com/graphics/2015-doj-and-police-violence.

critical theorists.[143] For example, Kimberlé Crenshaw has made a similar observation about anti-discrimination law, noting that it "has largely succeeded in eliminating the symbolic manifestations of racial oppression, but has allowed the perpetuation of material subordination of Blacks."[144]

Because the law is not neutral or objective but actually perpetuates white supremacy, seeking change through liberal legal reform will result in "ephemeral" victories and "substantial" risks.[145] In addition, reforms are often inadequate because reformers often underestimate the pervasiveness of racism and other biases ingrained in the law.

REFORM VERSUS TRANSFORMATION

The fact that pattern and practice investigations may work somewhat, sometimes is a reason that they should be encouraged, because working "somewhat, sometimes" in this context means that the police kill and hurt fewer people.

Crisis 3, the police–community relations articulation, is addressed, in an imperfect, possibly short-term, and very expensive way, by the U.S. Justice Department's interventions in local police departments. Reformers should continue to press for these investigations, fully aware of their shortcomings. The work they do is both essential and stopgap. They prevent some people from being beaten and killed by the police. But they will not resolve Crisis 4 problems identified by the movement for black lives. Pattern or practice investigations, and other liberal reforms, will not bring about the extreme change in American criminal justice necessary to end over-policing, mass incarceration, and the vast racial disparities.

Indeed, in some instances, reform gets in the way of change because it placates and takes energy and focus away from the actual transformative work. Recall, for example, that in Los Angeles, after the Justice Department intervention, more than two-thirds of the black and Latino citizens felt that the police are doing a good or excellent job.[146] Recall also the statistics that suggest that huge racial inequities continue to exist, in a city that is 10 percent African American.[147]

BLACKS IN LOS ANGELES
(AFTER THE FEDS)

- 10 percent of population
- 22 percent of stops
- 31 percent of arrests
- 34 percent of "categorical" use of force
- 43 percent of injury reports in "takedowns"

In essence, the Chokehold remains in full effect in the City of Angels—even after a $300 million federal intervention.[148] People of color remain disproportionately the victims of police violence. In this sense the LAPD is not doing good or excellent work for the black and Latino citizens they are supposed to serve and protect. But the federal intervention makes the minority residents feel better about what the police are doing.

A related dynamic occurred in Prince George's County, Maryland. After the Department of Justice intervention, the number of complaints about use of force decreased. At the same time, however, the use of force by the police actually *increased*. In other words, the police used force more and yet received fewer complaints about it.[149]

Reform has a pacification effect. It calms the natives even when they should not be calm.[150] "False consciousness" is the term some theorists have used to describe the tendency of liberal reforms to "dupe those at the bottom of the social and economic hierarchy" with promises of "equality, fairness, and neutrality."[151]

In the context of civil rights and anti-discrimination law, Kimberlé Crenshaw warned that the "limited gains" of civil rights legislation could "hamper efforts of African Americans to name their reality and to remain capable of engaging in collective action in the future."[152] Even though civil rights laws passed in the 1960s succeeded in breaking down some formal barriers, subtle and invidious forms of discrimination persisted. Moreover, the *perception* of progress may have mollified communities of color and sapped the energy needed for a continued push for substantive equality.

A newsletter from the Department of Justice's Community Oriented Policing's office, in an article entitled "The Case for Procedural Justice: Fairness as a Crime Prevention Tool," describes the work of the leading procedural justice scholar: "Professor Tom Tyler of Yale Law School, [has] identified several critical dimensions of procedural fairness: (1) *voice* (the perception that

your side of the story has been heard); (2) *respect* (perception that
system players treat you with dignity and respect); (3) *neutrality*
(perception that the decision-making process is unbiased and
trustworthy); (4) *understanding* (comprehension of the process
and how decisions are made); and (5) *helpfulness* (perception
that system players are interested in your personal situation to the
extent that the law allows)." [153]

The problem with all the focus on perceptions about the police
is that it can cloak aggressive policing in enhanced legitimacy, and
it has the potential to blunt the momentum for rising up against
overcriminalization, wealth inequality, and white supremacy.

Tracey Meares, a law professor at Yale, argues that we should
encourage "rightful policing"—police officers should not only
obey every constitutional requirement and administrative rule;
they should also "comport themselves in ways that confer dignity
on those with whom they interact and otherwise treat people with
respect." [154] In this framing, the ideal form of policing is both lawful and legitimate. [155]

Of course Professor Meares is correct that police officers
should be polite and comply with the law in their encounters with
citizens. But lawfulness and legitimacy are not enough. If existing law is too tolerant of police violence, then "rightful policing"
might fail to address the substantive shortcomings of the criminal justice system. Any procedural justice reforms need to be accompanied by substantive reforms if they are to have an impact
beyond public relations.

President Obama's Task Force on 21st Century Policing provides a way forward. The proposals in the final report were a mix-
ture of procedural justice and more substantive proposals.

First, the Task Force urged "law enforcement agencies [to]
adopt procedural justice as the guiding principle . . . for . . . their
interactions with rank and file officers and with the citizens they
serve." [156] The first of the report's six "pillars" was "Building
Trust & Legitimacy," and the Task Force proposed a number of

procedural justice reforms, from transparency measures to track-ing the level of trust in the community.[157]

At the same time, the final report included a number of sub-stantive proposals that addressed or at least acknowledged deeper issues. Examples include independent investigations of deadly-force incidents, bans on racial profiling, and the establishment of civilian review boards.[158] Moreover, the Task Force acknowl-edged that the criminal justice system "alone cannot solve many of the underlying conditions that give rise to crime," and that policymakers must "address the core issues of poverty, education, health, and safety."[159] White supremacy does not make the gov-ernment's list of issues that policymakers must address, but polic-ing will never be adequate until we address inequality.

THE WAY FORWARD

Barack Obama was wrong when he said, "What happened in Ferguson may not be unique, but it's no longer endemic. It's no longer sanctioned by law or by custom."[160] What happened in Fer-guson is both endemic and sanctioned by law.

President Obama came closer to the truth in another speech about race, this one made on the fiftieth anniversary of the "Bloody Sunday" police violence in Selma, Alabama. There he said:

> What greater expression of faith in the American experi-ment than this, what greater form of patriotism is there than the belief that America is not yet finished, that we are strong enough to be self-critical, that each successive generation can look upon our imperfections and decide that it is in our power to remake this nation to more closely align with our highest ideals?[161]

"Remaking" the country sounds more like a radical project than a liberal one. Yet it is exactly what must be done for people of color to be as free as white people. The system is now working the way it is supposed to, and that makes black lives matter less. That system must be dismantled and the United States of America must, in President Obama's words, be "remade." The final chapter of this book suggests a beginning. But first I want to give some practical advice to African American men who find themselves in the snares of the Chokehold.

7

If You Catch a Case: Act Like You Know

If you are an African American male, police and prosecutors are waiting for you. Watching and regulating the conduct of black men is a major part of their work. Cops are eager to stop and frisk you. They are looking for a reason to arrest you. This will improve their reputation on the force and their precinct's numbers on Compstat, a management system used by major police departments to track crime. If they make enough stops and arrests, they might make detective. Prosecutors too are working to enroll you in the system. When I did that work I got the most credit for winning convictions, which I obtained mainly by forcing defendants to plead guilty. If the judge sentenced somebody to substantial time in prison, I got high fives all around the office.

This is how the Chokehold works. But there are things that you can do to disrupt its grip. You should resent having to do these things. They severely curtail your rights as a citizen of the United States, and as a free human being. The final chapter of this book is about how to bring down this entire system.

In the meantime, if you want to avoid getting caught up in the snares of the Chokehold, here is a guide to navigating the system. And if you do catch a case, here is advice from a former prosecutor about how to manage the criminal process. And not just any prosecutor, but an African American male prosecutor who has had the same kind of bad interactions with the police as many of my brothers. I've been stopped and frisked by cops more times than I can count; I have been thrown against a car by police twice; I have been arrested, and I have been prosecuted myself, for a crime that I did not commit. I beat my case and if what I did can be of any use to anyone else who has caught a case I am happy to share it.

HOW TO NOT GET STOPPED

If the police want to stop you, they can almost always find a reason. Remember, under the "reasonable suspicion" legal standard that allows the police to detain you temporarily, you do not have to be doing anything illegal. As a practical matter, "reasonable suspicion" can be anything that strikes the police as unusual or that makes you stand out. In addition, in cities like New York and Baltimore, courts have found that if cops don't have a reason to stop you, they can just make one up—with little fear of consequences.[1]

So the task is to make the police not want to stop you, to cause them to lose interest in you, to turn yourself into the invisible man. There is some obvious stuff: Don't drink alcohol or smoke weed in public places. Don't ride in a car or hang out on the street with people who might have guns or drugs on them. Understanding that cops use low-level misdemeanor offenses as a way to catch black men, you have to exercise proper caution.[2] No riding a bike on the sidewalk. As an African American man, you are better off peeing in your pants than urinating outside.

But you already know those things. Most of what attracts the police to you is subtler. Here are some other things that are suspicious to the police. These tips come from police officers and defense attorneys. I don't mean that these factors provide legal reason for the cops to stop you. Rather, they draw attention. They extend the hard stare to active surveillance.

Three or more black men in a car at any time
Black man in a new or late-model car
Black man in a black SUV

Black man in a car with tinted windows
Black man with a white woman
Black men in a group laughing too loudly
Black men play-fighting or joking around physically
Black men raising their voices
Black men in any sort of disagreement or argument
Black man running fast
Black man in a hoodie
Black man with low pants
Black man with a T-shirt that says "Black Lives Matter"
"Racial incongruity"—a legal term meaning being in a
    place where members of your race usually are not

The law of stop and frisk enforces a conformity about race but
also restricts any kind of standing out from the crowd. "Suspiciousness" is an ideological bundle of sticks. It discourages acting
different from everybody else, looking weird, or not living up to
a police officer's expectations about how a black man should act.
The cops don't only enforce the criminal law; they also enforce
the politics of respectability.

Many will rebel. The black teenagers with their pants hanging
down their behinds know that it makes the police look at them
extra hard. They do it anyway, in the name of free expression.
Mad respect. But if you do not want to deal with the cops you
must understand that the country African American men live in
is not free.[3] So basically don't stick out. And if you are unfortunate
enough to attract the attention of an officer, you must find a way
to send the message, without a word, that you are safe. There is
a specific way you should, as an African American man, look at
a cop. You want, just by your gaze, to communicate respect and
deference, but not fear, which is interpreted by the police as a
sign that you are guilty of something. You have to demonstrate
not only that you are safe but also that you are compliant. This is
an actor's trick. Of course when a cop is trying to decide whether
you should be detained, you are afraid. And, to preserve your own

sense of self-worth, you should not actually feel compliant. What is required, though, is a performance, to keep you safe. The gaze is everything. Practice at home or with a friend.

It is usually not a good idea to run or otherwise attempt to evade cops. As discussed in chapter 3, this gives the police a legitimate reason to stop you, even if they did not have one before. Indeed the only situation in which you should even consider running is if you know you have contraband on you, or you know the cop does not like you, and you think that if you run, you will not be chased. In Baltimore, for example, the word on the street is that the cops don't chase most people who run.[4] That is why Freddie Gray took off when he saw the cops. He didn't have anything illegal on him; he probably just did not feel like being bothered that day.

So, again, if the practice of your hood is that the cops don't chase folks, running might occasionally make sense for a brother. But even in those places, unless you have contraband, it's probably safer to take your chances with staying put. Running will, at minimum, draw the attention of the police to you, and for an African American man that is never a good thing.

HOW TO PREVENT A STOP FROM TURNING INTO AN ARREST

None of the above worked and you have been stopped. There's still a good chance things will work out; most stops don't turn into arrests. Here's what you can do to be one of the lucky ones.

The following tips apply to people who get stopped by the police in public. If the cops come to your house with a warrant for your arrest, you're going down. Skip ahead to the section about how to find a good lawyer. But most people get arrested on the street, following a stop. And, drum roll please, here is some rare good news for black people about the police. In cities where studies have been done, African Americans who are stopped are less likely to be arrested than white people.[5] This is because the police frequently use any dumb excuse to stop a black person, whereas they are more likely to stop a white person for something that actually is suspicious, and which leads to an arrestable offense.

Okay enough good news, now back to the regularly scheduled programming. Much of what you think about how the police are supposed to treat you is wrong. No, they don't have to tell you why you are being stopped. If you end up getting arrested, they do not even have to explain what crime you are being arrested for.[6] If you get patted down, they don't have to get someone of your same gender to do it. A female cop can frisk a man, and a male cop can frisk a woman. In twenty-four states, if cops ask for identification, you have to produce it, or you get arrested. These states are listed in the endnotes.[7]

These tips for avoiding arrest are not foolproof. If the cops want to arrest you, maybe because they have a quota to meet, they will. However, if it's just a routine stop for a petty misdemeanor, the cops usually don't care too much about letting you go. It's not like they think they would be letting a hardened criminal loose. As we have seen, police stops don't have much to do with public safety.

The most important thing you need to know is this: A stop is a masculinity contest between you and the police.[8] You must let the cops win. It's all about machismo, regardless of whether the cops are male or female. They are stopping you to demonstrate their dominance of the street. Here's how you pretend like you acquiesce:

Address the police as "Officer," "Sir," and "Ma'am." Never raise your voice. Don't make jokes or communicate any kind of irreverence. Do not let the police provoke you—even if they are treating you with contempt. Unless the police start hitting you, do not ask bystanders to record the stop. Don't object if people are recording, it's a good thing, and you should do the same thing for another brother or sister. But at this moment, when you are trying not to be arrested, if you yell for someone to start recording, it will make the police angry. This is not a time for civil liberties. This is a time for being dominated by the state, and acting like you like it.

The cops will ask you a bunch of nosy questions, like "Where are you going?" and "What are you doing?" and "Who do you know around here?" They will want you to name names and provide addresses. They usually ask how many times you have been arrested, and if you are on probation or parole. Say as little as possible, but answer the questions they can find out by running a computer check.

Never admit to any offense other than a traffic infraction. If you actually committed the traffic infraction, admit that. But any criminal offense—regardless of whether you did it—you should remain silent. It's just like you hear on TV: anything you say can and will be used against you.

Police lie. It's perfectly legal.[9] If they have separated you and your friend, and they tell you your friend has implicated you, do not believe them. If they say, "Just admit you broke the law and we will not arrest you," do not believe them. If they say they know you were acting in self-defense or that somebody just gave you the drugs to hold, do not trust them.

It is best not to assert too many rights. If you are not sure whether you actually are being detained, politely ask, "Officer, am I free to go?" If they say "no," don't ask them what their reasonable suspicion is. Do not, at this point, ask to see an attorney (you don't have a right to one during a stop anyway). Do not ask if their body camera is on. Don't ask why they are touching your private parts or going in your pockets. Never tell cops, "You can't do this." It sets them off, and, under the law of the streets, yes, they can.

Here is one major exception to the recommendation that, during a stop, you do not assert your rights. If you have contraband in your possession—illegal drugs or a gun—and the cops ask if they can search, you must politely say no. This may seem obvious, but police claim people who are carrying say "yes" all the time.

Can that be true? Not always. Sometimes, in court, the police say there was consent and the defendant says there was not. If there is a credibility contest between the police and a defendant, judges almost always believe, or pretend like they believe, the cop. You, the black suspect, do not get the benefit of the doubt.

But, according to police officers that I trust (not necessarily trust on the street; I mean I trust them to give me the real deal), it's quite common for people who possess illegal materials to agree to be searched.[10] This is stupid, don't do it. My cop friends theorize that the suspect consents because he thinks that if he says "yes" the police will not actually search him, or thinks that when the cops find the contraband, they will give the suspect a break because he consented to the search. None of this is true.

There is some information you can volunteer that might make a difference. If you have a close family member or friend who is a police officer, let them know that. "Close" meaning you know his or her cell phone number by heart and you can tell the officer to call that person right then and there to vouch for you.

If you have a job, let the cop know. Ask if you can show them your work ID. The same goes if you are a student.

For men, crying almost never helps, and often makes things worse. Women, particularly white women, have more latitude but even then it depends on the officer. It should be reserved as a last resort, when the officer is opening up the handcuffs.

IF YOU ARE ARRESTED

As far as cooperating with the police to get them to let you go, game over. They are not going to unarrest you. Everything from this point on is adversarial. The cops are officially out to get you. Your job is to give them as little to work with as possible.

This starts with being physically 100 percent submissive. Your tone should remain quiet and respectful, even during the more invasive search of your body and your immediate surroundings that the police are allowed to do once they have arrested you. Don't threaten to call the chief of police, your city councilperson, the NAACP, or the local news. Hold your hands out for the handcuffs. Bow your head down to get in the squad car.

Your performance has now become more difficult because you are angry and even more frightened. But things will get much worse if you pick up a charge of resisting arrest or assault on a police officer. That's usually a felony, even if the crime you are being arrested for is a misdemeanor. Being taken into custody for a low-level offense is extremely unpleasant and inconvenient but odds are, even if you are convicted, you will not go to prison, unless you have several other convictions under your belt. And there is still a possibility that the prosecutor will drop the charges after the arrest. But if you catch a charge of resisting arrest, all of that goes out of the window. You might as well start deciding what you are pleading guilty to.

To avoid that additional charge, understand that cops can be sensitive, even prickly, when it comes to their own personal space being invaded. Ironic, I know. But any physicality on your part can be misinterpreted.[11] So when you are arrested, you have to communicate to the police that your body is theirs to work with.

Supreme Court Justice Sonia Sotomayor, in a biting critique of the Court's case law, outlined what happens next at the jail: "The police officer can finger you, swab DNA from the inside of your mouth, and force you to shower with a delousing agent, while you lift your tongue, hold out your arms, turn around, and lift your genitals. Even if you are innocent, you will now join the 65 million Americans with an arrest record and experience the 'civil death' of discrimination by employers, landlords, and who ever else conducts a background check."[12]

Probably the most famous Supreme Court decision of all time is *Miranda v Arizona*.[13] Everybody knows that when you get arrested, the police read you this warning:

1) You have the right to remain silent.
2) Anything you tell the police can be used against you in court.
3) You have the right to an attorney.
4) If you cannot afford an attorney, the government will provide one for you.

But these rights don't work the way you think. Technically the police do not have to read you your Miranda warnings. To be precise, if they want to introduce any of your post-arrest statements in a trial, they are required to first give you the Miranda warnings. They usually do. But if they don't give you the warnings, it's not like that's a get out of jail free card. It just means that they can't use your statements in court. And, thanks to the Chokehold, there are several exceptions that allow un-Mirandized statements to be used.[14]

In any event, don't talk. Let me put that more strongly. Shut the fuck up. Don't admit to anything other than what can be found on your driver's license. It does not matter if you are innocent. Every time they ask you a question about what happened say, "I invoke my right to a lawyer."

This is the hardest rule to follow. When I was arrested, I did not follow it myself. I should have known better, but I thought, as an attorney, I could talk my way out of it. Plus I was innocent. So what happened after I made my case to my arresting officer? My lawyer ass was locked up and taken to the holding cell along with all the other black men who had been arrested that day.

When you assert your right to counsel, do not expect the cops to get you a lawyer. They never do that. Honestly if you said to the average police officer, get me an attorney, she would have no idea what to do. All Miranda requires is that if you invoke your right to counsel, the police have to leave you alone. That is why it is so important to claim your right to a lawyer. The Supreme Court has said that if you only invoke your right to silence, the police can badger you by, under certain circumstances, going back later to ask if you have changed your mind.[15] But if you say you need a lawyer, the police aren't supposed to say another word to you about your alleged crime.[16]

WHO SHOULD YOU CALL?

In many jurisdictions you don't have a right to make a telephone call. That's an urban myth. But at some point after you are booked—which means driven to the police station or courthouse, mug shot taken, fingerprinted, searched once again—the police usually let you make a call. To whom should you direct it?

If you already have a lawyer, or have the knowledge and financial resources to get a good one immediately, call that person. He or she can try to get the prosecutor to delay filing charges until the lawyer does a quick investigation of the case. This usually does not work, but it is worth a shot. But most people charged with crimes are poor and they do not have an attorney on retainer. In that case call your mother. Or your partner, sibling, or best friend. The person who is going to stop everything to address the mess your life has just become. They need to do what they can to try to get you out of jail as soon as possible. The longer you sit in jail, the worse your outcomes are likely to be.

Special shout-out to mothers, partners, siblings, and best friends: go back and read the section in chapter 2 about how many outstanding warrants there are. Those warrants are for people who failed to appear in court. If you had bailed that person out, you just lost your money. Don't hock everything you own to raise bail for a person you don't have confidence will actually show up in court. Yes, I know the guy who is locked up will be pissed. But if you think that there is a significant risk he will miss the court date, it makes not only his situation but also your own worse. The Chokehold is insidious. This is how it tears families apart.

When a person gets a call that someone they care about has been arrested and is locked up, the natural inclination is to go to the police station. This is a bad move. The cops are not going to let a visitor see the dude prior to his appearance in court. But if it's a serious case, and the mother or girlfriend shows up at the station, a detective might try to interview her, asking questions like, "Did you see your son last night? Where did your boyfriend tell you he was going?" Just as anyone who has been arrested should never talk to the cops, anyone who is trying to help the guy should also not talk to the cops. Nothing good can come of it.

Here are the three things a person can do that are most helpful for someone who has just been arrested:

1) Call a lawyer right away; in addition to telling the lawyer what you know about the case, tell her every good thing you can think of about the person who has been arrested, including whether he has a job or is in school, is close to his family, attends church, and is active in the community. All of this will help the attorney try to get the guy released.

2) If there are witnesses to the arrest, put together a list of their names and contact information. Do not interview the witnesses yourself and never write down anything they have told you, because the prosecutor could try to subpoena any statements you have recorded. Just give the names of the witnesses to the defense attorney.

3) Show up at the courthouse for the "arraignment." That's the hearing where the formal charges are read and, by law, it has to happen within forty-eight hours of the arrest. The defendant will know you are there, but make sure the defense attorney knows who you are. You are there to provide moral support to your dude, and for the judge to see you when she is trying to decide whether to set bail or release the dude pending trial. The fact that somebody showed up for the defendant sometimes makes a difference to the judge.

PUBLIC DEFENDERS VERSUS PAY LAWYERS

Many people think of public defenders as inferior lawyers. I get a lot of emails and calls from people charged with serious crimes who think their case is going down because the judge appointed a public defender to represent them. They automatically assume a private attorney is better. Sometimes loved ones of people in this situation are willing to do whatever it takes—like mortgaging their house—to retain a pay lawyer. This is often a terrible idea.

Public defenders are often the best lawyers you could have. If you are a poor person charged with a felony in the District of Columbia, the Bronx, or San Francisco, pray that the judge appoints the public defender to represent you. Other jurisdictions where you are most likely better off with a public defender include Harlem, Oakland, Philadelphia, Miami, West Palm Beach, Seattle, and the states of New Hampshire and Colorado. And if you are charged with a federal crime, most federal public defender offices will provide you with top-notch representation.

There are some kinds of cases that public defenders have more experience with than any other lawyers, including serious felonies like homicide and robbery.

When I was a young lawyer, I worked at what is probably the best white-collar criminal defense firm in the country. If I was charged with tax evasion or making an illegal campaign contribution, I would hire that firm. But Mike Tyson, the former boxing champion, made a mistake when he retained that firm to defend him against rape charges. That's not a crime that the attorneys there had much experience with defending.[17] Tyson was convicted, and sentenced to six years in prison. It's hard to know whether he would have had a different outcome if he had been represented by an attorney with the background of a public defender, but experience certainly makes lawyers better, and public defenders have more practice defending street and violent crime than lawyers at fancy law firms do.

Of course not every public defender is great. When they don't do a good job, it is often because their offices don't get the resources they need. In any event, most poor people are not represented by public defenders but rather by court-appointed lawyers. These are private attorneys who support themselves by taking these kinds of cases. Many are excellent lawyers who have the same kind of experience and local courthouse knowledge as public defenders.

But some of them are awful. If you get appointed one of the lousy ones, you are screwed. You have no choice in the lawyer the judge appoints. If you complain, it is extremely unlikely that the judge will appoint another attorney to represent you. Your options are limited. If the charges are serious, this is the time to consider hiring a pay lawyer. For many people charged with crimes, however, this is not a realistic option.

Hope that you live in one of the few places where appointed lawyers earn a decent wage. One study found that a 1 percentage point change in the wage gap between appointed attorneys and private lawyers reduces the probability of being found guilty by about 4 percentage points. Hope also that your appointed lawyer is not a rookie. The same study found that attorneys with just one more year of experience won sentences for their clients that were five months shorter.[18]

Let's keep it real. If you have major concerns about your appointed lawyer, and you can somehow pull together the cash to pay an experienced lawyer big bucks to represent you, you should hire that lawyer. One study found that defendants represented by private lawyers received sentences that were three years shorter than those represented by public defenders.[19] It may be that prosecutors offer better deals to those clients because they think private lawyers will spend more time on the defense than lawyers who mainly represent poor people.

If you are in a position to retain a lawyer, you should interview him or her just the way you would anyone else you are hiring to do important work for you. Make sure the person has experience in criminal cases, and that he or she knows their way around the courthouse where your case is being heard. Ask the attorney how long it takes her to return calls to clients, and how she keeps clients up to date about developments in their cases. Get the names of three people she has represented in criminal cases and call those people for a reference. If the attorney cops an attitude about any of this, that's a good sign you should not hire him or her. These are the kinds of questions that rich people ask when they select a lawyer, and you should expect the same quality of service. Trust me, brother, there will be times when it will feel like everybody else in the courtroom assumes you are guilty, and most people outside the courtroom too, and you need a defense attorney who treats you with the respect you deserve.

Some brothers still suffer from the mind-set that it's better to have a white lawyer, or a Jewish lawyer. The theory is that those attorneys are more connected, or better at coming up with defenses, or that judges and juries will like them better. This is white supremacist hogwash. There is no evidence to support the claim that lawyers of certain ethnicities or faiths get better outcomes for their clients. Of course you want an attorney who will be a good negotiator with the prosecutor and who has a proven track record. It's just that being white or Jewish is not a good proxy for that skill set.

Be clear that I am not saying that race and gender don't matter in the courtroom. Every chapter in this book suggests that they do matter, hugely. The point is that the Chokehold means the odds are against you, and you need a defense attorney who is going to fight like hell. It's silly and counterproductive to make group-based assumptions about which lawyers will do so, based on their race or religion.

There is, however, one situation in which a lawyer's race or gender might tip the scale in favor of hiring her. Depending on what crime you are charged with, you might need to prove to a jury that you are not a racist or sexist. A man who is prosecuted for sexual assault, for example, might be better off represented by a female defense attorney.[20] A white person charged with a hate crime against an African American might select an African American lawyer. Even in these cases, gender and race should not be the only consideration. It's just that if you are lucky enough to have a choice in who represents you—and most people charged with crimes are not—and you have a jury trial, your lawyer's gender or race could help send the right message to the jury.

BE THAT NEEDY CLIENT

Jeff Adachi runs one of the best criminal defense firms in the country. He is the elected public defender in San Francisco. Adachi is a brave man. He took the Harvard implicit bias test, which demonstrated that he has unconscious prejudices against African Americans. He admits the same is probably true for the lawyers who work for him, as it is for most attorneys, and it might impact the way they represent black defendants.[21] Adachi is taking steps to reduce the bias, like having his lawyers get to know their clients as people and asking themselves whether they would treat a case differently if the defendant were white.

But most lawyers are not so proactive about their prejudices. They don't even know they have them. How can you make sure that your attorney is representing you the same way he would a white dude? This is not just an issue for appointed attorneys. Even pay lawyers sometimes don't devote the necessary resources to your case.

You have to motivate your lawyer. You do this in two ways. First, you make sure the lawyer knows you as a person and hopefully likes you. Attorneys take an oath to represent all their clients zealously, but zeal is a difficult commodity to distribute in equal portions. If your attorney finds you rude, disrespectful, or irrational, she may not go to the mat for you the way you need her to. If, however, you show her photos of your children or discover you are both NBA fans, she will remember something about you other than what happened on one of the worst nights of your life.

Second, you must be demanding. If enrolling the attorney as your friend is the carrot, the stick is being vigilant about the specific things she is doing to give you the best representation at every stage of the process. Yes, it's checking up on her, but your lawyer should be okay with it as long as you don't come across like you think she is part of a conspiracy to lock you up. Just let her know you are extremely anxious, as anyone should be when their freedom is in the hands of a prosecutor or judge.

There are certain things that an excellent defense attorney should do. They are what criminal defense lawyers do for rich people. Unless there is some really good reason that she carefully explains, your lawyer should do these three things for you:

1) If you are being held in jail, your lawyer should file a motion for your release. She should ask the judge to dismiss the charges. Your lawyer will lose. Judges almost never drop charges that prosecutors have brought, in part because the "probable cause" legal standard for bringing charges is relatively low. But many judges will allow a hearing, which means that a police officer or other witness will have to testify under oath about the circumstances of your arrest. This gives you and your attorney information that you otherwise would not have about the strength of the prosecution's case.[22]

2) Ask the prosecutor for "discovery" and "Brady." "Discovery" is information about the case that the prosecution is required to turn over at some point before the trial. The rules and timetable vary depending on the jurisdiction, but it usually includes a list of the prosecution's witnesses, any statements they have made, and police reports pertaining to the arrest. "Brady" is any evidence the police or prosecutors have that is favorable to you and relevant to whether you will be found guilty or not guilty. Under the law, the prosecution has an obligation to share this with you, but of course it's up to them to decide whether it meets the criteria.[23] As you can imagine, prosecutors tend to be stingy with what they disclose. And even when they illegally withhold evidence prosecutors are rarely sanctioned. As federal judge Alex Kozinski wrote in 2013, "Brady violations have reached epidemic proportions in recent years."[24] But your lawyer

should still ask because if you have an ethical prosecutor, he might hand over evidence that has the potential to set you free.

3) Hire an investigator. Otherwise the only version of the facts is going to come from you and the police. In the experiences of many people who have been charged with crimes, including me, the police lie. Some witnesses, especially so-called snitches who are cooperating with the prosecution in return for some favor, often lie as well.[25] A good investigator can interview witnesses who might have another version of what happened. In my criminal case, my lawyer hired an investigator who was a former D.C. cop, and some officers were willing to talk to him even though they never would have talked to my lawyer.

WHAT TO TELL YOUR LAWYER

Your lawyer probably will not ask you if you are guilty. She does not need to know and she does not want to know. But she does have to be aware of what the evidence against you is. Based on what you tell her, and what the prosecution is required to reveal about its case, she will put together a defense.

She does not personally have to think you are innocent in order to defend you. What attorneys call "factual guilt" means that you committed the offense you are charged with. A good defense attorney does not much care if this is true. "Legal guilt" means that the prosecution proved, beyond a reasonable doubt, that you committed the offense. There is often a wide gap between factual guilt and legal guilt, and effective defense attorneys exploit that gap to win your case.[26]

At the same time, your attorney cannot allow you to testify in court to something that you have told her is not true. She risks losing her law license if she sponsors perjured testimony.[27] So, for example, if you have previously told her that when you saw the police coming, you threw the weed out of the car window, you cannot, at trial, testify that you never had any weed, unless, for some reason, the facts have become clearer in your mind. If that is the case, let your lawyer know that what you told her at first was inaccurate. But even if you did toss the weed, this does not mean that you have to plead guilty. You can still go to trial. Your lawyer would probably advise you to exercise your Fifth Amendment right not to testify, and she would try to poke holes in the government's case, for example by attacking the credibility of the police. This is the good part about the criminal justice system not being an actual search for truth, and you may as well make it work for you.

GOING TO COURT: A STYLE GUIDE

When I was a prosecutor we used to laugh at the way some defendants dressed for court. They made our jobs easy because they looked guilty. They wore baggy pants, white T-shirts, gold chains, or some other urban style that you might see teens wearing on the subway. That is not a good look if you are trying to avoid going to jail. Even "casual Friday" outfits like nice jeans or khaki pants and sneakers hurt your case.

When a black man has his fate in the hands of a judge or jury, he needs to wear a suit. The District of Columbia Public Defender Service, one of the best in the country, has a closet of jackets and ties for its clients who don't own them. At a minimum, male defendants should wear a nice pair of slacks and a button-down shirt. And my public defender friends swear by polished shoes for their clients. Judges and jurors notice things like that.

If you have braids or locs, cut them off. They'll grow back. You need prosecutors and judges to exercise whatever mercy their miserly hearts can muster. You do this by getting them to relate to you. People who become prosecutors and judges are conservative, socially if not always politically. Don't distract them with hair that offends their parched standards of respectability. It's hard enough getting them to see past your black skin.

SHOULD YOU SNITCH?

The prosecution might offer you a deal if you help them make a case against somebody else who they want to lock up more than they want to lock you up. The first thing you need to figure out is if you accept the offer, are you going to "get got" or is somebody in your family going to "get got." If cooperating with the government puts you or your loved ones in jeopardy, do not do it. It's a hard-knock world out there, and the truth is the prosecutor is more interested in winning his case than he is in protecting you. If he cared that much about you, he would not be prosecuting you in the first place. You are in the best position to assess the risks, and if you have any doubt about your safety, turn the offer down.

If you think that you can cooperate with the prosecution and be safe, then you need to make sure that the deal is worth it. Ask your lawyer exactly what difference it would make in your case's outcome if you snitch compared to if you don't snitch. Sometimes the most the prosecutor can do is recommend to the judge that you get a reduced sentence. Your defense attorney should indicate, based on her experience, how likely it is that the judge would follow the prosecutor's recommendation.

Finally, you should help the prosecution only if you think it's the right thing to do. Sometimes people cooperate because they think the person the prosecution is going after really did something wrong and deserves punishment. In general, however, the way the prosecutors use snitches can be a little bit lazy and a little bit sleazy. Prosecutors are not sure they have enough evidence to get a conviction, so they basically bribe someone to be a witness. If the deal is good enough, some people are tempted to lie. Studies show that one of the most common reasons for wrongful convictions, including in death penalty cases, is dishonest testimony by snitches. You don't want to participate in this unsavory practice unless you can tell the truth. You never want to put another brother or sister in prison by lying about their guilt. But the irony is, as discussed next, sometimes you might want to lie about your own guilt, in order to go home sooner.

SHOULD YOU COP A PLEA? THE TRAGEDY OF KALIEF BROWDER

Kalief Browder was an innocent man. An innocent man who should have pled guilty. Then he might still be alive.

Kalief was sixteen years old when he was arrested for robbing a man of his backpack in the Bronx, New York.[28] Kalief had been walking home from a party when NYPD officers stopped and frisked him. The victim, who was sitting in the police car, first said Kalief had robbed him that night, and then changed his mind and said it hadn't been that night, but two weeks prior. Still Kalief was arrested, and bail was set at $3,000, which his family could not afford. And so he sat in Riker's Island, the notorious New York City jail.

For almost three years. The trial kept being delayed. During two years of this time, Kalief was held in solitary confinement. Kalief always insisted on his innocence. At one point, after he had been locked up for more than two years, the prosecution offered him a deal: If he would plead guilty to two misdemeanors, the judge would sentence him to time served, and he could go home that day. Kalief said he could not plead guilty to a crime he had not committed. His specific words to the judge were "I'm alright."[29]

But Kalief was not "alright." Videos from the jail security cameras show him being brutally assaulted, once by a group of inmates and another time by a prison guard. After he had been incarcerated for more than one thousand days, the prosecution summarily dismissed the case.[30] Kalief finally went home. But the two years in solitary confinement had changed him, as it changes virtually everyone who suffers it. Kalief had a hard time coping with life on the outside, just as he had not been able to cope on the inside. On the morning of June 6, 2015, Kalief tied bedsheets to his neck and jumped to his death from the second story of his mother's home.

Read the tragedy of Kalief Browder as a cautionary tale. Sad and repulsive as it may seem, for some people, pleading guilty might be the best decision, even if they did not commit the crime. The presumption of innocence is just words on paper. Many people, including many judges and jurors, think if you have been arrested you are guilty. This makes going to trial risky, especially for African American men. Prosecutors exploit this bias when they plea-bargain by not really giving the defendant much of a break. They know that if you go to trial and lose, you will get a lot more time than if you had accepted the plea—even if the plea offer is not generous.

For this reason, almost everyone who is prosecuted for a crime ends up pleading guilty. Ninety-five percent, to be exact. If you think that you get a raw deal because you are African American, you are correct. Virtually every study has demonstrated that white men get better plea offers than black men. But prosecutors have so much discretion it will be virtually impossible for your lawyer to prove you are getting treated worse because you are black, even though everyone knows it's true.[31]

IF YOU GO TO TRIAL

I understand why Kalief did not want to plead guilty because I felt the same way. When I was arrested, the prosecutor offered me "diversion," which meant that I could do community service and then the case would be dismissed. But to be approved for diversion, you have to admit you committed the crime. Since I had not committed the crime, I could not bring myself to do that, and so I went to trial. To make that decision, I used a kind of cost-benefit analysis that I would recommend to you.

You and your lawyer should make an informed decision based on the risk of conviction if you go to trial, and what the consequences of being found guilty would be. The main consequence is usually more jail time than if you pled guilty. Technically, it is unconstitutional to punish people for exercising their right to a jury trial, but this right is meaningless. If the vast majority of defendants did not plead guilty, American criminal justice would grind to a halt. There are far too many criminal cases for all of them to go to trial, which presumably would be the result if there were not a severe penalty attached to losing. Michele Alexander, who wrote *The New Jim Crow*, wrote an op-ed in the *New York Times* suggesting that if many more defendants started exercising their right to a jury trial, it would create a productive chaos in the criminal process system that would force lawmakers to deal with mass incarceration.[32]

As a prosecutor, I bluffed about the strength of the government's case all the time. Your lawyer should be able to assess the strength of your defense compared to other cases she has tried. She will tell you that you never know what a jury is going to do, and she is right. But if you have confidence in her skills as a trial attorney, and she thinks you have a decent case, you should seriously consider going to trial.

Like Kalief, I am an African American man, but otherwise I had a lot of advantages that he did not. I retained the best lawyer in the city, a former public defender named Michele Roberts. We hired a former police officer as our investigator, and as far as we could tell, the prosecution didn't have a strong case. We thought my chances of being acquitted were very good. My jury was predominately African American. We would make sure they knew that I was a well-educated lawyer. It is the kind of thing that should not matter to a jury, but any experienced trial attorney will tell you it actually does. You have to present yourself as the kind of black man who does not belong in jail.

At my trial, we also had character witnesses testify who were high-status members of the community. Your attorney should try to do the same for you. A minister, teacher, or neighborhood elder who knows you well can help the jury see you as a human being and not the black thug the prosecutor is doing his damnest to invoke.

If I lost my case, the consequences of conviction would have been personally devastating. I would have lost my job as a prosecutor, and it would have been difficult to find another job as an attorney. On the other hand, even if I were convicted, it was very unlikely that I would have been sentenced to prison for a first-time misdemeanor.

I was innocent as well, but that was not the most important thing. Innocent people get convicted in criminal court every day. And, every day, guilty people get set free.

The truth is that most defendants who go to trial lose. In recent years state prosecutors have won 85 percent of their felony cases and almost 90 percent of their misdemeanor cases.[33] Federal prosecutors lose only one out of every ten cases.

The numbers change some depending on the jurisdiction. The conviction rate has averaged approximately 84 percent in Texas, 82 percent in California, 72 percent in New York, 67 percent in North Carolina, and 59 percent in Florida.[34]

If you decide to go to trial, the next big decision is whether you should take the stand. It's your call, but listen carefully to your attorney's advice. If you have serious prior convictions, she will probably advise you to take the Fifth. Even if you don't, she will be concerned that the prosecutor's cross-examination will make you look guilty. As a prosecutor, I was really good at this. If the defendant was an African American male, and pretty much all of them were, I would get up in his face, or at least as close to him as the judge would let me, and try to set him off.

I would ask the defendant a series of detailed questions about his testimony designed to throw him off and make it look like he was lying. I was good at this because I did it every day. The defendant, on the other hand, did not have much experience in criminal trials and he was already stressed out because his freedom was on the line. Just know that an effective trial lawyer can make even an innocent person look guilty.

So I guess it was poetic justice when, during my own trial, the prosecutor tried the same tactic with me. The damn thing is it almost worked. He got me so worked up during his cross-examination that I became surly and aggressive when I answered his questions. I fell directly into the trap he had laid for me. During a break, my lawyer told me to lose the attitude. For the remainder of the cross, I was cool and collected, or at least that is what I tried to convey to the jury.

If you do take the stand, it's time for the performance of your life. You should practice your testimony in advance. Ask your attorney to go through the questions she is likely to ask you and the questions the prosecutor will probably ask on cross-examination. If the jury perceives you are lying, they will hold that against you. Borrow a trick that cops use and look at the jury, not your lawyer, when you answer her questions. Don't use street slang. It's okay to be nervous but you have to be calm and polite to everybody, even the prosecutor. During the prosecutor's cross-examination, you just want to get in and get out. Don't say any more than asked. If a question can be answered "yes" or "no," that is the only answer you should give.

You have to make the judge or jury care about you. It helps if your partner, mother, and grandmother are sitting in the front row, as conservatively dressed and well mannered as possible.

You have positioned yourself so that whether you get convicted depends on how you come across to the twelve people in the jury box, but a "not guilty" verdict is not the only measure of success. All you need is at least one juror to take your side, and then there is a hung jury, which basically means you won. The prosecutor can bring the case again, but unless it's a serious charge, they usually do not. And if your lawyer pokes enough holes in the government's case, the jury foreperson might come back with those magic words: "Your Honor, we the jury find the defendant not guilty." Good luck, brother.

IF YOU LOSE

Sorry, my dude. A lot of brothers have been in this situation. At the moment, more than 500,000 to be exact.[35]

SENTENCING

Have people show up. Your parents, relatives, and friends. Probably not young children, because the judge might feel like you are trying to manipulate her, or that you are a poor parent to expose them to your sentencing. See if you can get former teachers, employers, and faith leaders to write letters. You will probably get to make a statement. As always, practice in advance. Express regret and contrition.

SHOULD YOU APPEAL?

You're probably going to lose. Your chances of winning on appeal are even less than your chances of winning at the trial level. The prosecution wins almost 90 percent of criminal appeals.[36]

CONCLUSION

If this chapter reads like a nightmare, it is because that's exactly what the criminal system is for an African American man. You have no rights that a cop is bound to respect. You do not live in the same country as a white person. That has to change. *Chokehold*'s final chapter discusses the revolution brothers desperately need.

8

Woke: Unlocking the Chokehold

There just has to be a new system of reason and logic devised by us who are at the bottom, if we want to get some results in this struggle that is called "the Negro revolution."

—Malcolm X

The United States is a country of gross racial inequality. The Chokehold means that African American men, like African American women and many other groups, are not full citizens. Their lives are not afforded the same dignity and respect as white lives.

Black men living in high-poverty neighborhoods are particularly at risk for violence—as harm doers and as victims, from the police and from each other.

None of this is new. African Americans have never been free. African Americans have never been safe. Liberal reforms, such as anti-discrimination laws, have not brought long-term change. Civil rights laws have helped stigmatize discrimination but have barely blunted its effect. Black people have always been on the bottom. Other groups—Irish, Italians, Jews, Chinese, Eastern Europeans—have come later and surpassed African Americans in opportunity and achievement.[1]

One might have thought that Barack Obama's presidency would herald the pinnacle of African American success. Some progress was made. Obama appointed many African Americans to high office, including the first African American attorney general and many federal judges. The Justice Department investigated more police departments for misconduct than all of the previous administrations combined. Black unemployment decreased from 12.7 percent when Obama took office to 8.3 percent in September 2016.[2]

But black unemployment remained twice white unemployment, as it has been for decades. The percentage of African Americans who live below the poverty line actually went up, from 25.8 percent in 2009 to 26.2 percent in 2012.[3] In 2013, according to the *Wall Street Journal*, the Small Business Administration granted less than 2 percent of its loans to African American businesses — the lowest amount in its history. During the George W. Bush administration, by contrast, 8 percent of SBA loans went to black-owned businesses.[4] Black family net worth declined during Barack Obama's presidency, to a thirty-year low, even as white families' net worth increased during this same period.[5]

Obama's presidency brought about nothing approaching the racial reconciliation he had campaigned on. Instead Obama's second term was marked by viral videos of police killing and beating up unarmed African Americans. From the ashes of Ferguson rose the most radical and intersectional civil rights movement in African American history. The movement for black lives has put the world on notice that the Chokehold is not sustainable. The United States has been here before, with black-led resistance to slavery and the old Jim Crow. What African Americans do, every century or so, is to save this country's soul. For blacks this has been tiresome and unrewarding work. Racial subordination has simply been refashioned from slavery to convict leasing to segregation to mass incarceration. Now is the time to disrupt the wretched cycle once and for all. Let this be the last time blacks reinvent this country without crushing white supremacy.

ABOLITION: THE THIRD GIFT

The language of "reconstruction" can't be employed without considering what preceded it—abolition. We abolished the institution of
slavery. We abolished legalized segregation. If we want a third Reconstruction to take place, the abolition of prisons should be on the
table.[6]

—Mychal Denzel Smith, author and activist

If I ruled the world, I'd free all my sons. I'd open every cell in Attica
and send them to Africa.[7]

—Nas and Lauryn Hill, hip-hop artists

Prison, like the Chokehold, has a literal and symbolic meaning
for African American men. Prison is the place where approximately 1 million black people live, making them among the most
incarcerated groups in the history of the planet. As a metaphor,
prison is a dumping ground for people for whom society has no
use—human garbage.[8] The symbolic and literal came together
in 2012 when Orange County, California, issued a press release
entitled "Waste Management Partners with Police to Fight Crime
and Watch Neighborhoods." The press release announced a
"Waste Watch" training program during which garbage truck
drivers partnered with police to look for "suspicious activity."[9]

U.S. prisons are built for black men, and black men will be
free, literally and figuratively, only when prisons are no more.
The Chokehold means that white supremacy is embedded in
every aspect of the peculiar institution, from who is admitted to
the kinds of conduct they are locked up for to how long they stay
to how they are treated while there.

Our moral justification for forcing human beings to live in
cages is that they have freely chosen to do wrong. But the United
States has never had the capacity to make those judgments on a
non-racial basis and it is hard to imagine that it ever will. So we

have to stop it. Abolition does not mean that people who broke the law would be ignored by the government. It only means that the intervention would not be to lock them in a cage. Instead we must figure out whether there is anything essential that incarceration does, and, if so, are there other ways that can be accomplished?

Incarceration, for people of all races and genders, is violent and dehumanizing. Ending it will make the United States a more just nation. Think of prison abolition as the third gift people who fight for African American freedom will have provided to the country, after they defeated slavery and the old Jim Crow.

I get it. Prison abolition sounds crazy, reckless, and unsafe. The cage is the ultimate mediation of our anxiety about African American men. The Chokehold scares us into thinking that releasing black male criminals from jail would endanger us all. But here's an essential fact you need in order to open your mind to abolition: fewer than one in five people who are in prison are there for homicide or a sex crime.[10] If we think of those as the most dangerous crimes, we understand that prison is not mainly about protecting us from perilous offenders. Even if we are uncertain about the best intervention for the small group of inmates who are likely to seriously harm others on the outside, we can begin the abolitionist project by focusing on alternatives for the 80 percent of inmates who have not committed the most severe offenses.

This is not just a pie in the sky hypothesis. A recent study by New York University's Brennan Center for Justice notes: "Over the last decade, 27 states have reduced both imprisonment and crime together. From 1999 to 2012, New Jersey and New York reduced their prison populations by about 30 percent, while crime fell faster than it did nationally. Texas decreased imprisonment and crime by more than 20 percent during the same period. California, in part because of a court order, cut its prison population by 27 percent, and violence in the state also fell more than the national average."[11]

The Brennan Center estimates that almost 40 percent of people in prison could be released today with little impact on public safety. Its analysis is based on the fact that approximately 25 percent of prisoners are serving time for low-level offenses like drug possession and minor property crimes. Another 14 percent of inmates are, according to the report, serving time for more serious offenses but have been locked up so long that incarcerating them more would not have any additional public safety benefit. Just releasing this 40 percent would save taxpayers $200 billion over twenty years. That would be enough to hire 327,000 new schoolteachers.[12]

One concern about abolition is that criminals would not receive the punishment they deserve. When people have caused harm, the community has a right to expect accountability and that steps will be taken to prevent any more harm. But those goals are not necessarily tied to prison. Indeed in some ways prison is counterproductive to their achievement.

Common Justice is a Brooklyn-based program that diverts people charged with violent crime from prison to an intense treatment program that includes making amends with victims. In order for a defendant to participate in Common Justice, his or her victim has to consent. Ninety percent of victims do consent, not because they feel compassionate toward the people who have harmed them but because people who live in tough Brooklyn neighborhoods most desire safety and justice, and they understand that prison rarely delivers those. Participants in Common Justice are forced to acknowledge the harm that they have caused and to make amends to the people they hurt. It's agonizing; sometimes people in the middle of treatment say that being locked up would have been easier. And it works better: people who successfully complete the program are much less likely to pick up another charge than people who have been incarcerated.

Common Justice was founded by Danielle Sered, a white woman who grew up in Chicago during the 1990s.[13] Sered committed crimes and ended up, at fifteen years old, arrested for grand auto theft. The judge sentenced her to six months on probation. Her accomplice, who was a black man, got six years in prison.

That experience taught Sered that white privilege itself brings a sort of prison abolition. White people don't get locked up, or get less time, for the same conduct that sends black people to prison. When we wonder what would be the effect if most people who break the law were not locked up, we can look at white folks as an example of a community where that is already the case.

Another kind of abolition is selected by more than half of all victims of violent crime. They choose not to call the police.[14] What this means is that for most people who survive violence, doing nothing is a preferable option to involving the state. This choice starts to make sense when you consider the fact that 60 percent of people who have done time end up returning to prison within eighteen months of their release.[15] The Chokehold has so distorted our sense of reality that the high rate of recidivism of people who have been incarcerated is used to justify even more incarceration. Some people don't understand that it is really the system that has failed to rehabilitate or provide meaningful opportunities for people coming home from prison. Instead they blame the recently released inmate for not learning whatever lesson the system was ill equipped to teach him in the first place. So judges usually sentence defendants who have been locked up previously to even more time for a new offense. Danielle Sered jokes that this is like taking your car to a repair shop where the mechanic not only fails to fix your car but actually makes it worse, and then charges you even more to repair the additional damage that he has caused.

ONE CELL AT A TIME:
THREE ACTIONS TOWARD ABOLITION

As a practical matter, almost nobody, including me, would be prepared today to release every incarcerated person. The legal scholar Allegra McLeod, one of the most important abolition theorists, writes that it should be understood not as "an immediate and indiscriminate opening of prison doors" but rather "a gradual project of decarceration, in which radically different legal and institutional regulatory forms supplant criminal law enforcement." [16]

Here are three suggestions for things activists could advocate for right now that would start the move toward decarceration to abolition. First, the maximum punishment for every criminal offense in the United States should be reduced to twenty-one years in prison.[17] This is already the law in Norway for any offense other than war crimes and genocide. Sentencing in the United States is much longer than it needs to be for any reasonable purpose. One in nine prisoners is serving a life sentence. In state prisons, another 10 percent of inmates are serving sentences longer than twenty years.[18] For every crime, the United States locks people up longer than most other countries. For example, American sentences for burglary are from two to four times longer than in England.[19] In 2010, approximately 125,000 people jailed in the United States were age fifty-five or older.[20] U.S. inmates are incarcerated for so long that many prisons operate assisted living facilities for elderly inmates. This is not only very expensive for taxpayers, it is wasteful spending as well. We know that prisoners who are older than fifty are extremely unlikely to commit another crime if they are released.[21]

Second, we should reduce the number of offenses you can be sent to prison for, beginning with decriminalizing low-level offenses. Every year about 10 million people get locked up for misdemeanors.[22] These are offenses like driving with a suspended license, drug possession, minor assault, vandalism, and shoplifting. Decriminalization is a way of ratcheting down the police super power to arrest. Instead the police would give you a ticket, like they do now for most traffic offenses. The reader may recall that many of the arrest warrants that were issued in Ferguson, Missouri, were for failure to pay fines. To avoid this scenario, lawmakers should restrict the police from any arrests related to failure to pay a fine or show up in court in response to a citation. Otherwise, decriminalization would not be so different from criminalization.[23] Cyrus Vance, the district attorney of Manhattan, took a step in the right direction, ending arrests in cases for minor offenses such as taking two seats on the subway, public urination, or walking down the street with an open container of liquor.[24] But we need to go much further, by not allowing anyone to be jailed for any crime that is currently punished with less than one year in prison.

When fines are imposed, they should be based on income. Rich people should have to pay more and poor people less. "Day fines" is the legal term for penalties that are based on a percentage of a person's actual income. So, for example, a millionaire might have to pay $10,000 for a misdemeanor offense, someone who makes $100,000 a year would pay $1,000, and someone who makes $10,000 would pay $100—all for the same offense. This would be a more fair and equitable way of punishing people than requiring everyone to pay the same amount, no matter how rich or poor they are. Some European nations have limited incarceration in part by relying more on fines as a form of punishment. Their experience has been that having to pay money works better than incarceration to prevent many kinds of crime.[25]

The third action is likely to be the most controversial. We should stop spending so much money on the police and instead invest those funds in community health care. Almost 80 percent of people in prison suffer from either addiction or mental illness.[26] It's commonplace to say that prisons are now the largest mental health providers in the country, but "warehouses" would be more descriptive. Correctional facilities are simply not equipped to treat the mental health and substance abuse issues that most incarcerated folks have. That may be one reason why the leading cause of death in prison is suicide—in 2013, for example, 34 percent of all deaths in prison were the result of inmates killing themselves.[27] Imagine if the $16 billion authorized in the Crime Bill of 1994 for prison construction and hiring police had gone instead to providing mental health services.

If cities were required to reduce the size of their police forces, what would happen to public safety? Probably not much. Remember that the vast majority of arrests are for low-level misdemeanor offenses. If we decriminalize these offenses, we reduce much of the work that police do now. The truth is that the police do not prevent or solve most crime.[28] If you tell them that your smartphone was stolen or your purse snatched, it is extremely unlikely that the cops are going to get it back. In the experience of many citizens, they don't even try. Studies demonstrate that a visible police presence might prevent some property crimes but does not make much of a difference at stopping violent crime.[29] Violent crime has gone down dramatically in recent years. But cops should not get credit for that good news, considering that it has fallen not just all over the country, where many different styles of policing are used, but indeed all over the Western world.[30]

Still some people cling to the belief that when trouble arises it's best to dial 911. The reality is that in moments of extreme trauma and stress, calling a person with a gun and the power to arrest often makes things worse, not better. Vulnerable groups all over the United States, including survivors of domestic abuse and transgendered people, are now engaged in projects creating alternatives to policing for keeping safe, including neighborhood patrols and having trained and respected members of the community intervene in times of crisis.[31]

Putting some of the billions of dollars that we spend on policing into health care, education, and job training would not only be a major step toward abolition, it could yield immediate tangible benefits to African American men, who would have fewer of the Chokehold's enforcers to contend with. As we have seen, the police are no friend to the black man. This is true in part because many officers have what President Obama's Task Force on 21st Century Policing described as a "warrior" mind-set. This is not just a figure of speech. Obama used his executive power to limit a program that allowed military surplus weapons to be provided to local police departments. He banned the Pentagon from giving cops grenade launchers, militarized aircraft, and bayonets. But departments could still receive other material, like armored tanks, intended to be used against foreign enemies.

Obama's policing commission recommended police officers think of themselves as "guardians" rather than warriors. Even as the number of officers is significantly reduced, there are two qualifications that should have special significance when new officers are hired, because they are associated with more peaceful officers. First, police departments should be at least 50 percent female. Now approximately 88 percent of officers are male.[32] Research indicates that female cops are more likely to de-escalate conflict and less likely to shoot.[33] The *Washington Post* reported that, from 2006 to 2016, of the fifty-four officers prosecuted for unlawful shootings, only two were women.[34] Studies done in Denver, Indianapolis, Washington, D.C., and Kansas City demonstrate that female officers are significantly less likely to be the subject of excessive force complaints.[35]

The other important qualification for officers is a college degree. Cops with more education are less likely to use force and are better at problem solving.[36] A frequently cited study by Jayson Rydberg and William Terrill of Michigan State University found other advantages to a college education, including that more educated cops exhibit better acceptance of minorities and are less likely to be involved in unethical behavior. By this point in the book, the reader may be so familiar with the perverse consequences of the Chokehold that she thinks no fact about how twisted the U.S. criminal process is would surprise her. But here is one, related to intellectual qualifications for being a cop, that still might. Did you know that you can be rejected from being a police officer because you are too smart? The Wonderlic Cognitive Ability Test is used by many police departments throughout the country to assess the learning and problem solving abilities of applicants. The highest score you can get is 50, and most cops score between 20 and 27. Robert Jordan applied to the New London, Connecticut, police department and was turned down, because he received a 33 on the test. The police department rejected applicants who scored above a 27, because it felt they would not be happy being cops. Jordan sued, and the United States Court of Appeals for the Second Circuit affirmed the police department's decision, stating that, "Even if unwise," the upper limit on test scores "was a rational policy instituted to reduce job turnover and thereby lessen the economic cost involved in hiring and training police officers who do not remain long enough to justify the expense."[37]

To get started on the path to abolition, we don't have to have all the answers right now. The first two abolitions—of slavery and U.S. apartheid—took decades. What is needed right now is the resolve for transformation. The present system is cruel, racist, and unsustainable. Our vision must contain a robust view of freedom and democracy in which no African American man—indeed no human being—is locked in a cage. When we make that commitment, we—activists, scholars, faith leaders, workers—will build on existing models of providing safety and accountability in ways that best serve families and communities.

HOW TO GET WHAT WE NEED:
THEORIZING BLACK RESISTANCE

The movement for black lives started as a response to violence against African American men. Formations like Black Lives Matter and One Million Hoodies for Justice rose up in reaction to George Zimmerman's killing of Trayvon Martin.[38] Now the platforms of many of these organizations have broadened to include radical critiques of the government and, especially, of white supremacy.[39] Some Black Lives Matter activists have championed liberal reforms like federal investigations of police departments and local or federal prosecutions of police officers.[40] But this is not the best use of the time and creativity of activists. As I have demonstrated in chapter 6, that kind of liberal reform does not address the central problems the movement for black lives has articulated; indeed in some ways liberal reforms exacerbate the problems.

Activists need to decide how much of their focus should be on improving the criminal justice system versus ending white supremacy. The political scientist Marie Gottschalk has documented how other countries have reduced prison populations without addressing the root causes of crime.[41] The movement for black lives might be able to accomplish short-term fixes in which the police are less brutal and fewer people get locked up. But that's not good enough.

In order for transformation to occur, the movement must look far beyond the police. Until we address the larger structural issues, racial subordination will just reproduce itself, as it has now evolved from slavery to segregation to mass incarceration.

This does not mean, however, that work on criminal justice reform does not have a place in the movement. Civil rights strategies like suing police departments are useful for getting ordinary people "woke," when they see how bad things really are and how resistant the system is to change. Fighting the good fight—even for small goals—is empowering. There are psychic benefits that inspire the community mobilization that is likely necessary for the radical activists to achieve their goals. The historian Michael Klarman has observed, "Not only did the civil rights movement have to overcome black hopelessness and fearfulness, but sometimes it was necessary as well to undo the psychological damage that the ideology of white supremacy had inflicted on those blacks who had internalized its lessons."[42] My suggestion, then, is not that people in the movement for black lives give up on criminal justice reforms; rather, activists should have a coherent perspective on what old-school liberals can and cannot do in terms of achieving the movement's ultimate goals.

For many years, civil rights organizations like the NAACP were reluctant to address criminal justice issues. Thurgood Marshall, before he became the first African American on the Supreme

Court, was the leader of the NAACP Legal Defense Fund. He allowed the NAACP to represent only innocent defendants.[43] In 1943, a case came across his desk involving a sixteen-year-old African American boy who had been sentenced to death for rape and had tried to break out of prison. Marshall refused to represent him because the boy was "not the type of person to justify our intervention."[44] According to Harvard professor Randall Kennedy, this cautiousness was motivated by respectability politics: By "distanc[ing] as many blacks as far as possible from negative stereotypes used to justify racial discrimination against all Negroes," civil rights organizations sought to strengthen the reputation of at least some African Americans and take away some of the rationale for discriminatory policies.[45] All the mainstream civil rights organizations selected clients in the same way, which means that they largely stayed away from criminal justice issues, even though that was the site of some of the worst racism. The Black Panther Party was a major exception; advocating for criminal justice reform was one of its major platforms from its inception in 1966.[46] Articles about police, intelligence agencies, and criminal justice dominated its newsletter, averaging about 30 to 40 percent of the content.[47] Still, most black organizations wanted nothing to do with people who were not seen as respectable, especially criminals. In *The New Jim Crow*, Michelle Alexander calls out the "relative quiet" of the "civil rights community's response to the mass incarceration of people of color."[48]

Things started to change in the 1990s. With one in three young black men catching a criminal case, the Chokehold could no longer be ignored. Some civil rights organizations began openly criticizing the war on drugs. Kweisi Mfume, the president of the NAACP, signed an open letter to the secretary general of the United Nations, calling for a public health rather than criminal approach to drug abuse.[49] The campaign to end the sentencing disparity between crack and powder cocaine enrolled most of the major civil rights organizations, including the NAACP, the NAACP Legal Defense Fund, the ACLU, the National Council of La Raza, the Leadership Conference on Civil Rights, and the Lawyers Committee for Civil Rights Under Law.[50] Now traditional civil rights organizations have also embraced the cause of reforming the police.[51]

This leads to a suggestion about how labor might be employed in the most efficient way that capitalizes on various activists' strengths and resources. Let the traditional civil rights organizations focus on liberal reform. Groups like the NAACP, the NAACP LDF, National Council of La Raza, Mexican American Legal Defense and Educational Fund, the ACLU, and the Center for Constitutional Rights should be at the forefront of advocating for these kinds of interventions. The movement for black lives, however, should focus on the broader-scale transformation, such as imagining and advocating for prison abolition.[52] The final part of this book lays out some of the important work at hand.

FOR RUNAWAY SLAVES ONLY

This section is for the people who want to do more. It is for the radicals, the people who would have sat in at the lunch counters, the slaves who would have fought back, the folks who would have sheltered the runaways on the underground railroad, and the women and men who would have led the slave uprisings. You are the people who will do the most important work to unlock the Chokehold. You should not expect to be loved, admired, or even understood. Your heroic foremothers and forefathers were not either. In 1961, a Gallup poll asked Americans what they thought about demonstrations like sit-ins at lunch counters and freedom rides. Fifty-seven percent said it would "hurt the Negroes' chances of being integrated in the South." Only 28 percent said it would help. In 1963, a Gallup poll revealed that only 25 percent of citizens had a favorable opinion about the March on Washington. Shortly before Martin Luther King Jr. was assassinated in 1968, 50 percent of white people told Gallup that King was hurting the cause of Negro rights; only 36 percent said he was helping.[53] History will be your judge, as it has been of the freedom fighters before you.

If, as this book has suggested, the system is broke on purpose, as a means to control African Americans and devalue their lives, the system must be radically resisted and transformed. The movement for black lives is attempting to do so, but aspects of its resistance platform are under-theorized. This is not surprising in a social justice movement that is both new and explicitly decentralized in terms of leadership and decision making.[54]

How do racially unjust law and policy change? The traditional view is that minorities are supposed to lobby Congress or bring court cases asking for civil rights. That only works sometimes. Historically, legislators and judges sometimes have remedied racist law, but other times they have established and enforced it, for example in laws that allow slavery and in the present-day police super power cases. The way democracy is practiced in the United States provides the majority with a lot of power to wreak havoc upon unpopular groups, and white people have used this tool to their full advantage. Judges are supposed to protect racial minorities from the tyranny of the majority, but the U.S. Supreme Court refuses to allow judges to do anything unless there is smoking gun evidence of racism.[55] When the majority disguises its bias, or is not even aware of it, people of color get no protection from the Constitution. Harvard Law School professor Lani Guinier proposed some new models, based on how voting works on corporate boards, to allow minorities to have more influence, but this was considered so controversial the Senate refused to confirm her to head the Justice Department's Civil Rights Division.

Law is a tool. It can be used to enforce racism, and it can be used to try to remedy racism. The most infamous racist laws in the United States are laws that supported slavery and laws that enforced de jure segregation. Then the law changed, to abolition of slavery and segregation. Slavery, after almost 250 years, was outlawed by the U.S. Congress when it ratified the Thirteenth Amendment to the Constitution.[56] The Supreme Court, however, receives the credit for ending enforced segregation, in *Brown v. Board of Education*.[57] The struggle of African Americans, and many concerned others, to crush both the "peculiar institution" of slavery and Jim Crow segregation is well known and shall not be rehearsed here.

Rather, I will make three observations, each toward an assessment of how and why the law changed from oppressing blacks to abolition. First, the end of slavery and legal segregation were brought about, in part, by violence and lawbreaking by abolitionists. There are important differences, though, in the course of conduct that accomplished the Thirteenth Amendment and that led to the *Brown* decision. Slavery was ended because of violence, and not just any violence but war, and not just any war but the Civil War—the bloodiest, most destructive conflict in American history.[58] Prior to the War Between the States, abolitionists lobbied lawmakers and brought court cases and appealed to public sentiment. In the end, however, the brute force of rifles and bayonets was the most direct cause of the liberation of 4 million African American slaves. In comparison, ending legally enforced segregation was less bloody. The Supreme Court, in *Plessy v. Ferguson*, decided in 1896, declared that Jim Crow laws were constitutional.[59] Early in the next century, a group of black lawyers, including Charles Hamilton Houston and Thurgood Marshall, began an effort to change the Court's mind. This time the means of converting the law was not war but rather a carefully calculated series of legal arguments, made in state courts and designed, ultimately, to undermine the Supreme Court's analysis in *Plessy*.[60] This effort proved successful, eventually. The Supreme Court, in *Brown v. Board of Education*, decided in 1954, ordered the end of laws requiring segregation in public education.[61] Next, civil rights leaders turned to the federal legislature. Their goal was a sweeping civil rights law that would eliminate the remaining vestiges of formal discrimination in the law. To influence Congress to pass such a law, traditional methods were employed, including lobbying and "horse trading." In addition, some civil rights leaders encouraged breaking the law, through the practice of "civil disobedience." People who subverted the law, for example, by disobeying laws that they believed were unjust, sometimes were treated violently by the police. Some extreme examples were prominently publicized and helped create the political climate that accelerated passage of the Civil Rights Act of 1964 and of the Voting Rights Act of 1965.[62]

The second observation is that the first two abolitions took a long time. Although the evil of slavery and segregation seems obvious now, changing the law was a protracted and difficult struggle. The fight to end slavery in the United States persisted for more than two hundred years; efforts to end American apartheid required, in the most charitable assessment, "only" one hundred years. During these centuries of struggle, millions of black people lived lives of unspeakable pain, waiting for relief from the political and judicial branches.

The third point is that there has always been diversity of opinion in the minority community about ways to respond to oppressive laws, or indeed, even whether the laws are oppressive. Some African Americans did not feel insulted by the "separate but equal" statutes. Even among blacks who believed that the Jim Crow laws were racist, the idea of openly defying those laws was very controversial. Most African Americans, including southerners, did not engage in subversive tactics, like civil disobedience, that involved breaking the law. In fact, some blacks discouraged the tactic, because of legitimate concern about white backlash.[63]

WHAT IS THE ROLE OF LAWBREAKING IN
THE MOVEMENT FOR BLACK LIVES?

In reference to you, colored people, let me say God has made you free. Although you have been deprived of your God-given rights by your so-called Masters, you are now as free as I am, and if those that claim to be your superiors do not know that you are free, take the sword and bayonet and teach them that you are—for God created all men free, giving to each the same rights of life, liberty and the pursuit of happiness.

—Abraham Lincoln, speech to freed slaves

Obama, change gon' come or I'm gonna buy the whole hood [guns] on me.

—Jay-Z[64]

Activism by radicals invariably posits that unless there is change, there will be violence against the state. It's not so much a threat as a description of the vulnerability of any oppressive institution. "What happens to a dream deferred?" the famous Langston Hughes poem asks. "Does it dry up like a raisin in the sun? . . . *Or does it explode?*"[65] People in the movement for black lives should build consensus on what their comfort level is with lawbreaking and subversive tactics to create change. Without a strategy, there is a danger that the widespread anger at police in the black community could take a sinister turn.

Several prominent hip-hop artists, for example, have imagined the possibility of fighting back as a response to police violence. In 2015, Kendrick Lamar, one of the most critically acclaimed hip-hop artists, appeared on the television program *Saturday Night Live*. His performance was just a few weeks after a grand jury had refused to bring charges against the police officer who killed Eric Garner by placing him in a chokehold. Lamar changed the lyrics to one of his songs to say, "I put a bullet in the back of the head of the police."[66] Eminem, the world's best-selling hip-hop artist, has referred to himself as "the criminal cop killing, hip hop villain."[67] In "Shootout," Nas describes taking the life of a police officer.[68] Harvard recently named an endowed fellowship in Nas's honor.[69]

There's a history here—of hip-hop artists whose characters spit homicidal lyrics about the police and who, far from ostracized, are embraced by the masses. In the late 1980s, Dr. Dre rose to fame with NWA's "Fuck tha Police," which fantasizes about the execution of a racist cop.[70] Dre's recent collaboration with Apple to market his Beats headphones positions him to be hip-hop's first billionaire.[71] A few years later, the band Body Count, fronted by hip-hop legend Ice-T, caused a huge controversy with its song "Cop Killer."[72] Ice-T responded by saying, "I'm singing in the first person as a character who is fed up with police brutality. I ain't never killed no cop. I felt like it a lot of times. But I never did it."[73] Ice-T later portrayed a cop on *Law and Order: SVU*.

It's tempting to think of the enmity that hip-hop directs at the police as hyperbolic, consistent with the genre's over-the-top, rambunctious ethos. But an essay by James Baldwin, published in 1960, reminds us that hip-hop's message is as real as the streets. In "Letter from Harlem," Baldwin described a cop patrolling the ghetto and "facing, daily and nightly, people who would gladly see him dead, and he knows it. There is no way for him not to know it; there are few things under heaven more unnerving than the silent, accumulating contempt and hatred of a people."[74]

The threat of violence, and other forms of lawbreaking, has animated a range of political and cultural responses to the police treatment of African Americans. After unarmed black men were killed in Ferguson, Baltimore, and Charlotte, for example, activists took to the streets, defying curfews, not obtaining permits, and destroying property, including police vehicles and privately owned businesses. After these acts, activists won some concessions, including federal intervention in Ferguson and prosecution of police officers in Baltimore.[75] In this sense, the lawbreaking may have been productive.

Belief in the moral righteousness of violence as a means of protesting and changing unjust laws is part of U.S. history. Violent protests of the Stamp Act (1765) and the Townshend Acts (1767) helped launch the American Revolution. After the war was won, Thomas Jefferson wrote, "God forbid we should ever be twenty years without such a rebellion. . . . And what country can preserve its liberties, if its rulers are not warned from time to time, that this people preserve the spirit of resistance? Let them take arms. . . . The tree of liberty must be refreshed from time to time, with the blood of patriots and tyrants."[76]

Steeped in the rhetoric of American rebellion, African American rebels have existed since slavery. Notable slave uprisings include the Stono Rebellion in South Carolina (1739), an attempted attack on New Orleans (1811), and the Nat Turner insurrection in Virginia (1831).[77] Significantly, none of the American slave rebellions proved successful. *Africana: The Encyclopedia of the African and African American Experience* states, regarding the Nat Turner incident, "Like other slave uprisings in the United States, it caused enormous fear among whites but did not seriously threaten the slave regime."

One of the things we most remember about activists in the last major racial justice campaign in the United States is their stance on violence. Martin Luther King Jr. and his followers famously advocated nonviolence. At the same time, Malcolm X and black nationalist formations like the Black Panther Party embraced self-defense "by any means necessary" and specifically disavowed the pacifism of King.[78]

At what point is violence acceptable as a tactic for achieving racial justice? Is this a moral question or just a strategic one? Consider the case of Denmark Vesey. He was a free black man who attempted, in 1822, to organize a rebellion among South Carolina slaves. The plan was to burn the city of Charleston, kill the whites, steal ships, and escape to Haiti. The plan was thwarted by an informant, and thirty-five blacks, including Vesey, were executed. In 2001, the city of Charleston approved funds to erect a monument in Vesey's honor.[79] Some whites protested, but the South Carolinians who regarded Vesey as a hero carried the day.

The Denmark Vesey case reveals an interesting disjunction between morality and efficiency. Denmark Vesey's plan was surely impractical; no American slavery rebellion ever was successful. Yet Vesey's inefficiency does not seem to have negated his heroism.

The Chokehold, however, is a different kind of injustice than slavery. It may be that violence, including violence against civilians, is morally permissible to combat extraordinary racial discrimination (for example, slavery or genocide) but not "ordinary" racial subordination, like the ways that African American people are policed and jailed. Would violence be acceptable if the majority of African American men were incarcerated? When, if ever, does the subordination caused by the Chokehold reach the point where African Americans can make a morally justifiable decision to "live free or die"?[80] These are questions with which the movement for black lives must seriously engage. I want to suggest that violence against police officers, or any other persons, is unjustified, on moral grounds and because it would hurt the movement. Understanding the role of lawbreaking in overturning the old Jim Crow, however, should inspire a more open-minded perspective on other kinds of resistance, including civil disobedience, demonstrations at police stations and prisons, and disruptions of organizations and alliances that benefit from the Chokehold.

DONALD TRUMP AND THE
"PRODUCTIVE APOCALYPSE"

Our great African American President hasn't exactly had a positive impact on the thugs who are so happily and openly destroying Baltimore!

—Donald Trump tweet, 12:38 a.m., April 28, 2015

In *The New Jim Crow*, published in 2010, Michelle Alexander wondered about the implications of the recently elected Barack Obama. On the one hand, it was "an extraordinary opportunity." On the other hand, there were aspects of Obama's record that raised alarm, including his appointments of Vice President Joe Biden and Chief of Staff Rahm Emanuel, who had been enthusiastic supporters of the war on drugs. In addition, Alexander worried that African Americans "who are most oppressed by the current caste system . . . may be the least likely to challenge it, now that a black family is living in the White House." [81]

In large part, Alexander's concerns were prescient. As we have seen, the United States did not make as much progress on racial justice during the Obama presidency as many had hoped. Obama was not pressured by civil rights organizations because black leaders did not want to be seen as piling on to the considerable pushback he got from racists who were unhappy to see an African American chief executive.

Now, as for all but eight years of U.S. history, a white family is back in the White House. There were stark differences in the appeals to voters made by Donald Trump and his Democratic challenger Hillary Clinton. Clinton realized she needed a strong turnout of African American voters to help defeat Donald Trump, who, like every Republican candidate for the previous fifty years, was likely to receive the majority of the white vote. Yet Clinton was regarded with suspicion by some in the African American community, especially young people inspired by the movement for black lives. She was seen as complicit in President Bill Clinton's endorsement of policies that, during the 1990s, helped create mass incarceration. Most infamously, in a move right out of the Chokehold handbook, Hillary Clinton warned the nation, in 1996, about "the kinds of kids that are called 'super-predators.' . . . No conscience, no empathy, we can talk about why they ended up that way, but first we have to bring them to heel."

So it was no surprise that during the primary campaign of 2016, Clinton was called to task. Movement activists interrupted her rallies and fund-raisers. Leading public intellectual Ta-Nehisi Coates announced he was voting for Bernie Sanders, Clinton's rival in the Democratic primary, because he was "very, very concerned" about Clinton's record during her husband's presidency.[82] Michelle Alexander wrote an article for *The Nation* titled "Why Hillary Clinton Doesn't Deserve the Black Vote."[83] During the general election, some activists even floated the idea that a Trump victory would be a "productive apocalypse" because it would inspire a people's revolution.[84]

In response, Hillary Clinton embraced the movement. She uttered the words "black lives matter" well before even Barack Obama did.[85] Clinton campaigned with the "Mothers of the Movement," African American women who had lost children to police violence.[86] Trump, on the other hand, called people protesting police violence a "threat" and accused them of calling for "death to the police."

As the whole world knows, Donald Trump won. As I have suggested, given the power of the Chokehold, this is unlikely to shift local police practices. The optics are quite different, however, in a way that can advance the cause of the movement for black lives. A progressive president such as Hillary Clinton might have been if she had defeated Trump creates a sense of optimism, or at least forbearance, among activists. Let's wait and see, the sense is, if the reforms—the Justice Department investigations, the body cams, the bipartisan coalitions to reduce incarceration—will work.

Trump's victory, on the other hand, occasioned no such hope. Rather, it exposed the fact that things are unlikely to get better unless the people demand change. In the Marxist expression, the contradictions are heightened. Many people feel that they have more to be angry about even if, in pragmatic terms, they do not, because the Chokehold operates in largely the same way in a Democratic administration as a Republican one.

There is an interesting correspondence between Donald Trump's description of the African American community and that of the movement for black lives. Both agree that the state of African Americans is dire, and unlikely to improve absent radical change. Campaigning for president, Trump asked African Americans, if they voted for him, "What the hell do you have to lose? . . . You're living in poverty, your schools are no good, you have no jobs, 58% of your youth is unemployed—what the hell do you have to lose?" [87] The platform of the movement for black lives demands "an end to the war on black people" and states, "We take as a departure point the reality that by every metric—from the hue of its prison population to its investment choices—the U.S. is a country that does not support, protect or preserve Black life." [88]

In either view, it is not so much that the apocalypse has arrived but rather, for African Americans, that it has been here all along. It is up to every American of goodwill to determine whether, this time, the apocalypse will be productive and cause a critical mass to rise up and demand transformation. Until the Chokehold is unlocked, African American men will never be free, and, in the words of Supreme Court Justice Sonia Sotomayor, "our justice system will continue to be anything but." [89]

ACKNOWLEDGMENTS

This book has been a long time coming. It started out, several years ago, as a guide to the criminal justice system for African American men, but then Trayvon Martin was killed. A guide to the criminal justice system would not have saved Trayvon; he was shot down just walking home from the store after buying some candy. Then came Michael Brown, also walking in the street; Sandra Bland, driving her car; Eric Garner, allegedly selling cigarettes on the street corner; and Freddie Gray, minding his own business in his own neighborhood, to name only a few of the black people who were killed for no reason and treated in life and death more like criminals than the people who killed them—not one of whom has gone to prison. The movement that rose up to avenge their deaths inspired me. In the language of the movement for black lives, I got "woke." *Chokehold* is the result. More than anything I hope *Chokehold* honors the lives of those fallen sisters and brothers and advances the project to mark their deaths as the start of a revolution.

It takes a posse to write a book. I am fortunate to belong to a few. *Chokehold* was nurtured at the African American Policy Forum's Social Justice Writers Workshop, an annual gathering of race women and men in Negril, Jamaica. We eat ackee and codfish, write, read each other's work, meet in the Atlantic Ocean for two hours to workshop papers, and eat jerk chicken. Deepest gratitude to Kimberlé Crenshaw, Luke Harris, and Devon

Carbado for creating and sustaining this beloved community. They made *Chokehold* a better book, along with the others who joined us in the ocean, including Sahar Aziz, Khaled Beydoun, Laura Flanders, Marcus Hunter, Kiese Laymon, George Lipsitz, Darnell Moore, Priscilla Ocen, Marlon Peterson, Andrea Richie, and Alvin Starks.

The men of Positive Change, at Maryland's Jessup Correctional Institution, blessed me with an insightful reading of the entire manuscript. Much respect, my brothers, and stay strong.

The Criminal Justice Roundtable is a yearly gathering of some incredible criminal law scholars. What a privilege to present chapters to the group in meetings at Harvard and Stanford. Shout-out to Tracey Meares, Carol Steiker, and David Sklansky for the opportunity, and to the members of the roundtable for the amazing feedback.

The John Mercer Langston Conference is a formation of black male law professors and those brothers were some of my best, and toughest, critics. High fives to all the participants in my workshop, especially Mario Barnes, Charlton Copeland, and Terry Smith.

In addition to the posses, cash money and time off from the 9–5 gig helped *Chokehold* get done. Georgetown University Law Center, my wonderful academic home, provided a sabbatical and summer research grants. Dean Bill Treanor always has my back.

Mad props to my friends and colleagues who commented on draft chapters. I shared my stuff with these folks because they are some of the smartest and most generous people I know, and I got way better than I gave. Thank you to Amna Akbar, Sharon Dolovich, Jeff Fagan, Katherine Franke, Justin Hansford, Bernard Harcourt, Kris Henning, Eisha Jain, Corinna Lain, Adam Levitin, Judith Lichtenberg, David Luban, Scott McAbbe, Allegra McLeod, Tracey Meares, Sherally Munshi, Gary Peller, Catherine Powell, Andrea Roth, Stephen Rushin, Michael Seidman, Ted Shaw, Abbe Smith, Gerry Spann, Carol Steiker, Peter Tague, Kendall Thomas, Deborah Tuerkheimer, Robin West, and Patricia Williams.

My research assistants are the best. Alexander Galicki, Eric Glatt, Bradford Ham, Suraj Kumar, Will McAuliffe, Sonia Tabriz, Daniel Walsh, Chase Whiting, and Edward Williams all went beyond the call of duty. Georgetown Law students Jessica Lyn Davis, Garrett Thomas, and Adi Williams also made contributions, as did Monica Martinez, my faculty assistant.

Big up to the peeps who generously shared their ideas, experiences, and encouragement, especially Deleso Alford, Alvaro Bedoya, Donovan Chamberlayne, Angela Jordan Davis, Tamara Lawson, Eric Lotke, and Robert Patterson. The Raben Group has been an invaluable partner in introducing *Chokehold* to the world. Robert Raben and Donald Gatlin are my top dawgs.

I presented works in progress of various chapters at the University of Alabama School of Law, Arizona State University's Sandra Day O'Connor College of Law, University of Florida Levin College of Law, Fordham Law School, Georgetown University Law Center, George Washington University Law School, and the University of Richmond School of Law. Many thanks to the participants in those sessions.

The New Press is the publisher a writer dreams of. Sometimes it seemed as if Diane Wachtell and Ellen Adler believed in this project even more than I did. I am grateful to everyone at The New Press for their support and their diligent work on *Chokehold*, and to Diane and Jed Bickman for their superb editing.

My friends gave me hugs and bought me drinks, offered tough love when I needed it (and a few times when I really didn't), and showed so much support. Paul McPherson, Mark Brown, Jayne Jerkins, Dana Lintz, Scott McAbbe, Brenda Morris, Uche Onwuamaegbu, Ron Ross, Myron Smith, Mark Srere, and Verna Williams — thank you for the love.

My mother, Lindi Butler-Walton, is my biggest supporter, followed by my sister Kimberly Butler. Every page of this book is a product of the love they have shown me all my life. Jonell Nash, my father's partner, and Elmo "Walt" Walton, my mother's husband, both made their transitions as I worked on this book. They supported my work and, more importantly, loved my parents fiercely, and I know that, in the great beyond, they are still taking good care of us.

My father, the actor Paul Butler, used his art to show the world the joy and pain of being a black man in the United States of America. Daddy was a race man through and through. He loved black people and believed in us and he loved me and believed in me. This book is dedicated to him.

NOTES

Introduction: Broke on Purpose

1. See Civil Rights Division, "Investigation of the Ferguson Police Department," U.S. Department of Justice, March 4, 2015, available at www.justice.gov/sites/default/files/opa/press-releases/attachments/2015/03/04/ferguson_police_department_report.pdf; Charlie Leduff, "What Killed Aiyana Stanley-Jones?," *Mother Jones*, November/December 2010; Mark Berman and Wesley Lowery, "Former South Carolina Police Officer Who Fatally Shot Walter Scott Indicted on Federal Civil Rights Violation," *Washington Post*, May 11, 2016; David A. Graham, "The Mysterious Death of Freddie Gray," *The Atlantic*, April 22, 2015; Annie Sweeney and Jason Meisner, "A Moment-by-Moment Account of What the Laquan McDonald Video Shows," *Chicago Tribune*, November 25, 2015; Carol Cole-Frowe and Richard Fausset, "Jarring Image of Police's Use of Force at Texas Pool Party," *New York Times*, June 8, 2015; Timothy Williams and Mitch Smith, "Cleveland Officer Will Not Face Charges in Tamir Rice Shooting Death," *New York Times*, December 28, 2015; Cheryl Corley, "The Driving Life and Death of Philando Castile," NPR, July 15, 2016.

2. Nick Wing, "Donald Trump Says 'Police Are the Most Mistreated People' in America," *Huffington Post*, January 14, 2016; Reena Flores, "Donald Trump: Black Lives Matter Calls for Killing Police," CBS News, July 19, 2016.

3. See Ta-Nehisi Coates, "The Black Family in the Age of Mass Incarceration," *The Atlantic*, October 2015.

4. See Ta-Nehisi Coates, "Nonviolence as Compliance," *The Atlantic*, April 27, 2015; Kristina Marusic, "From Peaceful Protests to Violent Uprisings, Here's What History Can Teach Us About the Baltimore Riots," MTV News, April 28, 2015; German Lopez, "Riots Are Destructive, Dangerous, and Scary—but Can Lead to Serious Social Reforms," Vox, September 22, 2016.

5. See "On the Stop-and-Frisk Decision: *Floyd v. City of New York*," *New York Times*, August 12, 2013; Civil Rights Division, "Investigation of the Baltimore City Police Department," U.S. Department of Justice, August 10, 2016, available at www.justice.gov/opa/file/883366/download; Civil Rights Division, "Investigation of the Ferguson Police Department," U.S. Department of Justice,

March 4, 2015, available at www.justice.gov/sites/default/files/opa/press-releases /attachments/2015/03/04/ferguson_police_department_report.pdf; Sari Horwitz, Mark Berman, and Mark Guarino, "Justice Dept. Launches Investigation into Chicago Police Department," *Washington Post*, December 8, 2015; Joel Rubin, "Justice Department Warns LAPD to Take a Stronger Stance Against Racial Profiling," *Los Angeles Times*, November 14, 2010; Civil Rights Division, "Investigation of the Cleveland Division of Police," U.S. Department of Justice, December 4, 2014, available at www.justice.gov/sites/default/files/opa/press -releases/attachments/2014/12/04/cleveland_division_of_police_findings_letter .pdf; Community Oriented Policing Services, "Collaborative Reform Initiative: An Assessment of the San Francisco Police Department," U.S. Department of Justice, October 2016, ric-zai-inc.com/Publications/cops-w0817-pub.pdf.

6. Paul Butler, "The System Is Working the Way It Is Supposed To: The Limits of Criminal Justice Reform," *Georgetown Law Journal* 104 (2016): 1419, 1446.

7. "Los Angeles Police Reconsider Using Chokehold," *New York Times*, September 3, 1991.

8. Conor Friedersdorf, "Eric Garner and the NYPD's History of Deadly Chokeholds," *The Atlantic*, December 4, 2014.

9. See Susanna Capelouto, "Eric Garner: The Haunting Last Words of a Dying Man," CNN, December 8, 2014; Jim Dwyer, "Two Fatal Police Encounters, but Just One Video," *New York Times*, August 5, 2014; Jen Chung, "NYPD Strips Badge, Gun from Cop Involved in Fatal Chokehold," *Gothamist*, July 20, 2014; Al Baker, J. David Goodman, and Benjamin Mueller, "Beyond the Chokehold: The Path to Eric Garner's Death," *New York Times*, June 13, 2015; Massimo Calabresi, "Why a Medical Examiner Called Eric Garner's Death a 'Homicide,'" *Time*, December 4, 2014; Josh Voorhees, "Of Course It Happened Again," *Slate*, December 3, 2014; James Queally, "Man's Death After Apparent Chokehold by NYPD Officer to Be Probed," *Los Angeles Times*, July 18, 2014.

10. *City of Los Angeles v. Lyons*, 461 U.S. 95 (1983).

11. Public Enemy, *It Takes a Nation of Millions to Hold Us Back* (Def Jam Records, 1988).

12. See Sahar F. Aziz, "Policing Terrorists in the Community," *Harvard National Security Journal* 5 (2014): 147; Kaaryn Gustafson, "Degradation Ceremonies and the Criminalization of Low-Income Women," *UC Irvine Law Review* 3 (2013): 101; Khiara M. Bridges, "Privacy Rights and Public Families," *Harvard Journal of Law and Gender* 34 (2011): 113; Joseph William Singer, "Well Settled?: The Increasing Weight of History in American Land Claims," *Georgia Law Review* 28 (1994): 481; Frances Ansley, "Doing Policy from Below: Worker Solidarity and the Prospects for Immigration Reform," *Cornell International Law Journal* 41 (2008): 101; "Sustaining Tiered Personhood: Jim Crow and Anti-Immigrant Laws," *Harvard Journal on Racial and Ethnic Justice* 26 (2010): 163; Leigh Goodmark, "Transgender People, Intimate Partner Abuse, and the Legal System," *Harvard Civil Rights-Civil Liberties Law Review* 48 (2013): 51; Dylan Vade, "Expanding Gender and Expanding the Law: Toward a Social and Legal Conceptualization of Gender That Is More Inclusive of Transgender People," *Michigan Journal of Gender and Law* 11 (2005): 253; Sunny Woan, "White

Sexual Imperialism: A History of Asian Feminist Jurisprudence," *Washington and Lee Journal of Civil Rights and Social Justice* 14 (2008): 275.

13. Paul Butler, "Black Male Exceptionalism? The Problems and Potential of Black Male–Focused Interventions," *Du Bois Review* 10 (2013): 485.

14. Akasha Gloria T. Hull, Patricia Bell Scott, and Barbara Smith, *All the Women Are White, All the Blacks Are Men, but Some of Us Are Brave: Black Women's Studies* (New York: Feminist Press at the City University of New York, 2015).

15. Kimberlé Williams, Andrea J. Ritchie, Rachel Anspach, Rachel Gilmer, and Luke Harris, "Say Her Name: Resisting Police Brutality Against Black Women," African American Policy Forum and Center for Intersectionality and Social Policy Studies, 2015, 28.

16. See Michelle Alexander, *The New Jim Crow: Mass Incarceration in the Age of Colorblindness* (New York: The New Press, 2012).

17. See *Floyd v. City of New York*, 959 F. Supp. 2d 540 (S.D.N.Y. 2013).

18. Lisa L. Miller, "Violence and the Racialized Failure of the American State," *Lawyers, Guns & Money*, December 8, 2014, available at www.lawyers gunsmoneyblog.com/2014/12/violence-racialized-failure-american-state-guest -post-lisa-m-miller.

19. See Tracey Meares, "A Third Reconstruction?," *Balkinization*, August 14, 2015, balkin.blogspot.com/2015/08/a-third-reconstruction.html.

20. Robin Morgan, "Goodbye to All That," maanmittauslaitos.files.wordpress .com/2011/02/robin20morgan20-20goodbye20to20all20that.pdf.

1: Constructing the Thug

1. See Rachel D. Godsil and Alexis McGill Johnson, "Transforming Perception: Black Men and Boys," American Values Institute, March 2013.

2. See Pamela M. Casey et al., "Helping Courts Address Implicit Bias," National Center for State Courts, 2012, B-2, B-6.

3. The character used in chapter 1's text is merely a representative character and not necessarily one that was used in the study. For the full study, see Keith Payne et al., "An Inkblot for Attitudes: Affect Misattribution as Implicit Measurement," *Journal of Personality and Social Psychology* 89 (2005): 277.

4. See Godsil and McGill Johnson, "Transforming Perception: Black Men and Boys."

5. Fredrick Kunkle, "'Walking While Black' Can Be Dangerous Too, Study Finds," *Washington Post*, October 26, 2015.

6. Jason Okonofua and Jennifer L. Eberhardt, "Two Strikes: Race and the Disciplining of Young Students," *Psychological Science* 26:5 (April 8, 2015).

7. John Edgar Wideman, "The Seat Not Taken," *New York Times*, October 6, 2010.

8. Jamie Reidy, "That Seat Is Not Taken: Why Black Men Love Southwest Airlines," *The Good Men Project*, March 14, 2012.

9. More explicit types of training also have very promising effects. For instance, subjects who undergo forty-five minutes of intensive practice at rejecting

stereotypes—clicking "No" when viewing a black face paired with a stereotypi-cal description—showed a resulting reduction in implicit bias. Researchers liken the training (which cannot be accomplished more quickly) to practicing a new physical skill. To review this study, see Kerry Kawakami et al., "Just Say No (to Stereotyping): Effects of Training in the Negation of Stereotypic Associations on Stereotype Activation," *Journal of Personality and Social Psychology* 78:5 (May 2000).

10. See Antonya M. Gonzalez, Jennifer R. Steele, and Andrew S. Baron, "Re-ducing Children's Implicit Racial Bias Through Exposure to Positive Out-Group Exemplars," *Child Development* (July 8, 2016).

11. Jennifer L. Doleac and Benjamin Hansen, "Does 'Ban the Box' Help or Hurt Low-Skilled Workers? Statistical Discrimination and Employment Out-comes When Criminal Histories Are Hidden," *Social Science Research Network* (July 1, 2016): 5.

12. Ibid., 23.

13. Ibid., 6.

14. The data presented in figure 1 concerns race and is not disaggregated by gender. As a point of reference, females commit about 10 percent of violent crime in the United States.

15. "Scientists define stereotypes as the beliefs and opinions people hold about the characteristics, traits, and behaviors of a certain group (Allport, 1954; Macrae, Mile, Bodenhausen, 1994; Hilton & Von Hippel, 1996). Stereotypes often cause us to make assumptions (both negative and positive) about people based upon superficial characteristics (Schneider, 2004). They also tend to be self-perpetuating, which leads to their deep entrenchment." See Godsil and Mc-Gill Johnson, "Transforming Perception: Black Men and Boys."

16. Christopher Ingraham, "Three Quarters of Whites Don't Have Any Non-White Friends," *Washington Post*, August 25, 2014.

17. On local news shows, blacks are disproportionately portrayed as criminals, and whites as victims. See Brooke Gladstone, "Racial Bias in Crime Reporting," *On the Media*, WNYC, June 5, 2015 (reporting on Nazgol Ghandnoosh, "Race and Punishment: Racial Perceptions of Crime and Support for Punitive Policies," *The Sentencing Project*, 2014).

18. Ibid.

19. "Racial Attitudes Survey," Associated Press, October 29, 2012.

20. Nia-Malika Henderson, "White Men Are 31 Percent of the American Population. They Hold 65 Percent of All Elected Offices," *Washington Post*, Oc-tober 8, 2014.

21. Although there may be some problems with these data—as crime statis-tics are not always disaggregated into violent and nonviolent crimes, perpetrator statistics are not always disaggregated by gender, and data on Latino and His-panic offenders is not always reported—it is possible to measure violent crimes sorted by race, and homicides sorted by race and gender. See Jon Greenberg, "Sally Kohn: 'White Men Account for 69 Percent of Those Arrested for Violent Crimes,'" *Politifact*, *Punditfact*, April 2, 2015.

22. This figure was calculated by deriving from the total number of white victims of violent crimes (2,788,600) the percent who perceived their attacker to be black (15.4% = 429,444), *subtracting* violent incidents of rape and sexual assault (19,293), *dividing* by the total white American population (196,678,913), *and multiplying* by 100 to arrive at 0.20854 percent. For the data used to calculate violent crimes, see "Criminal Victimization in the United States, 2008 Statistics Tables," Bureau of Justice Statistics, May 2011, table 42. For total white American population, see "QuickFacts," United States Census Bureau, April 1, 2010.

23. This figure was calculated by deriving from the total number of black victims of violent crimes (570,500) the percent who perceived their attacker to be black (64.7% = 369,146), *subtracting* violent incidents of rape and sexual assault (34,842), *dividing* by the total black American population (38,901,938), *and multiplying* by 100 to arrive at 0.85935 percent. For the data used to calculate violent crimes, see "Criminal Victimization in the United States, 2008 Statistics Tables," Bureau of Justice Statistics, May 2011, table 42. For total African American population, see "QuickFacts," United States Census Bureau, April 1, 2010.

24. "Sexual Violence Facts at a Glance," Centers for Disease Control and Prevention, 2012.

25. Walt Hickey, "Everyone Is Freaking Out About the $1.5 Billion Powerball, and the Stats Agree," *FiveThirtyEight*, January 12, 2016. "Consistently participating in a lottery with a very negative expected value is a great way to lose a lot of money over a period of time." Ibid.

26. Derek Thompson, "The 11 Ways That Consumers Are Hopeless at Math," *The Atlantic*, July 6, 2012.

27. See Phillip Atiba Goff et al., "Not Yet Human: Implicit Knowledge, Historical Dehumanization, and Contemporary Consequences," *Journal of Personality and Social Psychology* 94:2 (February 7, 2008).

28. Jill Leovy, *Ghettoside: A True Story of Murder in America* (New York: Spiegel & Grau, 2015), 6.

29. "Read Darren Wilson's Full Grand Jury Testimony," *Washington Post*, November 25, 2014.

30. Khalil Gibran Muhummad, *The Condemnation of Blackness: Race, Crime, and the Making of Modern Urban America* (Cambridge, MA: Harvard University Press, 2010).

31. Quote from David Levering Lewis, Khalil Gibran Muhammad, *The Condemnation of Blackness: Race, Crime, and the Making of a Modern Urban America* (Cambridge, MA: Harvard University Press, 2010).

32. "Black men consider a number of problems facing them severe, and are harshly critical of the priorities of black men as a group. For example, they are critical of what they see as black men's insufficient emphasis on education, health, family, and work. . . . In just about every area, black men are their own harshest critics as well as the most optimistic that things will get better." See "A Review of Public Opinion Research Related to Black Male Achievement," The Opportunity Agenda, October 30, 2011, 57.

33. Ibid., 70.

34. Ibid., 71.

35. Amy Zimmerman, "Diddy's Crazy Rap Sheet: From Attacking a Record Exec to His Alleged Kettleball Assault," Reuters, June 23, 2015.

36. "Racial, Ethnic, and Gender Disparities in Federal Sentencing Today," United States Sentencing Commission, 2015.

37. See Devah Pager, "Double Jeopardy: Race, Crime, and Getting a Job," *University of Wisconsin Law Review* 2 (2005).

38. Ryan Gabrielson, Ryann Grochowski Jones, and Eric Sagara, "Deadly Force, in Black and White," *ProPublica*, October 10, 2014. There has been criticism of the validity of the FBI's data by David Klinger, who said that FBI data had serious shortcomings regarding its inclusiveness. Ibid.

39. Ibid.

40. "Policing and Homicide, 1976–98: Justifiable Homicide by Police, Police Officers Murdered by Felons," Bureau of Justice Statistics, March 2001, 12.

41. Ibid.

42. Criteria of an officer-involved shooting: (1) The individual discharging the firearm is a sworn officer, either on or off duty; (2) the discharge of the firearm involves another human being; and (3) the discharge of the firearm is intentional (unless someone other than the officer is injured). Discharges in which someone other than the officer is injured are also counted as OISs even if the discharge is accidental.

43. See twittercounter.com/pages/100 (last viewed September 8, 2015). Note, also, that twenty accounts in the top one hundred are organizations (e.g., Facebook, Uber, Real Madrid).

44. See fanpagelist.com/category/top_users/ (last viewed September 8, 2015). Note, also, that approximately thirty accounts in the top one hundred are organizations (e.g., Facebook, Uber, Real Madrid).

45. It is important not to overstate this point. Accusation of involvement in a violent crime, particularly if a white person is the victim, can doom an African American man's career. The comedian Bill Cosby went from being one of the most respected men in America to one of the most despised when long-standing allegations that he sexually assaulted women received significant attention in the media. OJ Simpson, found civilly liable for killing his ex-wife and another person, might be the most unpopular person in the United States.

46. Interview of Public Enemy by John Leland, "Armageddon in Effect," *Spin*, September 1988.

47. Adrian Van Young, "Shots in the Dark: Interrogating Gun Violence in Fiction," *The American Reader*.

48. Martha Bayles, "Attacks on Rap Now Come from Within," *Wall Street Journal*, April 28, 2005.

49. DMX, "Party Up," 2001.

50. Phillip Atiba Goff et al., "The Essence of Innocence: Consequences of Dehumanizing Black Children," *Journal of Personality and Social Psychology* 106:4 (2014): 526.

51. "Black Boys Viewed as Older, Less Innocent than Whites, Research Finds," *American Psychological Association*, March 6, 2014.

52. Jamal Hagler, "8 Facts You Should Know About the Criminal Justice System and People of Color," Center for American Progress, May 28, 2015.

53. Thomas P. Bonczar, "Prevalence of Imprisonment in the U.S. Population, 1974–2011," Bureau of Justice Statistics Special Report, August 2003.

54. Joe Palazzolo, "Racial Gap in Men's Sentencing," *Wall Street Journal*, February 14, 2013.

55. Jennifer Eberhardt et al., "Looking Deathworthy: Perceived Stereotypicality of Black Defendants Predicts Capital-Sentencing Outcomes," *Association for Psychological Science* 17:5 (2006).

56. Ryan D. King and Brian D. Johnson, "A Punishing Look: Skin Tone and Afrocentric Features in the Halls of Justice," *American Journal of Sociology* 122:1 (July 2016).

2: Controlling the Thug

1. United States Department of Justice, Civil Rights Division, "Investigation of the Ferguson Police Department," March 4, 2015.

2. Ibid., 3.

3. Ibid.

4. Ibid., 81.

5. Nick Selby, "The Backlog: Misdemeanor Arrest Warrants in the USA," *Medium*, October 6, 2014.

6. James B. Comey, "Hard Truths: Law Enforcement and Race," February 12, 2015, https://www.fbi.gov/news/speeches/hard-truths-law-enforcement-and-race.

7. Thomas Frank, "Black People Are Three Times More Likely to Be Killed in Police Chases," *USA Today*, December 1, 2016.

8. Joel H. Garner and Christopher D. Maxwell, "Measuring the Amount of Force Used by and Against Police in Six Jurisdictions," National Criminal Justice Reference Service.

9. "2015 Law Enforcement Officer Fatalities Report," National Law Enforcement Officers Memorial Fund, December 2015. See also Bill Chappell, "Number of Police Officers Killed by Gunfire Fell 14 Percent in 2015, Study Says," National Public Radio, December 29, 2015.

10. "People Shot Dead by Police in 2015," *Washington Post*, last visited October 27, 2016.

11. "The Counted: People Killed by Police in the US," *The Guardian*, last visited October 27, 2016.

12. Kimberly Kindy et al., "Fatal Shootings by Police Are Up in the First Six Months of 2016, Post Analysis Finds," *Washington Post*, July 7, 2016.

13. William J. Bratton, "New York City Police Department Annual Firearms Discharge Report 2013," www.nyc.gov/html/nypd/downloads/pdf/analysis_and_planning/nypd_annual_firearms_discharge_report_2013.pdf

14. George Fachner and Steven Carter, "An Assessment of Deadly Force in the Philadelphia Police Department," Collaborative Reform Initiative, U.S. Department of Justice, 2015, 18, 26.

15. "New York Police Department Annual Firearms Discharge Report: 2013," Police Department, City of New York, October 2014, 57.

16. "2012 Use of Force Report with 2013 Statistical Overview," Los Angeles Police Department, 2013, 31.

17. John Rappaport, "An Insurance-Based Typology of Police Misconduct," University of Chicago Legal Forum, July 8, 2016.

18. Ibid., 8–9.

19. Ibid., 10.

20. Radley Balko, "How the Insurance Industry Could Reform American Policing," *Washington Post*, March 1, 2016.

21. Jamiles Lartey, "By the Numbers: US Police Kill More in Days Than Other Countries Do in Years," *The Guardian*, June 9, 2015.

22. Camelia Simoiu, Sam Corbett-Davies, and Sharad Goel, "Testing for Racial Discrimination in Police Searches of Motor Vehicles," *Social Science Research Network* (July 18, 2016): 15–16.

23. Ibid., 20.

24. Ibid.

25. *Utah v. Strieff*, 136 U.S. 2056, 2070–71 (2016) (Sotomayor, J., dissenting).

26. Devon W. Carbado, "Black-on-Blue Violence: A Provisional Model of Some of the Causes," *Georgetown Law Journal* 104: 1479 (2016).

27. See "National Longitudinal Survey of Youth: 1979 Cohort," U.S. Bureau of Labor Statistics.

28. Misdemeanor arrests vary across a given week, tending to peak on Wednesdays when police staffing for patrols is at its highest, and falling on Sundays, when police staffing is at its weekly low. See K. Babe Howell, "Broken Lives from Broken Windows: The Hidden Costs of Aggressive Order-Maintenance Policing," *N.Y.U. Review of Law & Social Change* (2009): 284.

29. In an opinion written by Justice Kennedy, the United States Supreme Court held that both obtaining and analyzing a defendant's DNA after arrest is permitted under the Fourth Amendment of the United States Constitution. See *Maryland v. King*, 133 S. Ct. 1958 (2013).

30. Robert M. Sanger, "IQ, Intelligence Tests, 'Ethnic Adjustments' and Atkins," *American University Law Review* 65:1 (November 21, 2015).

31. Ibid., 109–11.

32. Josh Salman, Emily Le Coz, and Elizabeth Johnson, "Florida's Broken Sentencing System," *Sarasota Herald Tribune*, http://projects.heraldtribune.com /bias/sentencing.

33. United States Department of Justice, Civil Rights Division, "Investigation of the Ferguson Police Department," March 4, 2015, 1.

34. Clyde Haberman, "Heroin, Survivor of War on Drugs, Returns with New Face," *New York Times*, November 22, 2015.

35. Katharine Q. Seelye, "In Heroin Crisis, White Families Seek Gentler War on Drugs," *New York Times*, October 30, 2015.

36. Ibid.

37. Nazgol Ghandnoosh, "Race and Punishment: Racial Perceptions of Crime and Support for Punitive Policies," *The Sentencing Project*, September 3, 2014.

38. Justin T. Pickett and Ted Chiricos, "Controlling Other People's Children: Racialized Views of Delinquency and Whites' Punitive Attitudes Toward Juvenile Offenders," *Criminology* 50:3 (August 2012).

39. Elaine B. Sharpe, "Politics, Economics, and Urban Policing: The Postindustrial City Thesis and Rival Explanations of Heightened Order Maintenance Policing," *Urban Affairs Review* 50:3 (2014).

40. Adam Hudson, "How Punitive and Racist Policing Enforces Gentrification in San Francisco," *Truthout*, April 24, 2015, http://www.truth-out.org/news /item/30392-how-punitive-and-racist-policing- enforces-gentrification-in-san-fran cisco.

41. News Release, *Mayor Lee Launches New Open311 Platform to Improve City's 311 Customer Service*, San Francisco Office of the Mayor, August 8, 2013, http://www.sfmayor.org/index.aspx?recordid 387 &page 846.

42. A family headed by a white high school dropout has more wealth than a family headed by a black college graduate. See Patricia Cohen, "Racial Wealth Gap Persists Despite Degree, Study Says," *New York Times*, August 16, 2015.

43. Justin Wolfers, David Leonhardt, and Kevin Quealy, "The Methodology: 1.5 Million Missing Black Men," *New York Times*, April 20, 2015.

44. Devah Pager, "The Mark of a Criminal Record," 2003, http://scholar. harvard.edu/files/pager/files/pager_ajs.pdf; Devah Pager, Bruce Western, and Bart Bonikowski, "Discrimination in a Low-Wage Labor Market: A Field Experiment," 2009, http://scholar.harvard.edu/files/bonikowski/files/pager-western-boni kowski-discrimination-in-a-low-wage-labor-market.pdf.

3: Sex and Torture: The Police and Black Male Bodies

1. *Terry v. Ohio*, 392 U.S. 1, n.13 (1968), quoting L. L. Priar and T. F. Martin, "Searching and Disarming Criminals," *Journal of Criminal Law, Criminology and Police Science* 45 (1954): 481.

2. Ray Rivera, Al Baker, and Janet Roberts, "A Few Blocks, 4 Years, 52,000 Police Stops," *New York Times*, July 11, 2010.

3. *Terry*, 392 U.S. 16–17.

4. *Terry*, 392 U.S. 1.

5. See Rachel Konrad, "New Documents Shed More Light on FBI's 'Carnivore,'" CNET, November 16, 2000, news.cnet.com/New-documents-shed-more -light-on-FBIs-Carnivore/2100-1023_3-248762.html.

6. Orin S. Kerr, "Internet Surveillance Law After the USA Patriot Act: The Big Brother That Isn't," *Northwestern University Law Review* 97 (2003): 607, 656 n.239.

7. Ibid., 19.

8. Ibid., 16–17.

9. Steven Pinker, "Decivilization in the 1960s," *Human Figurations: Long-Term Perspectives on the Human Condition*, July 2013, quod.lib.umich.edu/h/humfig

/11217607.0002.206/—decivilization-in-the-1960s?rgn=main;view=fulltext, explains that criminologists concluded that the crime surge was not explained by the demographic.

10. James Baldwin, *Nobody Knows My Name* (New York: Vintage Books, 1962).

11. Alex Elkins, "The Origins of Stop-and-Frisk," *Jacobin*, May 9, 2015, jacob inmag.com/2015/05/stop-and-frisk-dragnet-ferguson-baltimore.

12. Alex Elkins, "Fifty Years of Get-Tough Policies," *Popular Resistance*, July 19, 2014, available at www.popularresistance.org/fifty-years-of-get-tough-policies.

13. John Barrett, "*Terry v. Ohio*: The Fourth Amendment Reasonableness of Police Stops and Frisks Based on Less than Probable Cause," in *Criminal Procedure Stories* (Carol S. Steiker, ed., New York: Foundation Press, 2006), 295.

14. *Terry*, 392 U.S. 27.

15. Ibid.

16. Barrett, "*Terry v. Ohio*," n.35.

17. See John Q. Barrett, "Deciding the Stop and Frisk Cases: Look Inside the Supreme Court's Conference," 72 *St. John's Law Review* 749, 843 (1998) ("Justice Marshall, who as a newcomer to the Court was relatively uninvolved in the Court's internal arguments over the stop and frisk cases, all but stated in later cases that he had voted wrong in Terry").

18. *Terry*, 392 U.S. 38.

19. *Terry*, 392 U.S. 14–15.

20. *Terry*, 392 U.S. 1, n.11.

21. Butler, "The System Is Working the Way It Is Supposed To," 1419, 1447.

22. See Randall Kennedy, *Race, Crime, and the Law* (New York: Pantheon Books, 1997), 136–67.

23. *United States v. Weaver*, 966 F.2d 391 (8th Cir. 1992).

24. "Court Says US Border Inspections of Muslims Were Allowed," *International Herald Tribune*, November 26, 2007.

25. Rivera, Baker, and Roberts, "A Few Blocks, 4 Years, 52,000 Police Stops."

26. Jim Dwyer, "What Donald Trump Got Wrong on Stop and Frisk," *New York Times*, September 27, 2016.

27. New York Civil Liberties Union, "Stop-and-Frisk Data," 2016, www.nyclu .org/en/stop-and-frisk-data; Zollan Konno Youngs, Scott Calvert and Mara Gay, "New York City Major Crimes Fall to Lowest Record Level," *Wall Street Journal*, January 4, 2017.

28. See Vesla M. Weaver, "The Only Government I Know: How the Criminal Justice System Degrades Democratic Citizenship," *Boston Review*, June 10, 2014, bostonreview.net/us/vesla-m-weaver-citizenship-custodial-state-incarceration; Amy E. Lerman and Vesla M. Weaver, *Arresting Citizenship: The Democratic Consequences of American Crime Control* (Chicago: University of Chicago Press, 2014).

29. See, for example, Charles Lawrence, "The Id, The Ego, and Equal Protection: Reckoning with Unconscious Racism," 39 *Stan. L. Rev.* 317 (1987); Cynthia Lee, "Making Race Salient: Trayvon Martin and Implicit Bias in a Not Yet Post-Racial Society," 91 *N.C. L. Rev.* 1555 (2013).

30. Paul Butler, "Stop and Frisk: Sex, Torture, Control" in *Law as Punishment/Law as Regulation* (Austin Sarat, Lawrence Douglas, and Martha Umphrey, eds., Stanford, CA: Stanford University Press, 2011).

31. Ibid.

32. Ibid.

33. Ibid.

34. My analysis in this section was advanced by two seminal articles that explore sex, gender, and criminal procedure. Frank Rudy Cooper's "Who's the Man? Masculinities and Police Stops" asserts that police use *Terry* stops to stage "masculinity contests" with other men. Frank Rudy Cooper, "Who's the Man? Masculinities and Police Stops," Suffolk University Law School, available at papers.ssrn.com/sol3/papers.cfm?abstract_id=1257183. David A. Sklansky has argued that an unstated animus of the Supreme Court in deciding criminal procedure cases in the 1960s was concern about the anti–civil libertarian methods that police used to investigate homosexual "crimes." David Alan Sklansky, " 'One Train May Hide Another': Katz, Stonewall, and the Secret Subtext of Criminal Procedure," *UC Davis Law Review* 41 (2008): 875–934.

35. *Little v. United States*, 125 A.3d 1119 (2015).

36. Richard Goldstein, "What's Sex Got to Do with It? The Assault on Abner Louima May Have Been Attempted Murder, but It Was Also Rape," *Village Voice*, September 2, 1997.

37. For an analysis of depictions of criminal justice in hip-hop music, see Paul Butler, "Much Respect: Toward a Hip-Hop Theory of Punishment," *Stanford Law Review* 56 (2004): 983–1016.

38. NWA, "Fuck tha Police," *Straight Outta Compton*, Perf. Dr. Dre, Eazy-E, Ice Cube, and MC Ren (Priority/Ruthless, 1988).

39. Lupe Fiasco, "Daydreamin'," *Food and Liquor*, Perf. Lupe Fiasco (Atlantic, 2006).

40. Webbie, "Six 12's," *Savage Life 2*, Perf. Webbie, Mouse (Atlantic, 2008).

41. Nicholas Powers, "The Gropes of Wrath," *Village Voice*, March 20, 2007.

42. "Urban Dictionary: frisk," Urban Dictionary, May 31, 2009, available at www.urbandictionary.com/define.php?term=frisk.

43. Dead Prez, "Cop Shot," *Cop Shot (White Label)* 12, Perf. M-1, stic-Man (Loud Records, 2008).

44. The U.S. Supreme Court also supports this proposition. Sexual harassment in the workplace is governed by Title VII of the Civil Rights Act of 1964, which provides that "it shall be an unlawful employment practice for an employer to discriminate against any individual with respect to his compensation, terms, conditions, or privileges of employment, because of such individual's sex." Circuits developed conflicting perspectives regarding whether Title VII allows such a claim where an employee is sexually harassed by another employee of the same sex. Some circuits held that Title VII plainly does not recognize same-sex sexual harassment claims. See *Goluszek v. H. P. Smith*, 697 F. Supp. 1452 (ND Ill, 1988). Others held that such claims are actionable only if the harassment was motivated by sexual desire (that is, if the harasser was a homosexual). Compare *McWilliams v. Fairfax County Board of Supervisors*, 72 F.3d 1191 (4th Cir. 1996)

with *Wrightson v. Pizza Hut of America*, 99 F.3d 138 (4th Cir. 1996). Others took the approach that Title VII protected employees from all types of sexual harassment, regardless of the harasser's gender or sexual preference. See Doe by *Doe v. City of Belleville*, 119 F.3d 563 (7th Cir.1997). In *Oncale v. Sundowner Offshore Services*, 523 U.S. 75 (1998), the Supreme Court weighed in, deciding unanimously that Title VII did include protection from same-sex harassers, even if that discrimination was not sexually motivated.

45. Bernard E. Harcourt, "Unconstitutional Police Searches and Collective Responsibility," *Criminology and Public Policy*, 2004.

46. Jon B. Gould and Stephen D. Mastrofski, "Suspect Searches: Assessing Police Behavior Under the U.S. Constitution," *Criminology and Public Policy*, 2004.

47. *Njaka v. Wright County*, 560 F. Supp. 2d 746 (D. Minn. 2008).

48. Ibid.

49. Ibid., 756.

50. Ibid., n.12.

51. *Myers v. James*, 2004 U.S. Dist. LEXIS 25666 (E.D. La. 2004).

52. Ibid., 4.

53. Ibid., 3.

54. Ibid., 21.

55. *Marrie v. Nickels*, 70 F. Supp. 2d 1252 (1999).

56. Ibid., 1257.

57. Ibid.

58. Gary Stoller, "Poll: Most Fliers Bothered or Angered by TSA Pat-Downs," *USA Today*, November 23, 2010, available at www.usatoday.com/travel /flights/2010-11-23-airport-security-tsa-poll_N.htm (The pat downs "bother or anger 57% of adult fliers").

59. "Fliers Liken Pat-Downs to Sexual Assault," MSNBC, November 18, 2010, available at www.nbcnews.com/id/40257031/ns/travel-news/t/fliers-liken -pat-downs-sexual-%20assault/#.TpxtN97iGU8.

60. Kate Dailey, "TSA Screenings Worry Sexual Assault Survivors," *Newsweek*, November 17, 2010.

61. See Charles Krauthammer, "Don't Touch My Junk," *Washington Post*, November 19, 2010.

62. Michael E. Miller, "Cop Accused of Brutally Torturing Black Suspects Costs Chicago $5.5 Million," *Washington Post*, April 15, 2015.

63. Civil Rights Cases 109 US 3 (1883).

64. Groups other than African American men, including black women and Jews, were also subject to lynching.

65. Robert McFadden and Joseph P. Fried, "The Louima Case: The Overview; In Harsh Testimony's Wake, Officer Accused in Torture of Louima to Plead Guilty," *New York Times*, May 25, 1999.

66. Greg Ridgeway, "Analysis of Racial Disparities in the New York Police Department's Stop, Question, and Frisk Practices," *RAND Technical Report* (2007): 35–37, available at www.rand.org/content/dam/rand/pubs/technical_re ports/2007/RAND_TR534.pdf.

67. Paul Butler, "Stop and Frisk and Torture-Lite: Police Terror of Minority Communities," *Ohio State Journal of Criminal Law* 12 (2014): 57, 61.

68. David Luban, *Torture, Power, and Law* (United Kingdom: Cambridge University Press, 2014): 47.

69. Ibid., 53.

70. Butler, "Stop and Frisk and Torture-Lite: Police Terror of Minority Communities."

71. M. Gregg Bloche, "Torture-Lite: It's Wrong, and It Might Work," *New York Times*, May 27, 2011.

72. Susan Sontag, "Regarding the Torture of Others," *New York Times*, May 23, 2004.

73. Michel Foucault, *Discipline and Punish: The Birth of the Prison* (New York: Vintage Books, 1979).

74. Ibid., 42.

75. Ibid., 34.

76. *Illinois v. Wardlow*, 528 U.S. 119 (2002).

77. Ibid., 122.

78. Ibid., 125.

79. Butler, "Stop and Frisk: Sex, Torture, Control."

80. Ibid.

81. Ibid.

82. Ibid.

83. Ibid.

84. Jay-Z, "99 Problems," Perf. Jay-Z, *The Black Album* (Roc-A-Fella Records and Def Jam Records, 2003).

85. Ibid.

86. I. Bennett Capers, "Policing, Race, and Place," *Harvard Civil Rights-Civil Liberties Review* 44 (2009): 68–69.

87. "Terrorism," *Black's Law Dictionary* (9th ed. 2009).

88. Joseph Goldstein, "Kelly Said Street Stops Target Minors, Senator Justifies," *New York Times*, April 1, 2013. Commissioner Kelly subsequently submitted an affidavit to the court denying that he had ever suggested that black and Latino men were being targeted for stop and frisk. Id. The court's opinion found that in fact black and Latino men were targeted. *Floyd v. City of New York*, 959 F. Supp. 2d 540, 589.

89. Julie Dressner and Edwin Martinez, "The Scars of Stop-and-Frisk," *New York Times*, June 12, 2012.

90. Ibid.

91. Joseph Goldstein, "A Focus on 3 Encounters in a Stop-and-Frisk Trial," *New York Times*, March 19, 2013.

92. James Forman Jr., "Arrested Development: Why Conservatives Should Oppose Racial Profiling," *New America*, September 10, 2001.

93. Henry Louis Gates, "Thirteen Ways of Looking at a Black Man," *New Yorker*, October 23, 1995.

94. Rivera, Baker, and Roberts, "A Few Blocks, 4 Years, 52,000 Police Stops."

95. I. Bennett Capers, "The Crime of Loving: Loving, Lawrence, and Beyond," in *Loving v. Virginia in a Post-Racial World: Rethinking Sex, Race, and Marriage* (Kevin Maillard and Rose Cuison Villazor, eds., United Kingdom: Cambridge University Press, 2012): 114, 126–27.

96. Dionne Grayman, "For Our Sons Police Stops Are a Part of Growing Up," *Women's eNews*, October 2, 2010, available at www.womensenews.org/story /sisterspace/101002/our-sons-police-stops-are-part-growing.

97. *Terry*, 392 U.S. 14, n.1, 11.

98. Rivera, Baker, and Roberts, "A Few Blocks, 4 Years, 52,000 Police Stops."

99. Luban, *Torture, Power, and Law*, 48.

100. Butler, "Stop and Frisk and Torture-Lite: Police Terror of Minority Communities."

101. See Rachel Harmon, "The Problem of Policing," 110 *Mich. L. Rev.* 761 (2012).

102. New York Civil Liberties Union, "Stop-and-Frisk Data."

103. *Floyd v. City of New York*, 959 F. Supp. 2d 540.

104. Dwyer, "What Donald Trump Got Wrong on Stop and Frisk"; Zollan Konno Youngs, Scott Calvert, and Mara Gay, "New York City Major Crimes Fall to Lowest Record Level," *Wall Street Journal*, January 4, 2017.

105. *Daniels v. City of New York*, 138 F. Supp. 2d 562, 565 (2001).

106. *Terry*, 392 U.S. 35.

107. Ibid., 38.

4: Black Male Violence: The Chokehold Within

1. Niall McCarthy, "Homicide in Chicago Eclipse U.S. Death Toll in Afghanistan and Iraq," *Forbes*, September 8, 2016.

2. U.S. Bureau of Justice Statistics, "U.S. Prison Population Declined One Percent in 2014," September 17, 2015, available at www.bjs.gov/content/pub /press/p14pr.cfm.

3. Mary A. Johnson, "Crime: New Frontier—Jesse Jackson Calls It Top Civil Rights Issue," *Chicago Sun Times*, November 29, 1993.

4. Trent Baker, "Seahawks' Richard Sherman: If Black Lives Matter, Stop Black-on-Black Crime," *Breitbart*, September 17, 2015.

5. "A$AP Rocky Says Black-on-Black Crime Is Worse than Police Violence," YouTube, June 9, 2015.

6. Desire Thompson, "Stephen A. Smith's 'Black-on-Black Crime' Rhetoric Gets an Epic Response from Black Twitter, Hip-Hop Community," *News One*, July 22, 2015.

7. Yesha Callahan, "Jay-Z on Black-on-Black Violence: 'We Need to Understand That We're Kings and Queens,'" *The Root*, May 18, 2015.

8. Taylor Lewis, "Black Twitter Reacts to Kendrick Lamar's Ferguson Comments," *Essence*, January 12, 2015.

9. "This Artist Is Comparing Black on Black Crime to the KKK," BET.com, March 27, 2016, http://www.bet.com/news/national/2016/03/27/black-lives-matter-protests-national-civil-rights-museum.html.

10. Mary Carole McCauley, "'Kin Killin' Kin' Exhibit Opens at the Reginald Lewis Museum," *Baltimore Sun*, October 14, 2016, http://www.baltimoresun.com/entertainment/arts/bs-ae-lewis-kkk-20161014-story.html.

11. Alexia Cooper and Erica L. Smith, "Homicide Trends in the United States, 1980–2008," Bureau of Justice Statistics, 2012, table 1.

12. See Brian A. Reaves, "Violent Felons in Large Urban Counties," *Bureau of Justice Statistics Special Report*, 2006, table 4. As of the 2010 United States Census, white and Latino men outnumbered black males. See "2010 Census," U.S. Census Bureau. There were 96,766,981 white males, 25,618,800 Latino males, and 18,563,970 black males. See "Overview of Race and Hispanic Origin: 2010," U.S. Census Bureau, 2010, table 2.

13. See Ashby Jones and Arian Campo-Flores, "Crime Persists as a Grim Challenge for Blacks," *Wall Street Journal*, August 28, 2013. See also Cooper and Smith, "Homicide Trends in the United States, 1980–2008," 3, 11, 13. "Most murders were intraracial. From 1980 through 2008, 84 percent of white homicide victims were [murdered] by whites [and] 93 percent of black victims were [murdered] by blacks. [During this same period, blacks were disproportionately represented among homicide victims and offenders.] Blacks were [also] six times more likely than whites to be homicide victims and seven times more likely than whites to commit homicide."

14. Jones and Campo-Flores, "Crime Persists as a Grim Challenge for Blacks."

15. Lauren J. Krivo and Julie A. Phillips, "Social Fact: The Homicide Divide," *The Society Pages*, August 2, 2013.

16. Reaves, "Violent Felons in Large Urban Counties."

17. Ibid. Blacks were also responsible, according to these statistics, for 35 percent of rapes. Ibid. Because rape is reported significantly less than other violent crimes, I do not consider those statistics in this chapter. See, e.g., Katherine K. Baker, "Once a Rapist? Motivational Evidence and Relevancy in Rape Law," *Harvard Law Review*, 1997, 584. I intend in no way to detract from the violence of rape; my concern is that the rape statistics are not as reliable as those for other violent crimes.

18. See William J. Stuntz, *The Collapse of American Criminal Justice* (Cambridge, MA: Harvard University Press, 2011), 16–22. Stuntz notes that "high rates of black violence in the late twentieth century are a matter of historical fact, not bigoted imagination. . . . Race and crime were bound up together, as immigration and crime once were, only more so." Ibid., 21.

19. Brian O'Flaherty and Rajiv Seth, "Homicide in Black and White," *Journal of Urban Economics* 68(3): 215–230, available at http://www.columbia.edu/~rs328/Homicide.pdf (table 1).

20. "Black Homicide Victimization in the United States," Violence Policy Center, March 2016, available at http://www.vpc.org/studies/blackhomicide16.pdf.

21. Lynn Langton et al., "Victimization Not Reported to the Police, 2006–2010," *Bureau of Justice Statistics Special Report*, August 2012, available at www.bjs.gov/content/pub/pdf/vnrp0610.pdf.

22. *McCleskey v. Kemp*, 481 U.S. 279 (1987).

23. "Crime in the United States 2013," FBI Criminal Justice Information Services Division, 2014, tables 43A–C.

24. Susan Estrich, *Real Rape* (Cambridge, MA: Harvard University Press, 1987).

25. In general, African Americans are less likely to report violent crime than white Americans. Langton et al., "Victimization Not Reported to the Police," available at www.bjs.gov/content/pub/pdf/vnrp0610.pdf.

26. Danielle Paquette, "Giuliani: 'White Police Officers Wouldn't Be There If You Weren't Killing Each Other,'" *Washington Post*, November, 23, 2014.

27. Ian Simpson, "Prosecution of U.S. Police for Killings Surges to Highest in Decade," Reuters, October, 26, 2015.

28. See generally Jill Leovy, *Ghettoside: A True Story of Murder in America* (New York: Spiegel & Grau, 2015).

29. @Touré, Twitter (December 8, 2013, 6:23 p.m.).

30. In 2012, 33,780 people died in motor vehicle traffic crashes. See "Early Estimate of Motor Vehicle Traffic Fatalities for the First Half (Jan–Jun) of 2013," National Highway Traffic Safety Administration's National Center for Statistics and Analysis, U.S. Department of Transportation, 2013, table 1.

31. Memorandum for the President from Daniel P. Moynihan to President Nixon, January 16, 1970, 4.

32. Roger Casement's Online Comment to "Nixons's Drug War— Re-Inventing Jim Crow, Targeting the Counter Culture," *Thom Hartmann Program*, September 21, 2012, 11:47 a.m.

33. Larry Gabriel, "Joining the Fight: Not Your Grandfather's NAACP," *Detroit Metro Times*, August 10, 2011.

34. White people overestimate their risk of being victims of crime. See Lincoln Quillian and Devah Prager, "Estimating Risk: Stereotype Amplification and the Perceived Risk of Criminal Victimization," *Social Psychology Quarterly* 73:1 (2010).

35. Naomi Murakawa and Katherine Beckett, "The Penology of Racial Innocence: The Erasure of Racism in the Study and Practice of Punishment," *Law and Society Review* 44:3–4 (2010): 710.

36. "Black Homicide Victimization in the United States," Violence Policy Center.

37. Benjamin Wallace-Wells, "Baltimore After Freddie Gray: A Laboratory of Urban Violence," *New York Magazine*, November 30, 2015.

38. James Forman Jr., "Racial Critiques of Mass Incarceration: Beyond the New Jim Crow," *New York University Law Review* 87:1 (2012): 48.

39. E. Ann Carson, "Prisoners in 2014," Bureau of Justice Statistics, September 2015, 30, table 4.

40. Marc Mauer, "The Crisis of the Young African American Male and the Criminal Justice System," The Sentencing Project, April 1999, 3. As The Sentencing Project noted more recently, "if current trends continue, one of every three black American males born today can expect to go to prison in his lifetime." See "Report of The Sentencing Project to the United Nations Human Rights Committee Regarding Racial Disparities in the United States Criminal Justice System," The Sentencing Project, August 2013, 1.

41. Melissa S. Kearney et al., "Ten Economic Facts About Crime and Incarceration in the United States," The Hamilton Project, May 2014, 11.

42. Scholars and researchers often conduct "damage-centered" research, which documents the pain and brokenness of marginalized peoples and seeks to hold accountable those in power. Damage-centered research, however, espouses a problematic "theory of change" that reinforces a "one-dimensional notion of these people as depleted, ruined, and hopeless." See Eve Tuck, "Suspending Damage: A Letter to Communities," *Harvard Educational Review* 79:3 (Fall 2009): 409–27.

43. Hussein Abdilahi Bulhan, *Frantz Fanon and the Psychology of Oppression* (New York: Springer Science & Business Media, 1985), 163.

44. Evan McMurry, "CNN's Don Lemon Backs Up Bill O'Reilly: 'He Doesn't Go Far Enough' in Criticizing Black Culture," *Mediaite*, July 27, 2013.

45. Ibid.

46. David Remnick, "Going the Distance: On and Off the Road with Barack Obama," *New Yorker*, January 27, 2014.

47. "President Obama March on Washington Speech (video, transcript)," *Politico*, August 28, 2013.

48. Katherine Fung, "Don Lemon: Bill O'Reilly's 'Got a Point' About Black People (video)," *Huffington Post*, July 28, 2013.

49. Mario Luis Small et al., "Reconsidering Culture and Poverty," *ANNALS of the American Academy of Political and Social Science* 629 (2010): 2–3. Scholars, too, have re-focused on culture, including "asking questions about the role of culture in many aspects of poverty and even explicitly explaining the behavior of the low-income population in reference to cultural factors." The new generation of scholarship, though, "is often reluctant to divide explanations into 'structural' and 'cultural,' because of the increasingly questionable utility of this old distinction." Ibid.

50. "Hip-hop: Beyond Beats and Rhymes," Media Education Foundation, 2006, available at http://www.mediaed.org/transcripts/Hip-Hop-Transcript.pdf.

51. Regina Austin has pointed out that misogyny also "plays a substantial role in defining the persona of the Black male outlaw. In the mythology of Black banditry, women—like cars, clothing, and jewelry—are prized possessions." See Regina Austin, "The Black Community, Its Lawbreakers, and a Politics of Identification," *Southern California Law Review* 65 (1989): 1784–85.

52. The sociologist Michael Eric Dyson notes, "[T]he notion of violent masculinity is at the heart of American identity. The preoccupation with Jesse James and the outlaw, the rebel, much of that is associated in the American mindset, the collective imagination of the nation, with the expansion of the frontier. In the history of American social imagination, the violent man using the gun to defend his family, his kip and kin, becomes a suitable metaphor for the notion of manhood."

53. "Hip-hop: Beyond Beats and Rhymes," Media Education Foundation.

54. Ibid.

55. Alexia Elajalde-Ruiz, "Nearly Half of Young Black Men in Chicago Out of Work, Out of School: Report," *Chicago Tribune*, January 25, 2016; Ben Casselman, "How Baltimore's Young Men Are Boxed In," *FiveThirtyEight*, April 28, 2015.

56. See Tracey L. Meares, "Place and Crime," *Chicago-Kent Law Review* 73 (1998): 669, 678.

57. See Julie A. Phillips, "White, Black, and Latino Homicide Rates: Why the Difference," *Social Problems* 49:3 (2002): 352. In this article, Julie Phillips described a study that found "the associations between homicide and various measures of socioeconomic deprivation, such as poverty, unemployment, and family structure, are stronger for whites than for blacks." See also Graham C. Ousey, "Homicide, Structural Factors, and the Racial Invariance Assumption," *Criminology* 37:2 (May 1999).

58. Graham C. Ousey, "Homicide, Structural Factors, and the Racial Invariance Assumption," *Criminology* 37:2 (1999).

59. Steffensmeier et al., "Scope and Conceptual Issues in Testing the Race-Crime Invariance Thesis: Black, White, and Hispanic Comparisons," *Criminology* 48:4 (2010), available at www.ncbi.nlm.nih.gov/pmc/articles/PMC4233132.

60. Laura Sullivan et al., "The Racial Wealth Gap," *Demos*, 2015.

61. Ben Walsh, "Here's How the Government Could Close the Staggering Racial Wealth Gap," *Huffington Post*, February 22, 2016.

62. "Kids Count 2015 Data Book: State Trends in Child Wellbeing," Annie E. Casey Foundation, 2015, 15, figure 4.

63. Patricia Cohen, "Racial Wealth Gap Persists Despite Degree, Study Says," *New York Times*, August 16, 2015.

64. Max Ehrenfreund, "Wealthier Black Kids More Likely to Go to Prison than Poor White Kids," *Washington Post*, March 25, 2016.

65. Patrick Sharkey, "Sorry, Conservatives: America Is Not Even Close to Being a Colorblind Country," *The Week*, May 28, 2014.

66. Tracey L. Meares, "Norms, Legitimacy and Law Enforcement," *University of Oregon Law Review* 79:2 (2000): 394–95 (citing Mercer L. Sullivan, *"Getting Paid": Youth Crime and Work in the Inner City* (Ithaca, NY: Cornell University Press, 1989); Robert J. Sampson, "Urban Black Violence: The Effect of Male Joblessness and Family Disruption," *American Journal of Sociology* 93:2 (1987); Robert J. Sampson and William Julius Wilson, "Toward a Theory of Race, Crime, and Urban Inequality," in *Crime and Inequality* (John Hagan and Ruth D. Peterson eds., Stanford, CA: Stanford University Press, 1995), 37, 42.

67. Ta-Nehisi Coates, "The Case for Reparations," *The Atlantic*, June 2014.

68. Ibid.

69. Ibid.

70. Ibid.

71. See Phillips, "White, Black, and Latino Homicide Rates."

72. "White Supremacy," *Oxford American English Dictionary*.

73. See Frances Lee Ansley, "Stirring the Ashes: Race, Class, and the Future of Civil Rights Scholarship," *Cornell University Law Review* 74:6 (September 1989).

74. David Wade, "The Conclusion That a Sinister Conspiracy of Foreign Origin Controls Organized Crime: The Influence of Nativism in the Kefauver Committee Investigation," *Northern Illinois University Law Review* 16:2 (1996): 384.

75. Ira Katznelson, *When Affirmative Action Was White* (New York: W.W. Norton & Company, 2005), 17.

76. Ibid., 22.

77. David Leonhardt, Amanda Cox, and Claire Cain Miller, "An Atlas of Upward Mobility Shows Paths out of Poverty," *New York Times*, May 4, 2015.

78. Raj Chetty and Nathaniel Hendren, "The Impacts of Neighborhoods on Intergenerational Mobility," April 2015, available at http://www.equality-of-opportunity.org/images/nbhds_exec_summary.pdf.

79. Phillips, "White, Black, and Latino Homicide Rates," 349–374.

80. Sullivan et al., "The Racial Wealth Gap."

81. Lois Beckett, "How the Gun Control Debate Ignores Black Lives," *ProPublica*, November 24, 2015.

82. Ibid.

5: Do the Brothers Need Keepers?

1. Office of the Press Secretary, "Remarks by the President on 'My Brother's Keeper' Initiative," The White House, February 27, 2014.

2. Lizette Alvarez and Cara Buckley, "Zimmerman Is Acquitted in Trayvon Martin Killing," *New York Times*, July 13, 2013.

3. Michael D. Shear, "Obama Starts Initiative for Young Black Men, Noting His Own Experience," *New York Times*, February 27, 2014.

4. Jennifer Senior, "The Paradox of the First Black President," *New York Magazine*, October 7, 2015.

5. Office of the Press Secretary, "Remarks by the President on Trayvon Martin," The White House, July 19, 2013.

6. Compare Stephanie Condon, "Obama: Trayvon Martin Could Have Been Me 35 Years Ago," CBSNews, July 19, 2013, with Kirsten Powers, "Obama's Trayvon Remarks Struck Right Notes," *USA Today*, July 24, 2013.

7. Paul Butler, "Black Male Exceptionalism? The Problems and Potential of Black Male–Focused Interventions," *Du Bois Review* 10 (2013): 485, 486.

8. Ibid.

9. Troy Patterson, "The Extinction of the Black Man," *Slate*, October 26, 2012.

10. Perry Stein, "ACLU Questions Legality of D.C.'s Minority Male School Program: What About Black Girls?," *Washington Post*, May 9, 2016.

11. Amicus Curiae Brief for Respondents at 33, *Fisher v. Texas*, No. 11-345, 133 S. Ct. 2411 (2012).

12. Irin Carmon, "Valerie Jarrett Defends 'My Brother's Keeper' Against Criticism," MSNBC, June 18, 2014.

13. Butler, "Black Male Exceptionalism?," 497–498.

14. Ibid.

15. Ibid., 496–501.

16. Kimberlé Williams Crenshaw, "Black Girls Matter: Pushed Out, Over-policed and Underprotected," Center for Intersectionality and Social Policy Studies, 2015.

17. Wendy Wang, "Interracial Marriage: Who Is 'Marrying Out'?," Pew Research Center, June 12, 2015, available at http://www.pewresearch.org/fact-tank/2015/06/12/interracial-marriage-who-is-marrying-out.

18. Ta-Nehisi Coates, "My President Was Black," *The Atlantic*, January/February 2017.

19. James Comey, "Hard Truths: Law Enforcement and Race," remarks delivered at Georgetown University, February 12, 2015.

20. Butler, "Black Male Exceptionalism?," 485, 503–4.

21. Verna L. Williams, "Reform or Retrenchment? Single-Sex Education and the Construction of Race and Gender," *Wisconsin Law Review*, 2004, 68–69.

22. Ibid., 71.

23. Ibid., 72.

24. Butler, "Black Male Exceptionalism?"

25. Ibid.

26. David W. Chen, "Bloomberg Says Math Backs Police Stops of Minorities," *New York Times*, June 28, 2013.

27. Jonah Goldberg, "Discrimination and My Brother's Keeper," *National Review*, March 5, 2014.

28. Catharine MacKinnon, *Toward a Feminist Theory of the State* (Cambridge, MA: Harvard University Press, 1989).

29. "Letter of 250+ Concerned Black Men and Other Men of Color Calling for the Inclusion of Women and Girls in 'My Brother's Keeper,'" African American Policy Forum, May 30, 2014, available at www.aapf.org/recent/2014/05/an-open-letter-to-president-obama.

30. DeNeen L. Brown, "Harry Belafonte Challenges Phi Beta Sigma to Join Movement to Stop Oppression of Women," *Washington Post*, January 12, 2014.

31. Taryn Finley, "This Fact About Women of the Black Panther Party May Surprise You," *Huffington Post*, September 2, 2015.

32. Perception Institute, "Black Male Re-Imagined," 2013.

33. Question Bridge, available at http://questionbridge.com.

6: Nothing Works: Why the Chokehold Can't Be "Reformed"

1. James Baldwin, *No Name in the Street* (New York: Vintage, 1972), 149.

2. Bill O'Reilly, "President Obama and the Race Problem," Fox News, July 22, 2013.

3. Katherine Fung, "Don Lemon: Bill O'Reilly's 'Got a Point' About Black People," *Huffington Post*, July 28, 2013.

4. "Obama's Racial Identity Still an Issue," CBS News, November 27, 2007.

5. "Obama's Father's Day Remarks," *New York Times*, June 15, 2008.

6. Randall Kennedy, *Race, Crime, and the Law* (New York: Vintage, 1997), 19.

7. Ibid., 74.

8. Ibid., 69–70.

9. Ibid., 75.

10. Ginger Gibson, "Trump, in Law and Order Speech, Calls for African-American Support," Reuters, August 17, 2016.

11. Jeremy Diamond, "Trump: Democrats Have 'Failed and Betrayed' African-Americans," CNN Politics, August 17, 2016.

12. Michael Javen Fortner, *Black Silent Majority: The Rockefeller Drug Laws and the Politics of Punishment* (Cambridge, MA: Harvard University Press, 2015), 23.

13. James Forman Jr., "Racial Critiques of Mass Incarceration: Beyond the New Jim Crow," *New York University Law Review* 87:1 (2012): 38–42.

14. Michael R. Bloomberg, "'Stop and Frisk' Keeps New York Safe," *Washington Post*, August 18, 2013.

15. Ibid.

16. Ibid.

17. Alana Semuels, "How to Fix a Broken Police Department," *The Atlantic*, May 28, 2015.

18. Ibid.

19. "Mission," National Initiative for Building Community Trust and Justice, available at www.trustandjustice.org/about/mission.

20. Ibid.

21. Ibid.

22. "Eric Holder's Keynote Address: Shifting Law Enforcement Goals to Reduce Mass Incarceration," Brennan Center for Justice, September 23, 2014, available at www.brennancenter.org/analysis/keynote-address-shifting-law-enforcement-goals-to-reduce-mass-incarceration.

23. Eric H. Holder Jr., "Time to Tackle Unfinished Business in Criminal Justice Reform," *Washington Post*, February 27, 2015.

24. Ibid.

25. See Jim Abrams, "Congress Passes Bill to Reduce Disparity in Crack, Powder Cocaine Sentencing," *Washington Post*, July 29, 2010.

26. "Message from the Movement 4 Black Lives Policy Table," *The Movement for Black Lives*, available at www.movementforblacklives.org/message-from-the-movement-4-black-lives-policy-table.

27. "About the Black Lives Matter Network," Black Lives Matter, available at www.blacklivesmatter.com/about.

28. Ibid.

29. Alexander, *The New Jim Crow*, 1–2, 4.

30. Ibid., 15, 258.

31. Ibid., 258.

32. Ta-Nehisi Coates, *Between the World and Me* (New York: Spiegel & Grau, 2015), 103.

33. Ta-Nehisi Coates, "Other People's Pathologies," *The Atlantic*, March 30, 2014.

34. "Message from the Movement 4 Black Lives."

35. Dana Liebelson and Ryan J. Reilly, "Inside Hillary Clinton's Meeting with Black Lives Matter," *Huffington Post*, October 9, 2015.

36. Beyoncé, "Formation," YouTube, February 6, 2016.

37. Michael Powell, "Colin Kaepernick Finds His Voice," *New York Times*, September 13, 2016.

38. John Eligon and Scott Cacciola, "As Colin Kaepernick's Gesture Spreads, a Spirit Long Dormant Is Revived," *New York Times*, September 12, 2016.

39. Barack Obama, "Remarks at Morehouse College Commencement Ceremony," May 19, 2013.

40. Barack Obama, "Remarks by the President After Announcement of the Decision by the Grand Jury in Ferguson, Missouri," November 24, 2014.

41. Jill Leovy, *Ghettoside: A True Story of Murder in America* (New York: Spiegel & Grau, 2015), 6–7.

42. The President's Task Force on 21st Century Policing, "Final Report of the President's Task Force on 21st Century Policing" (2015), 58.

43. Ibid., 5.

44. Obama, "Remarks by the President After Announcement of the Decision by the Grand Jury in Ferguson, Missouri."

45. See Ta-Nehisi Coates, "The Case for Reparations," *The Atlantic*, June 2014.

46. "Message from the Movement 4 Black Lives Policy Table," *The Movement For Black Lives*, available at www.movementforblacklives.org/message-from-the-movement-4-black-lives-policy-table.

47. Charles R. Lawrence III, "The Fire This Time: Black Lives Matter, Abolitionist Pedagogy and the Law," *Journal of Legal Education* 65:2 (2015): 387.

48. For a critique of the celebratory tradition in evaluating race relations law, see Randall Kennedy, "Race Relations Law and the Tradition of Celebration: The Case of Professor Schmidt," *Columbia Law Review* 86:8 (1986).

49. Marina Vornovitsky, Alfred Gottschalck, and Adam Smith, "Distribution of Household Wealth in the U.S.: 2000 to 2011," United States Census Bureau (2014), 3.

50. Rakesh Kochhar and Richard Fry, "Wealth Inequality Has Widened Along Racial, Ethnic Lines Since End of Great Recession," Pew Research Center, December 12, 2014.

51. Drew Desilver, "Black Unemployment Rate Is Consistently Twice That of Whites," Pew Research Center, August 21, 2013.

52. Janelle Jones and John Schmitt, "A College Degree Is No Guarantee," Center for Economic and Policy Research, May 2014.

53. Margery Austin Turner et al., "Housing Discrimination Against Racial and Ethnic Minorities 2012," U.S. Department of Housing and Urban Development, June 2013, 1.

54. Ibid.

55. Ibid.

56. Lauren C. William, "Airbnb Has an Unsurprising Race Problem," *ThinkProgress*, May 7, 2016.

57. Benjamin G. Edelman, Michael Luca, and Daniel Svirsky, "Racial Discrimination in the Sharing Economy: Evidence from a Field Experiment," Harvard Business School Working Paper, No. 16-069, December 2015.

58. Ibid., 11.

59. Ibid., 12.

60. Marianne Bertrand and Sendhil Mullainathan, "Are Emily and Greg More Employable than Lakisha and Jamal? A Field Experiment on Labor Market Discrimination," *The American Economic Review* 94:4 (2004).

61. Michael S. Gaddis, "Discrimination in the Credential Society: An Audit Study of Race and College Selectivity in the Labor Market," *Social Forces* 93:4 (2014).

62. Ibid., 17.

63. Ibid., 17–20.

64. Devin G. Pope and Justin R Sydnor, "What's in a Picture? Evidence of Discrimination from Prosper.com," *The Journal of Human Resources* 46:1 (2009).

65. Jennifer L. Doleac and Luke C.D. Stein, "The Visible Hand: Race and Online Market Outcomes," *The Economic Journal*, 123:572 (2013).

66. Ibid., 490.

67. See, e.g., Naomi Murakawa, *The First Civil Right: How Liberals Built Prison America* (New York: Oxford University Press, 2014).

68. Devon W. Carbado, "Critical What What?," *Connecticut Law Review* 43:5 (2011): 1610.

69. Ian F. Haney López, "The Social Construction of Race: Some Observations on Illusion, Fabrication, and Choice," *Harvard Civil Rights Civil Liberties Law Review* 29:1 (1994): 3–4.

70. Ibid., 7.

71. Ibid., 1–7, 163–67.

72. Ibid., 35.

73. Ibid., 119.

74. Haney López defines racism as "racial status-enforcement undertaken in reliance on racial institutions," or actions that have "the effect of enforcing a racial status hierarchy." Ian F. Haney López, "Institutional Racism: Judicial Conduct and a New Theory of Racial Discrimination," *Yale Law Journal* 109:8 (2000): 1809–10.

75. Devon Carbado and Daria Roithmayr, "Critical Race Theory Meets Social Science," *Annual Review of Law and Social Science* 10:149 (2014): 151.

76. Derrick Bell, *Faces at the Bottom of the Well: The Permanence of Racism* (New York: Basic Books, 1992), ix. See also Carbado, "Critical What What?," 1613 (asserting that racism is "built into the constitutional architecture of American democracy").

77. Daria Roithmayr, "Barriers to Entry: A Market Lock-In Model of Discrimination," *Virginia Law Review* 86:4 (2000) 731–32.

78. See Richard Delgado, "Zero-Based Racial Politics and an Infinity-Based Response: Will Endless Talking Cure America's Racial Ills?," *Georgetown Law Journal* 80:5 (1992): 1884 ("Racism is not a mistake, like parking in the wrong space or believing that the solar system has eight planets; rather, it is a means of *subjugating another person or group*").

79. Gary Peller, *Critical Race Consciousness: The Puzzle of Representation* (New York: Taylor & Francis, 2012), 7.

80. Charles R. Lawrence III, "The Fire This Time: Black Lives Matter, Abolitionist Pedagogy and the Law," *Journal of Legal Education* 65:2 (2015): 387.

81. 347 U.S. 483 (1954).

82. The Civil Rights Act, Pub. L. No. 88-352, 78 Stat. 241 (1964).

83. The Voting Rights Act, Pub. L. No. 89-110, 79 Stat. 437 (1965).

84. Kimberlé Williams Crenshaw, "Race, Reform, and Retrenchment: Transformation and Legitimation in Antidiscrimination Law," *Harvard Law Review* 101:7 (1988): 1346.

85. Ibid., 1346–47. See also Carbado, "Critical What What?," 1607–8 (citing the abolition of slavery and Jim Crow, *Brown v. Board of Education* and massive resistance to school desegregation, and the reframing of Martin Luther King Jr.'s vision in terms of "color blindness" as three examples of the reform/retrenchment dialectic).

86. Derrick A. Bell Jr., "*Brown v. Board of Education* and the Interest-Convergence Dilemma," *Harvard Law Review* 93:3 (1980): 523.

87. Ibid., 523–25.

88. Ibid, 527.

89. Ibid., 527–28.

90. U.S. Department of Justice Civil Rights Division, "Investigation of the Ferguson Police Department," (March 4, 2015), 71.

91. Ibid., 5.

92. Ibid., 33, 78.

93. U.S. Department of Justice Civil Rights Division, "Department of Justice Report Regarding the Criminal Investigation into the Shooting Death of Michael Brown by Ferguson, Missouri Police Officer Darren Wilson," (March 4, 2015).

94. Ibid., 84.

95. Ibid.

96. See ibid. (citing *Loch v. City of Litchfield*, 689 F.3d 961, 966 (8th Cir. 2012) (holding that "even if a suspect is ultimately 'found to be unarmed, a police officer can still employ deadly force if objectively reasonable'") (quoting *Billingsley v. City of Omaha*, 277 F.3d 990, 995 (8th Cir. 2002)); *Reese v. Anderson*, 926 F.2d 494, 501 (5th Cir. 1991) ("Also irrelevant is the fact that [the suspect] was actually unarmed. [The officer] did not and could not have known this"); *Smith v. Freland*, 954 F.2d 343, 347 (noting that "unarmed" does not mean "harmless [*sic*]") (6th Cir. 1992)).

97. Ibid., 8.

98. Ibid., 84.

99. Ibid.

100. Ibid, 85.

101. See Christopher R. Green, "Reverse Broken Windows," *Journal of Legal Education* 65:2 (2015): 265.

102. U.S. Department of Justice Civil Rights Division, "Investigation of the Ferguson Police Department," 70–78.

103. U.S. Department of Justice Civil Rights Division, "Department of Justice Report Regarding the Criminal Investigation," 5.

104. John Eligon, "Ferguson Approves a Federal Plan to Overhaul Police and Courts," *New York Times*, March 15, 2016.

105. *United States v. Ferguson*, No. 4:16-cv-000180-CDP (March 17, 2016), 19–20 [hereinafter *Ferguson Consent Decree*].

106. Ibid., 23.

107. 434 US 106 (1977).

108. *Ferguson Consent Decree*, 21.

109. See, e.g., *Schneckloth v. Bustamonte*, 412 U.S. 218 (1973) at 219 ("It is equally well settled that one of the specifically established exceptions to the requirements of both a warrant and probable cause is a search that is conducted pursuant to consent").

110. *Ferguson Consent Decree*, 22.

111. 412 U.S. 218 (1973).

112. 536 U.S. 194 (2002).

113. *Ferguson Consent Decree*, 22.

114. Kimbriell Kelly, Sarah Childress, and Steven Rich, "Forced Reforms, Mixed Results," *Washington Post*, November 13, 2015.

115. 42 U.S.C. § 14141(a) (2012).

116. Stephen Rushin, "Federal Enforcement of Police Reform," *Fordham Law Review* 82:6 (2014), 3191.

117. Ibid., 3219–22.

118. Ibid., 3224–26.

119. Ibid.

120. Kelly, Childress, and Rich, "Forced Reforms, Mixed Results."

121. Ibid.

122. Christopher Stone, Todd Foglesong, and Christine M. Cole, "Policing Los Angeles Under a Consent Decree: Dynamics of Change at the LAPD," Harvard Kennedy School (2009).

123. Ibid., 6.

124. Ibid., 22.

125. Ibid.

126. Ibid., 24.

127. Ibid., i.

128. Ibid., ii.

129. Ibid., 34.

130. Ibid., 37.

131. Robert C. Davis, Christopher W. Ortiz, Nicole J. Henderson, Joel Miller, and Michelle K. Massie, "Turning Necessity into Virtue: Pittsburgh's Experience with a Federal Consent Decree," Vera Institute of Justice (2002), 55.

132. Ibid., 57.

133. Ibid., ii.

134. Semuels, "How to Fix a Broken Police Department."

135. Elliot Harvey Schatmeier, "Reforming Police Use-of-Force Practices: A Case Study of the Cincinnati Police Department," *Columbia Journal of Law and Social Problems* 46:4 (2013): 562.

136. Greg Ridgeway et al., "Police-Community Relations in Cincinnati," RAND Corporation (2009), 89–90.

137. Semuels, "How to Fix a Broken Police Department."

138. Nathalie Baptiste, "Urban Policing, Without Brutality," *American Prospect*, July 20, 2015.

139. Ibid.

140. Kelly, Childress, and Rich, "Forced Reforms, Mixed Results."

141. Rushin, "Federal Enforcement of Police Reform," 3235 ("Even when internal policies favor aggressive enforcement of § 14141, the DOJ has only initiated around three new investigations per year").

142. Samuel Walker, "Institutionalizing Police Accountability Reforms: The Problem of Making Police Reforms Endure," *Saint Louis University Public Law Review* 32:1 (2012).

143. See Alan D. Freeman, "Race and Class: The Dilemma of Liberal Reform," *Yale Law Journal* 90:8 (1981): 1882–84.

144. Crenshaw, "Race, Reform, and Retrenchment," 1331–32.

145. Ibid., 1335.

146. Stone, Foglesong, and Cole, "Policing Los Angeles Under a Consent Decree," i.

147. Ibid., 22.

148. Amy E. Lerman and Vesla M. Weaver, *Arresting Citizenship: The Democratic Consequences of American Crime Control* (Chicago: University of Chicago Press, 2014).

149. Kelly, Childress, and Rich, "Forced Reforms, Mixed Results."

150. Crenshaw, "Race, Reform, and Retrenchment," 1346–49.

151. Anthony E. Cook, "Beyond Critical Legal Studies: The Reconstructive Theology of Dr. Martin Luther King, Jr.," in *Critical Race Theory: The Key Writings That Formed the Movement* (Kimberlé Crenshaw, Neil Gotanda, and Gary Peller, eds., New York: The New Press, 1996), 85, 86. See also Mari J. Matsuda, "Pragmatism Modified and the False Consciousness Problem," *Southern California Law Review* 63:6 (1990): 1777 ("Subordination can obscure as well as illuminate self-knowledge").

152. Crenshaw, "Race, Reform, and Retrenchment," 1349.

153. Emily Gold and Melissa Bradley, "The Case for Procedural Justice: Fairness as a Crime Prevention Tool," *COPS Community Policing Dispatch* 6:9 (September 2013).

154. Tracey L. Meares, "The Good Cop: Knowing the Difference Between Lawful or Effective Policing and Rightful Policing—and Why It Matters," *William & Mary Law Review* 54:6 (2013): 1878.

155. Ibid., 1879 (presenting a graph with "Lawfulness" on the x-axis, "Legitimacy" on the y-axis, and "Rightful Policing" in the top right quadrant).

156. The President's Task Force on 21st Century Policing, "Final Report of the President's Task Force on 21st Century Policing," 1.

157. Ibid., 9, 16.

158. Ibid., 2, 19–29.

159. Ibid., 8.

160. Barack Obama, "Remarks by the President at the 50th Anniversary of the Selma to Montgomery Marches," March, 7, 2015.

161. Ibid.

7: If You Catch a Case: Act Like You Know

1. *Floyd v. City of New York*, 959 F. Supp. 2d 540, 560; United States Department of Justice Civil Rights Division, "Investigation of the Baltimore City Police Department" (August 10, 2016).

2. Allegra Kirkland, "How New York Ended up with 1.2 Million Open Arrest Warrants," *Talking Points Memo*, August 4, 2015.

3. Andre Perry, "Black Aesthetic, White Supremacy: Steven Perry's Tweet Needs Cutting More than Black Boys' Hair," *The Root*, June 15, 2016.

4. John Eligon, "Running from Police Is the Norm, Some in Baltimore Say," *New York Times*, May 10, 2015.

5. *Floyd v. City of New York*, 959 F. Supp. 2d 540, 573. See also Ian Ayres, "Racial Profiling & the LAPD: A Study of Racially Disparate Outcomes in the Los Angeles Police Department," ACLU of Southern California (October 2008).

6. *Devenpeck v. Alford*, 543 U.S. 146, 155 (2007) ("While it is assuredly good police practice to inform a person of the reason for his arrest at the time he is taken into custody, we have never held that to be constitutionally required").

7. States with "stop and identify laws" include: Alabama, Arizona, Arkansas, Colorado, Delaware, Florida, Georgia, Illinois, Indiana, Kansas, Louisiana, Missouri, Montana, Nebraska, Nevada, New Hampshire, New Mexico, New York, North Dakota, Ohio, Rhode Island, Utah, Vermont, and Wisconsin. For more information, see "When Can Police Ask for ID?," Flex Your Rights, available at www.flexyourrights.org/faqs/when-can-police-ask-for-id.

8. See Frank Rudy Cooper, "Who's the Man? Masculinities Studies, Terry Stops, and Police Training," *Columbia Journal of Gender and Law* 18:3 (2009).

9. *Oregon v. Mathiason*, 429 U.S. 492 (1977).

10. Marcy Strauss, "Reconstructing Consent," *Journal of Criminal Law and Criminology* 92:1 (2001).

11. *Town of Newton v. Rumery*, 480 U.S. 386, 418 n.23 (1987) (Stevens, J., dissenting) (quoting *Boyd v. Adams*, 513 F.2d 83, 88–89 (7th Cir. 1975)) ("The danger of concocted charges is particularly great because complaints against the police usually arise in connection with arrests for extremely vague offenses such as disorderly conduct or resisting arrest").

12. *Utah v. Strieff*, 136 S.Ct. 2056, 2070 (Sotomayor, J., dissenting).

13. *Miranda v. Arizona*, 384 U.S. 436 (1966).

14. See, e.g., *United States v. Patane*, 542 U.S. 630 (2004) (holding that the physical fruits of a Miranda-defective confession are admissible); *New York v. Quarles*, 467 U.S. 649 (1984) (holding that Miranda-defective confessions are admissible when there are overriding public safety considerations).

15. *Michigan v. Mosley*, 423 U.S. 96 (1975).

16. See, e.g., Brian Rogers, "In Jail, You Get One Phone Call. But What's the Number?," *Houston Chronicle*, March 11, 2015 ("Truth is, there is no constitutional right to use a phone when being booked into jail; the police allow those calls as a courtesy"). Some states have enacted laws guaranteeing arrestees the right to make telephone calls. See, e.g., Cal. Penal Code § 851.5 (West 2013)

("Immediately upon being booked and, except where physically impossible, no later than three hours after arrest, an arrested person has the right to make at least three completed telephone calls").

17. Thomas Stinson, "Tyson Defense Had Guard Down During First Week," *Baltimore Sun*, February 3, 1992.

18. Iyengar, Radha, "An Analysis of the Performance of Federal Indigent Defense Counsel," *National Bureau of Economic Research* (June 2007): 23.

19. Morris B. Hoffman et al., "An Empirical Study of Public Defender Effectiveness: Self-Selection by the 'Marginally Indigent,'" *Ohio State Journal of Criminal Law* 3:1 (2005): 241–42.

20. Peter W. Hahn and Susan D. Clayton, "The Effects of Attorney Presentation Style, Attorney Gender, and Juror Gender on Juror Decisions," *Law and Human Behavior* 20:5 (1996): 533, 537–38.

21. Jeff Adachi, "Public Defenders Can Be Biased, Too, and It Hurts Their Non-White Clients," *Washington Post*, June 7, 2016.

22. See, e.g., John McCurley, "Pretrial Motion to Dismiss: Ending a Criminal Case," Lawyers.com.

23. *Brady v. Maryland*, 373 U.S. 83 (1963).

24. *United States v. Olsen*, 737 F.3d 625 (9th Cir. 2013) (Kozinski, J., dissenting).

25. See, e.g., Christopher N. Osher and Jordan Steffen, "How Police Reliance on Confidential Informants in Colorado Carries Risk," *Denver Post*, April 17, 2015.

26. See Kent Roach, "Four Models of the Criminal Process," *Journal of Criminal Law and Criminology* 89:2 (1999): 682 ("The criminal trial is concerned not with factual guilt, but with whether the prosecutor can establish legal guilt beyond a reasonable doubt on the basis of legally obtained evidence").

27. Model Rules of Professional Conduct, Rule 3.3 (American Bar Association, 2016) ("A lawyer shall not knowingly . . . offer evidence that the lawyer knows to be false").

28. Jennifer Gonnerman, "Before the Law," *New Yorker*, October 6, 2014.

29. Ibid.

30. Ibid.

31. "Studies that assess the effects of race [on plea bargaining] find that blacks are less likely to receive a reduced charge compared with whites (Farnworth and Teske, 1995; Johnson, 2003; Kellough and Wortley, 2002; Ulmer and Bradley, 2006). Additionally, one study found that blacks are also less likely to receive the benefits of shorter or reduced sentences as a result of the exercise of prosecutorial discretion during plea bargaining (Johnson, 2003)." Lindsey Devers, "Plea and Charge Bargaining," United States Department of Justice Bureau of Justice Assistance (January 24, 2011), 3.

32. Michelle Alexander, "Go to Trial: Crash the Criminal Justice System," *New York Times*, March 10, 2012.

33. Eric Rasmusen, Manu Raghav, and Mark Ramseyer, "Convictions Versus Conviction Rates: The Prosecutor's Choice," *American Law and Economics Review* 11:1 (2009).

34. Peter J. Coughlan, "In Defense of Unanimous Jury Verdicts: Mistrials, Communication, and Strategic Voting," *The American Political Science Review* 94:2 (2000).

35. E. Ann Carson, "Prisoners in 2014," United States Department of Justice Bureau of Justice Statistics (September 2015), 15 ("An estimated 516,900 black males were in state or federal prison at yearend 2014, accounting for 37% of the male prison population").

36. Nicole L. Waters, Anne Gallegos, James Green, and Martha Rozsi, "Criminal Appeals in State Courts," United States Department of Justice Bureau of Justice Statistics (September 2015).

8: Woke: Unlocking the Chokehold

1. Khalil Gibran Muhammad has described how Progressive Era activists created settlement houses that provided services for European immigrants. Progressives emphasized "environmental theories of crime and delinquency" and "discounted crime statistics . . . in favor of humanizing European immigrants." Khalil Gibran Muhammad, *The Condemnation of Blackness: Race, Crime, and the Making of Modern Urban America* (Cambridge, MA: Harvard University Press, 2011), 7.

2. U.S. Bureau of Labor Statistics, "The Employment Situation—October 2016," U.S. Department of Labor, November 4, 2016, available at www.bls .gov/news.release/pdf/empsit.pdf; Tami Luhby, "Are Blacks Worse Off Under Obama, Like Trump Says?," CNN Money, March 15, 2016, available at money .cnn.com/2016/03/15/news/economy/blacks-trump-obama.

3. Ibid.

4. Ruth Simon and Tom McGinty, "Loan Rebound Misses Black Businesses," *Wall Street Journal*, March 14, 2014.

5. Rakesh Kochhar and Richard Fry, "Wealth Inequality Has Widened Along Racial, Ethnic Lines Since End of Great Recession," Pew Research Center, December 12, 2014, available at www.pewresearch.org/fact-tank/2014/12/12/racial-wealth-gaps-great-recession.

6. Mychal Denzel Smith, "The Senate's Bipartisan Criminal Justice Reform Bill Only Tackles Half the Problem," *The Nation*, October 14, 2015.

7. Nas feat. Lauryn Hill, "If I Ruled the World (Imagine That)," *It Was Written* (Columbia Records, 1996).

8. Professor Jonathan Simon, among others, has described prisons as "waste management" stations. See Jonathan Simon, *Governing Through Crime: How the War on Crime Transformed American Democracy and Created a Culture of Fear* (New York: Oxford University Press, 2009).

9. "Waste Management Partners with Police to Fight Crime and Watch Neighborhoods," February 10, 2010, available at www.wm.com/documents/pdfs -for-services-section/press-release-waste-watch-of-orange-county-ca.pdf.

10. Dr. James Austin and Lauren-Brooke Eisen with James Cullen and Jonathan Frank, "How Many Americans Are Unnecessarily Incarcerated?," Brennan Center for Justice, 2016.

11. Ibid.

12. Ibid.

13. "Common Justice," Vera Institute of Justice, available at www.vera .org/centers/common-justice.

14. Lynn Langston, Marc Berzofsky, Christopher Krebs, and Hope Smiley-McDonald, "Victimizations Not Reported to the Police, 2006–2010," United States Department of Justice Bureau of Justice Statistics (August 2012), 1. For a video about restorative justice (narrated by Sered), see "Restorative Justice: Why Do We Need It?," Brave New Films, September 13, 2016, available at www.you tube.com/watch?v=8N3LihLvfa0.

15. Matthew R. Durose, Alexia D. Cooper, and Howard N. Snyder, "Recidivism of Prisoners Released in 30 States in 2005: Patterns from 2005 to 2010," United States Department of Justice Bureau of Justice Statistics (April 2014), 1.

16. Allegra M. McLeod, "Prison Abolition and Grounded Justice," *UCLA Law Review* 62:5 (2015): 1161.

17. Dana Goldstein, "Too Old to Commit Crime?," *New York Times*, March 20, 2015.

18. Human Rights Watch, "Old Behind Bars," January 27, 2012, available at www.hrw.org/report/2012/01/27/old-behind-bars/aging-prison-population-united -states.

19. James Austin and Lauren-Brooke Eisen with James Cullen and Jonathan Frank , "How Many Americans Are Unnecessarily Incarcerated?," Brennan Center for Justice, 2016, www.brennancenter.org/sites/default/files/publications/Un necessarily_Incarcerated_0.pdf.

20. Human Rights Watch, "Old Behind Bars," available at www.hrw.org /report/2012/01/27/old-behind-bars/aging-prison-population-united-states.

21. KiDeuk Kim and Bryce Peterson, "Aging Behind Bars: Trends and Implications of Graying Prisoners in the Federal Prison System," Urban Institute, September 5, 2014.

22. See Alexandra Natapoff, "Misdemeanors," *Southern California Law Review* 85:5 (2012).

23. See Alexandra Natapoff, "Misdemeanor Decriminalization," *Vanderbilt Law Review* 68:4 (2015).

24. Ashley Southall, "Summonses, Not Arrests, for Small Crimes in Manhattan," *New York Times*, March 1, 2016.

25. Sally T. Hillsman, "Fines and Day Fines," *Crime and Justice* 12 (1990): 49–98.

26. Austin et al., "How Many Americans Are Unnecessarily Incarcerated?"

27. Ibid.

28. Martin Kaste, "How Many Crimes Do Your Police 'Clear'? Now You Can Find Out," NPR, March 30, 2015.

29. See, e.g., New York City Department of Investigation's Office of the Inspector General for the NYPD, "An Analysis of Quality-of-Life Summonses, Quality-of-Life Misdemeanor Arrests, and Felony Crime in New York City, 2010–2015," June 22, 2016.

30. See Michael Tonry, "Why Crimes Rates Are Falling Throughout the Western World," *Crime and Justice* 43 (2014).

31. See "Alternatives to Policing," Justice in Policing Toolkit, available at www.justiceinpolicing.com/beyond-policy/alternatives-to-policing.

32. Danielle Paquette, "One Way to Curb Police Brutality That No One Is Talking About," *Washington Post*, July 14, 2016.

33. Avril Alley, Linda Waugh, and Andrew Ede, "Police Culture, Women Police and Attitudes Towards Misconduct," July 1996, available at http://www.aic.gov.au/media_library/conferences/policewomen/alley.pdf.

34. Paquette, "One Way to Curb Police Brutality That No One Is Talking About."

35. Katherine Spillar, "How More Female Police Officers Would Help Stop Police Brutality," *Washington Post*, July 2, 2015.

36. Jason Rydberg and William Terrill, "The Effect of Higher Education on Police Behavior," *Police Quarterly* 13(1):92-120 (March 2010); Ben Stickle, "A National Examination of the Effect of Education, Training and Pre-Employment Screening on Law Enforcement Use of Force," *Justice Policy Journal* 13:1 (Spring 2016), available at http://www.cjcj.org/uploads/cjcj/documents/jpj_education_use_of_force.pdf.

37. *Jordan v. City of New London*, US Court of Appeals for the Second Circuit, No. 99-9188 (2000).

38. "About Us," Million Hoodies Movement for Justice, available at www.millionhoodies.net/about.

39. See, e.g., Brandon M. Terry, "After Ferguson," *The Point* (2015), available at www.thepointmag.com/2015/politics/after-ferguson.

40. See Amna A. Akbar, "Law's Exposure: The Movement and the Legal Academy," *Journal of Legal Education* 65:2 (2015): 355.

41. Marie Gottschalk, "America Needs a Third Reconstruction: The Problem of Mass Incarceration Is a Problem of High Inequality," *The Atlantic*, September 18, 2015.

42. Michael J. Klarman, *From Jim Crow to Civil Rights: The Supreme Court and the Struggle for Racial Equality* (New York: Oxford University Press, 2006), 88–89.

43. Randall Kennedy, *Race, Crime, and the Law* (New York: Vintage, 1997), 20.

44. Ibid., 20–21.

45. Ibid., 17.

46. Charles Earl Jones, *The Black Panther Party [Reconsidered]* (Baltimore, MD: Black Classic Press, 1998), 200–207.

47. Ibid.

48. Alexander, *The New Jim Crow*, 224.

49. "UNGASS: Public Letter to Kofi Annan—Signatories," Drug Policy Alliance, available at www.drugpolicy.org/publications-resources/sign-letters/public-letter-kofi-annan/ungass-public-letter-kofi-annan-signato. See also Christopher S. Wren, "Anti-Drug Effort Criticized as More Harm Than Help," *New York Times*, June 9, 1998.

50. "Over 75 Groups and Law Professors Push Congress to Eliminate 100-to-1 Crack Sentencing Disparity," ACLU, April 29, 2009.

51. The NAACP advocates for "smarter results-based criminal justice policies" and "an end to racial disparities at all levels of the [criminal justice] system." NAACP, "Justice," available at www.naacp.org/programs/entry/justice. Groups like the National Council of La Raza and the ACLU have also pushed for criminal justice reform. National Council of La Raza, "Civil Rights & Criminal Justice," available at www.nclr.org/issues/civil-rights. ACLU, "Criminal Law Reform," available at www.aclu.org/issues/criminal-law-reform.

52. See Allegra M. McLeod, "Confronting Criminal Law's Violence: The Possibilities of Unfinished Alternatives," *Harvard Unbound* 8:3 (2013).

53. Elahe Izadi, "Black Lives Matter and America's Long History of Resisting Civil Rights Protesters," *Washington Post*, April 19, 2016.

54. See Jelani Cobb, "The Matter of Black Lives," *New Yorker*, March 14, 2016.

55. See, e.g., *Washington v. Davis*, 426 U.S. 229 (1976).

56. U.S. Const. amend. XIII, § 1.

57. *Brown v. Board of Education*, 347 U.S. 483 (1954).

58. Ta-Nehisi Coates, "What This Cruel War Was Over," *The Atlantic*, June 22, 2015.

59. *Plessy v. Ferguson*, 163 U.S. 537 (1896).

60. See Richard Kluger, *Simple Justice: The History of Brown v. Board of Education and Black America's Struggle for Equality* (New York: Vintage, 2004).

61. *Brown v. Board of Education*, 347 U.S. 483.

62. See, e.g., Taylor Branch, *Pillar of Fire: America in the King Years 1963–65* (New York: Simon & Schuster, 1998); Taylor Branch, *At Canaan's Edge: America in the King Years, 1965–68* (New York: Simon & Schuster, 2006); Clay Risen, *The Bill of the Century: The Epic Battle for the Civil Rights Act* (New York: Bloomsbury Press, 2014).

63. Simone Sebastian, "Don't Criticize Black Lives Matter for Provoking Violence. The Civil Rights Movement Did, Too," *Washington Post*, October 1, 2015.

64. Jay-Z, "A Billi," genius.com/Jay-z-a-billi-lyrics.

65. Langston Hughes, "Harlem" (1951).

66. Kendrick Lamar, "i (Live on SNL)," November 16, 2014, available at www.youtube.com/watch?v=sop2V_MREEI.

67. Eminem, "Till I Collapse," *The Eminem Show* (Aftermath / Interscope, 2002).

68. Nas, "Shootouts," *It Was Written* (Columbia Records, 1996).

69. Hiphop Archive & Research Institute at the Hutchins Center, "Announcing the Nasir Jones Hiphop Fellowship," July 12, 2013.

70. N.W.A., "Fuck tha Police," *Straight Outta Compton* (Priority / Ruthless, 1988).

71. See Kim Gittleson, "Dr. Dre: The First 'Hip-Hop Billionaire'?," BBC News, May 29, 2014.

72. Body Count, "Cop Killer," *Body Count* (Sire / Warner Bros., 1992).

73. "Rapper Ice-T Defends Song Against Spreading Boycott," *New York Times*, June 19, 1992.

74. James Baldwin, "Fifth Avenue, Uptown," *Esquire*, July 1960. The full essay is available at www.esquire.com/news-politics/a3638/fifth-avenue-uptown.

75. See Kimbriell Kelly, Sarah Childress, and Steven Rich, "Forced Reforms, Mixed Results," *Washington Post*, November 13, 2015.

76. Joyce Appleby and Terence Ball, eds., *Jefferson: Political Writings* (Cambridge: Cambridge University Press, 1999), 110.

77. Henry Louis Gates Jr., "What Were the Earliest Rebellions by African Americans?," *The Root*, April 22, 2013.

78. See, e.g., Stanley Crouch, "By Any Means Necessary," *New York Times*, September 10, 2006.

79. See Jon Wiener, "Denmark Vesey: A New Verdict," *The Nation*, March 11, 2002.

80. The well-known Negro spiritual "Oh Freedom" includes the words: "Before I'd be a slave I'd be buried in my grave." *Sing for Freedom: The Story of the Civil Rights Movement Through Its Songs*, 74–75 (Guy Carawan and Candie Carawan, eds., 1990). African American writer Toni Morrison explored this theme in the novel *Beloved*. See Toni Morrison, *Beloved* (1987).

81. Alexander, *The New Jim Crow*, 240–41.

82. Elahe Izadi, "Ta-Nehisi Coates Is Voting Sanders. How Big of a Problem Is This for Clinton?," *Washington Post*, February 10, 2016.

83. Michelle Alexander, "Why Hillary Clinton Doesn't Deserve the Black Vote," *The Nation*, February 10, 2016, available at www.thenation.com/article/hillary-clinton-does-not-deserve-black-peoples-votes.

84. DeRay Mckesson, "DeRay Mckesson: Why I'm Voting for Hillary Clinton," *Washington Post*, October 26, 2016, available at www.washingtonpost.com/posteverything/wp/2016/10/26/deray-mckesson-why-im-voting-for-hillary-clinton/?utm_term=.240f8d1dda4f.

85. Emma Margolin, "Hillary Clinton: 'Yes, Black Lives Matter,'" MSNBC, July 23, 2015, available at www.msnbc.com/msnbc/hillary-clinton-yes-black-lives-matter.

86. Amy Chozick, "Mothers of Black Victims Emerge as a Force for Hillary Clinton," *New York Times*, April 14, 2016, available at www.nytimes.com/2016/04/14/us/politics/hillary-clinton-mothers.html.

87. Tom LoBianco and Ashley Killough, "Trump Pitches Black Voters: 'What the Hell Do You Have to Lose?,'" CNN Politics, August 19, 2016.

88. "End the War on Black People," The Movement for Black Lives, available at https://policy.m4bl.org/end-war-on-black-people.

89. *Utah v. Strieff*, 136 S.C. 2056.

INDEX

Celebrating 25 Years of
Independent Publishing

Thank you for reading this book published by The New Press. The New Press is a nonprofit, public interest publisher celebrating its twenty-fifth anniversary in 2017. New Press books and authors play a crucial role in sparking conversations about the key political and social issues of our day.

We hope you enjoyed this book and that you will stay in touch with The New Press. Here are a few ways to stay up to date with our books, events, and the issues we cover:

- Sign up at www.thenewpress.com/subscribe to receive updates on New Press authors and issues and to be notified about local events
- Like us on Facebook: www.facebook.com/newpressbooks
- Follow us on Twitter: www.twitter.com/thenewpress

Please consider buying New Press books for yourself; for friends and family; and to donate to schools, libraries, community centers, prison libraries, and other organizations involved with the issues our authors write about.

The New Press is a 501(c)(3) nonprofit organization. You can also support our work with a tax-deductible gift by visiting www.thenewpress.com/donate.